Palgrave Studies in Pragmatics, Language and Cognition

Series Editors: **Richard Breheny** and **Uli Sauerland**
Series Advisors: **Kent Bach, Anne Bezuidenhout, Noël Burton-Roberts, Robyn Carston, Sam Glucksberg, Francesca Happé, François Recanati, Deirdre Wilson**

Palgrave Studies in Pragmatics, Language and Cognition is a series of high-quality research monographs and edited collections of essays focusing on the human pragmatic capacity and its interaction with natural language semantics and other faculties of mind. A central interest is the interface of pragmatics with the linguistic system(s), with the 'theory of mind' capacity and with other mental reasoning and general problem-solving capacities. Work of a social or cultural anthropological kind is included if firmly embedded in a cognitive framework. Given the interdisciplinarity of the focal issues, relevant research will come from linguistics, philosophy of language, theoretical and experimental pragmatics, psychology and child development. The series aims to reflect all kinds of research in the relevant fields – conceptual, analytical and experimental.

Titles include:

Anton Benz, Gerhard Jäger and Robert van Rooij (*editors*)
GAME THEORY AND PRAGMATICS

Reinhard Blutner and Henk Zeevat (*editors*)
OPTIMALITY THEORY AND PRAGMATICS

Siobhan Chapman and Billy Clark (*editors*)
PRAGMATIC LITERARY STYLISTICS

María J. Frápolli (*editor*)
SAYING, MEANING AND REFERRING
Essays on François Recanati's Philosophy of Language

Anamaria Falaus
ALTERNATIVES IN SEMANTICS

Corinne Iten
LINGUISTIC MEANING, TRUTH CONDITIONS AND RELEVANCE
The Case of Concessives

Mark Jary
ASSERTION

Ira Noveck and Dan Sperber (*editors*)
EXPERIMENTAL PRAGMATICS

Klaus Petrus (*editor*)
MEANING AND ANALYSIS
New Essays on Grice

George Powell
LANGUAGE, THOUGHT AND REFERENCE

Uli Sauerland and Penka Stateva (*editors*)
PRESUPPOSITION AND IMPLICATURE IN COMPOSITIONAL SEMANTICS

Uli Sauerland and Kazuko Yatsushiro (*editors*)
SEMANTICS AND PRAGMATICS
From Experiment to Theory

Hans-Christian Schmitz
ACCENTUATION AND INTERPRETATION

Belén Soria and Esther Romero (*editors*)
EXPLICIT COMMUNICATION
Robyn Carston's Pragmatics

Christoph Unger
GENRE, RELEVANCE AND GLOBAL COHERENCE
The Pragmatics of Discourse Type

Palgrave Studies in Pragmatics, Language and Cognition Series
Series Standing Order ISBN 978–0–333–99010–0 Hardback
978–0–333–98584–7 Paperback
(*outside North America only*)

You can receive future titles in this series as they are published by placing a standing order. Please contact your bookseller or, in case of difficulty, write to us at the address below with your name and address, the title of the series and the ISBN quoted above.

Customer Services Department, Macmillan Distribution Ltd, Houndmills, Basingstoke, Hampshire RG21 6XS, England

To renew, please telephone: **01904 770406**
with your ID Card Number
or email: **lc-helpdesk@yorkcollege.ac.uk**

Pragmatic Literary Stylistics

Edited by

Siobhan Chapman
University of Liverpool, UK

Billy Clark
Middlesex University, UK

palgrave
macmillan

First published 2014 by
PALGRAVE MACMILLAN

Palgrave Macmillan in the UK is an imprint of Macmillan Publishers Limited, registered in England, company number 785998, of Houndmills, Basingstoke, Hampshire RG21 6XS.

Palgrave Macmillan in the US is a division of St Martin's Press LLC, 175 Fifth Avenue, New York, NY 10010.

Palgrave Macmillan is the global academic imprint of the above companies and has companies and representatives throughout the world.

Palgrave® and Macmillan® are registered trademarks in the United States, the United Kingdom, Europe and other countries.

ISBN 978–1–137–02325–4

This book is printed on paper suitable for recycling and made from fully managed and sustained forest sources. Logging, pulping and manufacturing processes are expected to conform to the environmental regulations of the country of origin.

A catalogue record for this book is available from the British Library.

Library of Congress Cataloging-in-Publication Data
Pragmatic Literary Stylistics / edited by Siobhan Chapman, University of Liverpool, UK ; Billy Clark, Middlesex University, UK.
pages cm. — (Palgrave Studies in Pragmatics, Language and Cognition)
Summary: "Pragmatic Literary Stylistics considers the ways in which current theories of language in use and communicative processes are applied to the analysis, interpretation and definition of literary texts. The contributors draw on a wide range of contemporary pragmatic theories, including relevance theory, Gricean and neo-Gricean theory and politeness theory and utilise a variety of different types and genres of literary text in their analysis, including prose fiction, drama and poetry. An introductory chapter locates the book with respect to the history and current state of the field, and puts forward proposals for future direction. This book offers examples of some of the most important current types of interaction between pragmatics and literary stylistics which sets an agenda for the future of pragmatic literary stylistics and provides a foundation for future research and debate" — Provided by publisher.
Includes bibliographical references.
ISBN 978–1–137–02325–4 (hardback)
1. Linguistics in literature. 2. Language and languages in literature. I. Chapman, Siobhan, 1968– editor. II. Clark, Billy, editor.
PN56.L27P73 2014
809'.9334—dc23 2014019523

Contents

Figures

Contributors

Andrew Caink is Principal Lecturer in English Language and Linguistics at the University of Westminster. He has previously lectured at the universities of Durham, Lapland and Wolverhampton, and taught English Language in Finland, Poland and Bulgaria. His research interests are in literary pragmatics, particularly relevance-theoretic approaches to narrative and literary value, and theoretical linguistics, particularly generative syntax.

Siobhan Chapman is Professor of English at the University of Liverpool. She has previously taught at the universities of Newcastle and Kent. Her research and teaching interests are in the areas of pragmatics, particularly Gricean and neo-Gricean theory; philosophy of language, particularly twentieth century analysis; and stylistics, particularly the pragmatics of literature.

Billy Clark is Reader in English Language and Linguistics at Middlesex University. He has previously taught at Goldsmiths University of London, the University of Oxford and University College London. His research and teaching interests are in the areas of linguistic semantics and pragmatics, with a particular interest in relevance theory; stylistics; philosophy of language; and prosodic meaning.

Anne Furlong is Associate Professor at the University of Prince Edward Island. Her research applies relevance theory to literary interpretation and theatrical performance. Publications include '"It's not quite what I had in mind": Adaptation, faithfulness, and interpretation', 'The soul of wit', and 'A modest proposal: Linguistics and literary studies'.

Barbara MacMahon is Senior Lecturer in the English department at Sheffield Hallam University, and previously worked at the universities of Huddersfield, Northampton and León. She teaches and researches in literary linguistics and pragmatics, with particular interests in literary forms of metarepresentation and the role of sound patterning in poetry.

Lisa Nahajec is Lecturer in English Language at Liverpool Hope University. She has previously taught at Coventry University and the

University of Huddersfield. She teaches discourse analysis, media language and the structure of language and her research interests include pragmatics, stylistics and linguistic negation. Previous publications include 'Negation and the creation of implicit meaning in poetry' (*Language and Literature*).

Maria-Eirini Panagiotidou is Assistant Professor of Linguistics at West Chester University, USA. She holds a PhD in linguistics from the University of Nottingham, UK, and has taught at Virginia Commonwealth University and the University of Maryland, University College. Her research interests and publications lie in the areas of literary linguistics, cognitive poetics, intertextuality and ekphrastic poetry.

David Peplow is Lecturer in English Language at Sheffield Hallam University. His research interests are socio-linguistics and stylistics, and his teaching reflects this. He is currently leading an inter-disciplinary research project looking into the benefits of reading for care home residents. He studied for his PhD at the University of Nottingham, receiving full funding from the AHRC to conduct this research.

Ruth Schuldiner is a Postdoctoral Fellow in English at East Tennessee State University, having completed her doctorate at the University of Oxford. She has previously taught at the universities of Oxford and Westminster. Her teaching and research interests are focused on pragmatics and narrative, particularly in relation to the 19th-century novel.

Chantelle Warner is Assistant Professor of German and Applied Linguistics at the University of Arizona. Her research and teaching interests cross the fields of literary and linguistic study, focusing on the connections between style, pragmatics and social power. Her previous publications include *The Pragmatics of Literary Testimony: Authenticity Effects in German Social Autobiographies*.

1
Introduction: Pragmatic Literary Stylistics

Siobhan Chapman and Billy Clark

Pragmatics is an aspect of the study of language in use. It is concerned with how language users interact, communicate and interpret linguistic behaviour. Literary stylistics is the study of how close attention to language use can contribute to accounts of how texts are understood and evaluated. Yet despite the apparent overlaps and commonalities of interest between the two disciplines, there has, until now, been relatively little work that brings them together, or that explores the interface between them. This interface is central to the ten separate essays brought together in this volume, all representative of recent significant developments within the field that we are here naming 'pragmatic literary stylistics'.[1]

Pragmatic literary stylistics is developing within the framework of a broader range of work which has been termed the 'cognitive humanities' (examples of work in this area include: Turner 1998, 2006; Hogan 2003; Palmer 2004, 2010; Zunshine 2006, 2012; see also the recently established research network at: http://coghumanities.com). Like other areas of the cognitive humanities, pragmatic literary stylistics draws on a number of more established fields. Stylistics is an interdisciplinary enterprise which involves applying ideas from linguistics in the study of how texts are produced, understood and evaluated, and in addressing theoretical questions associated with this. It necessarily has many branches, both because of the wide range of genres, modes and purposes of the texts that are the object of study for stylistics, and because of the variety of frameworks from linguistics within which they can be analysed. Pragmatic literary stylistics is one such branch. Both adjectives are necessary to identify it; not all pragmatic stylistics focuses on literary texts, and not all literary stylistics applies ideas from pragmatics. The theoretical and analytical tools of stylistics in general and of pragmatic stylistics in particular can be applied to any kind of text. Literary texts, meanwhile, can be discussed in relation to a wide range of descriptive and analytical tools developed in linguistics, for instance, in relation to their semantic, grammatical, phonological or lexical properties. In principle all types of analysis might play a role in the discussion of any linguistic text and in practice any such discussion is likely to involve more than one type of analysis. The essays collected here are distinguished by the fact that some specific area of linguistic pragmatic theory plays a key role in their analysis of one or more literary text or texts.

In this introduction, we offer a brief overview of the development of pragmatic theory and of some of its main present-day branches. We consider some of the pioneering and the more recent ways in which individual researchers have experimented with applying different areas of pragmatic theory to the analysis of literary texts and we examine the very recent increase in interest in this area which is reflected in this collection. We then outline what we see as some of the fundamental assumptions, or underlying tenets, which characterise our understanding of pragmatic literary stylistics. It is these assumptions that we envisage will drive future initiatives and shape the future development of the field. The introduction concludes with brief summaries of the individual chapters.

The motivating force behind the initial establishment and the subsequent development of modern pragmatics was to find a systematic explanation for observable differences between literal, linguistic meaning (a notion which has been problematised in more recent work) and the meanings that particular utterances can convey in context. Individuals working in pragmatics have pursued such an explanation for a variety of reasons; they have variously been driven by philosophical, linguistic or sociological interests. But the shared goals of pragmaticists have been to establish the ways in which what words literally mean and what speakers may use them to mean may differ, to identify some principles or norms of language use which might explain those differences, and perhaps to offer some explanation as to why such differences typically occur in various communicative situations.

In the middle part of the 20th century, Oxford philosophers J. L. Austin and H. P. Grice separately established some central tenets and introduced some signal terminology of pragmatics. Work over the past several decades has questioned, revised and extended Austin's and Grice's specific ideas, but their work remains foundational to the discipline. Austin (1962) established the basis of what has become known as Speech Act Theory when he drew attention to what he saw as a generally overlooked distinction between what words mean, a matter of their form, and what they may be used to do, a matter of their function. Austin distinguished further between linguistic meaning (which he termed the 'locutionary act' on any occasion of speaking), the function of an utterance intended by the speaker (the 'illocutionary act') and the outcome, result or effect on the hearer of the utterance (the 'perlocutionary act'). To use one of Austin's own examples, if a speaker utters 'You can't do that', it is possible to report the locutionary act simply by stating what words were spoken and specifying the references of 'you' and 'that'. To report the illocutionary act, however, it is necessary to refer to what the speaker was doing in using those words: for instance 'He protested against my doing it'. To describe the perlocutionary act, it is necessary to describe what happened to the hearer next: 'He checked me', 'He stopped me', or perhaps 'He annoyed me' (Austin 1962: 102).

Grice (1975, 1989) distinguished 'what is said' on any particular occasion of utterance from 'what is implicated', introducing the technical term 'implicature' to describe the very specific type of non-literal meaning with which he was concerned. For Grice, implicatures typically arise as a result of a mutual, if tacit, expectation of cooperation between speaker and hearer; the hearer can justifiably assume that the speaker is abiding by a general principle of cooperation, which is further elaborated in terms of specific maxims relating to the quantity, quality and relation of information given and the manner in which that information is expressed. Apparently overt or ostentatious breaches, or 'flouts', of the conversational maxims, resulting in the need for the hearer to reconsider or reinterpret what has been said, will typically explain how and why many conversational implicatures occur. For instance, Grice suggests that a statement such as 'War is war', a tautology which is apparently entirely uninformative, flouts assumptions concerning the quantity of information speakers are expected to offer. Rather than simply dismiss this utterance as uncooperative, the hearer is likely to seek an alternative interpretation that is informative and therefore cooperative and will access various implicatures about the nature of war and the speaker's attitude to it (Grice 1989: 33).

Since Austin and Grice, pragmatics is usually divided into two groups: 'neo-Gricean' approaches such as those developed by Horn (1984, 1988, 1989, 2004) and Levinson (1987, 2000) which assume a set of principles sharing properties of Grice's maxims, and 'post-Gricean' approaches such as relevance theory (Sperber and Wilson 1986/1995) which do not. Neo-Gricean frameworks differ from each other in many specifics of terminology and in how they partition types of meaning, but they generally share a commitment to some version of the distinction between 'what is said' and 'what is implicated'. They attempt to establish general principles which explain the various ways in which these types of meaning may differ, while trying to reduce Grice's list of maxims to a more modest and more clearly motivated number; Horn's pragmatic system, for instance, has two principles, the Q-Principle and the R-Principle, while Levinson's has three, the Q-, I- and M-Principles. Approaches such as relevance theory are termed merely 'post-Gricean' since the pragmatic principles they propose are not 'maxim-like'. In the case of relevance theory, the two key principles are understood as law-like generalisations about human behaviour. The Cognitive Principle of Relevance is a generalisation about cognition in general (claiming that cognitive processes are geared towards the maximisation of 'relevance' as defined by the theory). The Communicative Principle is a generalisation about the processing of 'ostensive-inferential' communication (which is seen as giving rise to fairly precise expectations of relevance). A third area of work, on politeness (now often termed 'im/politeness' since the focus is as much on how utterances can be seen as impolite as on how they can be seen as polite), draws partly on Austin's classification of utterances into different types of speech acts and partly on Goffman's (1955) work on the notion of 'face' as adopted and developed in the work of Brown and Levinson (1987). It is usually associated with Gricean or neo-Gricean frameworks (see, for example, Culpeper 1996, 2011; Bousfield 2008; Bousfield and Locher 2008), but there has also been post-Gricean work on politeness (e.g. Escandell-Vidal 1996, 1998; Jary 1998; Nowik 2005, 2008; Christie 2007). Im/politeness theory is concerned with the various ways in which speakers may choose to defend or attack different aspects of their own face and that of other participants in a communicative situation, the consequences these choices have for how different types of acts are performed and their social impact.

These various branches of pragmatics are fundamentally theoretical in nature, concerned with general questions of how meaning is to be analysed, demarcated and explained. But each framework has been applied to a range of different text and discourse types, and almost from the start this has included the analysis of literary texts. Just a year after Grice's theory of conversation first appeared in published form, van Dijk suggested that the Gricean maxims 'partly concern the structure of the utterance itself, and might therefore be called "stylistic"' (van Dijk 1976: 44); he argued in favour of exploring the potential of a Gricean-style approach to the analysis of the interaction between writers and readers of literary texts. This type of approach has been sustained over the decades (e.g. Pratt 1977; Gautam and Sharma 1986; Cooper 1998; Blake 2002). As pointed out by Leech and Short (1981: 231–254), a Gricean approach can be applied both to interaction between writers and readers and to interaction between characters (any account of the latter, of course, being necessarily embedded within an account of the writer–reader interaction).

Similarly, the potential of relevance theory to offer insights into the reception and interpretation of literary texts was recognised from the start. Sperber and Wilson (1995: 202–224) discuss ways in which the theory can account for the effects of different stylistic choices and discuss the 'poetic effects' associated with weak implicatures. They do not themselves apply relevance theory to the analysis of any specific literary texts, but this was quickly taken up in subsequent work (e.g. Pilkington 1992, 2000; Blakemore 1993, 2008, 2009; Clark 1996, 2009; MacMahon 1996, 2001, 2007, 2009a, 2009b; Keeble 2005; Blass 2006; Bursey and Furlong 2006). There has, in contrast, been surprisingly little work in pragmatic stylistics situated within a neo-Gricean framework, but there is some evidence of a recent growth in interest in this area; for example, possible applications of neo-Gricean developments to literary stylistics have been explored by Israel (2011) and Chapman (2012).

Politeness theory has proved a valuable framework for analysing literary texts from a range of different genres. Work in this area has generally considered how awareness of and response to various types of face-related behaviour established in literary texts can affect how those texts are structured, narrated or constructed. Some of this work has focused on relationships that are established between narrators and readers, and how the presumed face needs of these two participants in the communicative interaction are addressed (e.g. Sell 1985; Simpson 1989). Other work has used politeness theory to describe and explain the development of relationships between characters, often the driving forces of change and of plot (e.g. Culpeper 1998; Blake 2002; Bousfield 2007; Bousfield and McIntyre 2011). While work on pragmatic literary stylistics has continued throughout the years, there has been an increased interest in this area in recent years and an associated increase in the variety of pragmatic frameworks employed and text types analysed. A Pragmatic Stylistics Special Interest Group was established at the Poetics and Linguistics Association in 2010 and has since run three workshops. This followed a one-off workshop at Middlesex University in 2008 and a number of workshops and conferences have focused on this area since, including a panel at the International Pragmatics

Association (IPrA) in Manchester in 2011, conferences in Nitra in 2008 and 2013, and a workshop at Sussex University in 2012. Morini (2009) developed a sustained analysis of a single author drawing on pragmatic theory. A mainstream stylistics journal, *Journal of Literary Semantics*, recently dedicated a special issue to inference and implicature in literary interpretation (Caink and Clark 2012).

There have, however, been surprisingly few publications which reflect the range of potential offered by pragmatic literary stylistics. Despite the appearance of it as an element of other texts (e.g. Lambrou and Stockwell 2007), we know of only one other edited collection focusing entirely on literary pragmatics (Sell 1991) and the present volume is the first collection to reflect the recent increased activity in this area. Apart from its relative novelty, the breadth of papers gathered in this volume represents a significant contribution to this developing research area. It contains work based on all of the approaches outlined above and concerned with the genres of prose, poetry and drama. It also exemplifies another type of broadening of interest in the field.

Like literary stylistics and other forms of stylistics in general, pragmatic literary stylistics has so far tended to focus on interpretation. This collection, too, includes a number of studies that concentrate on possible interpretations of specific literary texts, or on the elucidation of actual interpretations and responses from previous readers, critics and reviewers. However, the studies presented here reflect a recent broadening of the scope of work in this area and, as discussed below, the topics covered are not restricted to consideration of interpretations.

We have made several key assumptions in developing our own work on pragmatic literary stylistics and in preparing this volume. One is that the aim of pragmatic literary stylistics, like that of stylistics in general, is not to offer new readings or to suggest interpretations or evaluations that have not been identified by literary critics and other readers. Rather, the aim is to understand and explain how such readings, interpretations and evaluations arise, develop and spread. Most of the studies in this volume draw on what has been said by critics and reviewers of the texts under discussion. A striking feature of this approach is the way in which pragmatic theory can often explain and substantiate such responses and intuitive interpretations. The terminology and explanatory mechanisms developed in the largely theoretical and relatively abstract discipline of pragmatics are often capable of elucidating why readers respond to texts as they do. This is one way in which linguistic theory can profitably interact with the actual business of producing and interpreting language by actual users for communicative purposes. We should add that, despite this general assumption and perhaps in tension with it, we believe that ideas from pragmatics could potentially play a role in adjudicating between competing interpretations.

Another key assumption concerns theoretical and methodological eclecticism. There is a growing commitment in various branches of linguistic analysis to the idea that theorists and analysts should be open to a wide range of possible approaches, adopting frameworks which seem to help with addressing specific questions rather than sticking closely to one approach (see, for instance, Jeffries 2000). Like many stylisticians, we endorse this view and believe that different approaches should not necessarily be seen as 'competing' approaches from which a 'winner' needs to be chosen. Rather, we would suggest that specific approaches adopted should be those which seem to provide insights into the specific phenomena being considered. The final assumption we discuss here is our belief that work in pragmatic literary stylistics can constitute not only an application of specific pragmatic theories but also a way of shedding light on their nature and, to some extent, of testing them.

We are both aware of and interested in the apparent tensions between the assumptions identified above: that pragmatic literary stylistics is not in the business of generating interpretations but that it may nevertheless adjudicate between interpretations, and that pragmatic literary stylistics is rooted in theoretical eclecticism but is also a potential tool for testing and evaluating specific theories. We consider the discussion and possible resolution of these tensions to be important topics in the ongoing development of the discipline of pragmatic literary stylistics; we briefly expand on this below.

We are consistent with many other contemporary stylisticians in supporting the view that the task of stylistics is primarily to explain how different audiences arrive at the understandings that they do rather than to generate readings. While work in literary studies has often aimed to generate readings or interpretations, for example by considering texts in the light of particular frameworks adopted from elsewhere (such as psychoanalysis, Marxism or structuralism), work in stylistics aims rather to account for ways in which readers respond to texts whether or not they are aware of particular literary interpretative or linguistic frameworks. Pragmatic stylistics can play an important role here since it has something to say about how particular sets of contextual assumptions interact with linguistically encoded meanings to give rise to interpretations. Contrasting interpretations might arise when the contextual assumptions accessible to different readers are significantly different. An obvious example would be where allegorical interpretations depend on the accessibility of specific sets of contextual assumptions; for a recent discussion (in French) of a text with allegorical interpretations, see Hamilton and Crisp's (2013) discussion of Jean Paul Sartre's *Les Mouches*. *Les Mouches* is an adaptation of the Greek Electra myth (represented in Ancient Greek drama by Aeschylus, Euripides and Sophocles) which can be understood allegorically by audiences who notice connections with the occupation of France during the Second World War. Audiences without access to contextual assumptions about the occupation, and the fact that Sartre wrote his version during the period of the occupation, might not arrive at the allegorical understanding.

Despite our endorsement of this fairly standard view in stylistics, we believe that techniques from pragmatic stylistics might be used for the secondary task of developing arguments in support of particular readings. While such arguments have not been developed in much detail so far, Durant (2010) develops arguments about how ideas from the study of linguistic meaning in general can be used in developing understanding of particular kinds of contested meaning and of contributing to adjudications among contested interpretations. His discussion suggests further ways in which this might be achieved in future work. A key aspect of this work will involve consideration of the cultural contexts in which work is produced and understood, which is a topic addressed in some of the chapters gathered here (particularly those by Peplow and Warner).

As we have said, we also endorse arguments for theoretical eclecticism, such as those developed by Jeffries (2000). As Jeffries points out, the development of scientific theories is always an ongoing process. A new theory rarely invalidates all aspects of previous theories and is not generally assumed to be 'correct' or final. She takes as an example the emergence of Einstein's theory of relativity:

> One non-linguistic example of this is Newtonian physics, which was superseded by Einstein's theory of relativity. The Newtonian model still works for calculations within a certain range of space and speed, and to that extent is still used for practical purposes like aeroplane flight and even getting rockets to the moon. What Einstein did, however, was create the model needed for calculations of speed nearer to the speed of light and useful, therefore, for longer journeys into space.
>
> (Jeffries 2000: 5)

She goes on to suggest that we can even adopt assumptions we do not believe for some purposes, for example reasoning as if the Earth were flat when reading maps in many contexts.

When work in stylistics is concerned with specific aspects of production or response, the main aim is to account for the phenomenon being explored rather than to develop as accurate a theory as possible. The question to ask when analysing a text is not whether the theory being applied is 'correct' (strictly speaking, a better theoretical model than alternatives) but whether it helps to explain the particular features being considered. To take one simple example, we might be able to develop a useful account of an ironic utterance using either Grice's account, which is based on the assumption that irony flouts a maxim of quality (roughly, that the speaker is purporting to say something false in order to implicate an opposite proposition), or using the relevance-theoretic approach based on the notion of echoic use (roughly that the speaker is implicitly expressing a dissociative attitude to an implicitly attributed proposition). The decision about which framework to use for this purpose can be separated from the task of assessing how well each approach accounts for irony in general.

However, we also believe that stylistic analysis has a role to play in testing particular theoretical frameworks. To risk stating the obvious, any framework which constantly failed to be applicable in describing aspects of textual production or interpretation would not look convincing as a theoretical approach. More significantly, the resistance to analysis of particular phenomena might suggest amendments to current theories. It is easy, for example, to find examples of irony which cannot be accounted for using the traditional Gricean approach in which the communicator is seen as implicating the opposite of what she purports to be saying. Another example can be found in recent work by Carston (e.g. Carston 2010) which aims to develop the relevance-theoretic account of metaphor in the light of examples which do not seem to be fully accounted for by existing relevance-theoretic approaches. Examples she considers include extended metaphors where the literal understanding of expressions seems to play a role in comprehension.

An example in this collection is Chapman's application of neo-Gricean pragmatics to a particular issue in a particular literary text. The main analytical focus of the chapter is the potential of the text to communicate attitudes to a particular situation despite, or indeed because of, the fact that the situation is not addressed directly, or is described only in vague or nonspecific terms. But in its handling of this issue, the chapter lends support to fairly recent claims in the field of neo-Gricean pragmatics. Specifically, it endorses theoretical proposals that quantity implicatures, including what are sometimes known as scalar implicatures, are much more specific to particular communicative events, and dependent on wider stretches of context, than was originally recognised by, for instance, Horn.

Using pragmatic theories as approaches to literary texts shows that there are more than simply theoretical motivations, questions of economy and so on, in developing and evaluating pragmatic theory. Just as pragmatics can offer insights into the interpretation of literary texts, or explain the more intuitive insights of literary critics, so encounters with literary texts may suggest ways in which pragmatic theories can be developed, refined and adapted. One area where we envisage important developments in future work is in exploring the tension between the aims of developing specific analyses or understanding and of testing specific theoretical approaches.

In keeping with the diverse and wide-ranging properties of pragmatic literary stylistics discussed above, the chapters in this volume engage with a number of different pragmatic frameworks and a wide variety of different literary texts. As such they display something of the range of possible approaches and types of analysis of which pragmatic literary stylistics is capable, and of the types of critical and interpretative questions with which it can engage. But they also show certain recurrent topics or interests that are held in common by a number of different chapters. These include the use and interpretation of different types of negation, the significance of personal and social context to reader interpretation and the role of 'rereading' in literary interpretation and evaluation.

Andrew Caink's 'The art of repetition in Muriel Spark's telling' considers the function and interpretative possibilities of different types of repetition in prose fiction. Caink analyses passages from three of Spark's novels: *The Ballad of Peckham Rye, The Prime of Miss Jean Brodie* and *Loitering with Intent*. He discusses these in relation to repetition at three different levels: individual lexical repetition, sentential repetition and the repetition of larger sections of text, including repetitions-with-variation, a feature of the novels which Caink links to the oral storytelling tradition. Working within a relevance-theoretic framework, he is concerned with two sets of questions. First, he considers specific questions about the role of repetition in shaping Spark's distinctive style, in constructing her narratives and in manipulating her readers' responses to her novels in terms of the inferences they draw from them. Second, he considers questions about understanding and explaining the aesthetics of narrative in pragmatic terms. In both cases, he is concerned with the reader's contribution both to the structuring of an extended narrative and to the aesthetic effects that it achieves. Caink also uses his analyses of Spark's novels to consider the role of the non-spontaneous response of re-reading in literary reading and interpretation, in relation to pragmatic theory.

Siobhan Chapman's chapter, '"Oh, do let's talk about something else-": What is not said and what is implicated in Elizabeth Bowen's *The Last September*', employs a neo-Gricean approach, specifically the one developed by Horn (1972, 2006, 2007), to explore effects derived from things that are not said in Bowen's novel. Chapman focuses in particular on how important effects follow from avoiding direct discussion of a specific topic: the armed conflict in Ireland which is continuing in 1920 during the period in which the novel is set. The cases she examines most closely are those where the seriousness of the situation is implicitly denied or reduced and where implicatures follow from one or more characters not speaking. As Chapman points out, this phenomenon has been discussed by critics before but not analysed formally from a pragmatic stylistic point of view.

In 'Before and after Chekhov: Inference, interpretation and evaluation', Billy Clark draws both on personal and critical reactions, and also on the empirical evidence offered by his experiences of teaching final year undergraduates, in analysing responses to Chekhov's story *The Lady with the Little Dog*. He uses relevance theory in order to describe and explain some of the inferential processes that readers may employ in understanding and judging the story. The story itself makes an interesting subject for such a study because many readers report initially finding it trivial or unimpressive, before later coming to adjust their judgement of it and value it as an impressive piece of literary art. Clark uses a relevance-theoretic account of reader inferences to discuss and offer a possible explanation of the story's reception. He also explores two themes new to pragmatic literary stylistics: the differences between inferences made on first reading and those on subsequent readings of literary texts; and the extent to which inferential processes contribute to the evaluation of literary texts. Widening the discussion beyond the specific story by Chekhov, Clark draws on Sperber's (1996) ideas about the representation of cultural assumptions in order to discuss the ways in which specific literary texts are valued by individuals and by cultures. He argues that an account of individual inferential processes can contribute to explanations of this wider cultural process.

In 'Outsourcing: A relevance-theoretic account of the interpretation of theatrical texts', Anne Furlong argues that plays should primarily be understood and analysed as performances rather than as written texts. In support of her argument she focuses on two plays: Strindberg's *Miss Julie* and Ibsen's *A Doll's House*. She explores the ways in which relevance theory can explain not only some of the problems that these plays pose to directors and actors, but also some of the ways in which these problems might be addressed in performance. Furlong argues that 'non-spontaneous interpretation', which is aimed at maximal rather than optimal relevance, may play a significant part in directors', actors' and indeed playgoers' understandings of a play in performance. The 'outsourcing' of Furlong's title describes the process by which dramatists rely on both directors and actors to convey and in fact to determine at least part of their communicative functions. It is in performance, for instance, that evidence for interpretation provided by the text is supplemented by features such as prosody, movement, facial expression and spatial relations. Furlong argues that this process necessitates analysing performances as a whole in order to understand such collaboratively intended interpretations. It also points to the fact that students of literature should be taught to analyse and interpret plays as performances, rather than in the same ways as they would analyse purely text-based genres such as poetry and prose fiction.

Barbara MacMahon's discussion in 'Relevance theory, syntax and literary narrative' is centred on the analysis of an extended textual extract from A. S. Byatt's novel *The Children's Book*. MacMahon focuses on syntax, a strictly linguistic feature of her chosen text, but she argues that the effects of formal features such as this can be fully understood only in relation to pragmatics, concerned as the latter is with questions of communication and interpretation. She draws on relevance theory, with its emphasis on the interaction between linguistic form and context, and also on the concept of 'metarepresentation', taken from cognitive psychology (Cosmides and Tooby 2000; Sperber 2000), in her consideration of the effects of embedding various levels of narrative within a text. Her focus is on the ways in which Byatt constructs the contrasting characters and the voices of the two child protagonists. She analyses the syntactic structuring both of the directly reported speech attributed to the two children and also of those passages of the narrative that might be read as metarepresentative of thought, as free indirect thought attributed to one of the characters, which may function to establish narrator–character alignment. McMahon concludes that relevance theory is well placed to explain how the implications of choices in syntax at each level of representation in a text such as Byatt's novel can become available to the reader as relatively weaker or stronger implicatures. Such communicative possibilities are available in a variety of different genres of texts, but are particularly salient to the description and interpretation of prose fiction, because of its tendency to include embedded metarepresentations.

In 'Negation, expectation and characterisation: Analysing the role of negation in character construction in *To Kill a Mockingbird* (Lee 1960) and *Stark* (Elton 1989)', Lisa Nahajec is one of the contributors to this volume (along with Chapman and Schuldiner) to consider the implications and interpretative effects of different types of negation in literary texts. In this case, Nahajec focuses on the ways in which negative statements are used to defeat possible expectations about characters and thereby to construct specific alternative characterisations. She adopts Givón's (2001) account of negation as presuppositional, in that it introduces a pragmatic presupposition that the negated proposition is in some way expected or assumed, and uses the framework of Gricean pragmatics to explain the communicative effects of evoking but denying expected character traits. Nahajec gives an overview of work on linguistic negation and of work on characterisation, before analysing a passage from each of her chosen texts. Both passages focus on the description of a particular character and both make significant use of negative statements in the construction of those characters and, in the case of Lee's novel, of the first person narrator. Negative statements are, at least at the level of 'what is said', relatively uninformative, but they may nevertheless give rise to implicatures in context which are highly informative both about the expectations and assumptions of some 'ideal addressee' and about the features of a specific character in relation to these expectations. Moreover, the positive proposition which has been evoked but negated is not simply replaced by the implicated meaning, but is retained as the character is constructed in the ongoing discourse between narrator and reader.

In 'Intertextuality and the pragmatics of literary reading', Maria-Eirini Panagiotidou develops an approach based on work in cognitive linguistics (Evans 2006, 2009) to explore intertextuality understood primarily as a relationship between texts and readers. Intertextuality is established by the cognitive processes of readers and triggered by lexical items and the models they provide access to. Readers are seen as active agents giving rise to intertextuality and not merely passive receivers of authorial intentions, although the intentions of authors and cotextual factors, do, of course, also play a role in this process.

In '"I've never enjoyed hating a book so much in my life": The co-construction of reader identity in the reading group', David Peplow considers some ways in which readers respond to books beyond the initial reading, focusing on discussions carried out by members of a book group. He focuses on how identity is constructed and expressed in this context but also considers the nature of the language used and how interpretation and evaluation are affected by assumptions about taste and identity. The chapter contributes to the understanding of reading as a social activity and of how reading is affected by contextual factors beyond those generated by the text itself.

Ruth Schuldiner's chapter, 'The narrative tease: Narratorial omniscience, implicature and sensation in *Lady Audley's Secret*', shares with Chapman's chapter an interest in effects created by what is not explicitly communicated in a work of prose fiction. Taking a relevance-theoretic approach, Schuldiner shows that key aspects of the plot of *Lady Audley's Secret* are communicated implicitly and that the fact that they are implicated is salient to readers. The combination of an omniscient narrator and the absence of key information means that readers infer that the narrator is deliberately withholding key information. Schuldiner explores some of the effects of this technique, including a dark humour which follows from developing the narrative in this way. She also points out that this novel anticipates some key features of detective fiction developed in the work of Wilkie Collins (1868) and others.

Chantelle Warner's chapter, 'Literature as discourse and dialogue: Rapport management (facework) in Emine Sevgi Özdamar's "Blackeye and His Donkey"', shares with Peplow's chapter an interest in the relations between texts and social contexts. While Peplow focuses mainly on reading and reader discussions, Warner considers literary texts, and the act of writing, as dialogic acts contributing to the construction and management of face, identity and rapport. Warner uses ideas from a number of approaches, including relevance-theoretic pragmatics, but her approach is primarily based on ideas developed in work on politeness and impoliteness, most importantly the notions of facework, rapport and sociality rights. Adopting ideas developed by Bousfield (2008; Bousfield and Locher 2008), Culpeper (2011) and Spencer-Oatey (2004, 2005, 2007, 2009), she shows that Özdamar's vignette can be seen as an act of 'aggressive facework' which highlights a threat to her own face by the editors who invited her to write the piece and that the publication of the piece she submitted can be seen as an attempt by the editors to redress this. More generally, this chapter highlights the importance of considering literary writing as a social act and how focusing on these aspects of pragmatics can contribute to our understanding of literary discourse.

The range of topics covered by these chapters is broad, demonstrating that pragmatic approaches to literary stylistics can help to develop understanding of local writing and reading practice, of interpretation and evaluation, of the effects of specific textual phenomena, of texts as social acts and their role in the social practice of writers and readers. Each chapter combines the development of specific points and analyses with suggestions for further work along the lines developed in each case. Overall, the chapters demonstrate that work in pragmatic literary stylistics has significant contributions to make to pragmatic theory in general, to stylistics and to literary studies. The chapters collected here reflect the significant increase in work in pragmatic literary stylistics in recent years and also suggest new directions for significant and wide-ranging work in years to come.

Note

1. We are very grateful to Derek Bousfield and Dan McIntyre for helpful comments and suggestions on this introduction. We would also like to thank Olivia Middleton, Libby Forrest, Devasena Vedamurthi and other colleagues at Palgrave Macmillan for their help and positive encouragement while we prepared this collection.

2
The Art of Repetition in Muriel Spark's Telling

Andrew Caink

1 Introduction

This chapter focuses on repetition in extended prose fiction with a view to achieving two things. First, it seeks to capture significant facets of Muriel Spark's narrative style and draw out patterns in her exploitation of the reader's cognitive processes. Second, the interest is in developing a greater understanding of the aesthetics of an extended narrative in pragmatic terms from a relevance-theoretic perspective (Sperber and Wilson 1995; Clark 1996, 2013; Pilkington 2000). Given the nature of inferencing, we are therefore examining the contribution required of the reader in the construction of narrative and its aesthetic effects (Toolan 2001; Fabb 2002). I examine lexical, sentential and section repetition in three of Spark's most acclaimed novels and, in the final section, consider briefly a pragmatic account of re-reading (Furlong 1996, 2008).

The Ballad of Peckham Rye (Spark 1960; henceforth *Ballad*) recounts the influence of Dougal Douglas on the community of Peckham. Douglas is a figure who divides characters between those who are charmed by and those who are contemptuous of his novel methods and pronouncements. Employed by local factories to improve output, he is eventually 'run out of town'. One of the influences ascribed to Douglas is the disruption of Dixie and Humphrey's wedding ceremony with which the novel opens.

The Prime of Miss Jean Brodie (Spark 1961; henceforth *Prime*) focuses on the eponymous primary school teacher and a group of schoolgirls who remain under her influence throughout the thirties. The girls form an elite 'set' who are included in Brodie's intrigues with colleagues up until her forced resignation that results from the 'betrayal' of one of the girls,

Sandy. This character later enters a convent as Sister Helena and receives visitors during the late 1950s long after Brodie's death.

The narrative of *Loitering with Intent* (Spark 1981) centres on the intrigues of the Autobiographical Association, a club led by the dominating and manipulative Sir Quentin, and its secretary Fleur, the first person narrator. Fleur is a budding writer and the central premise of the novel is that characters and events begin to mirror characters and events in the novel she is writing. The trope is reminiscent of Spark's first novel, *The Comforters* (Spark 1957), in which a character, Caroline Rose, becomes aware that she is a character in a novel, hearing the typewriter and the repetition of her own thoughts.

Section 2 considers some aspects of Spark's use of lexical repetition and reviews a relevance-theoretic account of the effects of such repetition on the reader and the contribution it may make to the perception of narrative structure and inferred meanings. Sentential repetition in *Loitering with Intent* is the focus of Section 3 where the shift in likely inferences at each repetition are mapped out. Sections 4 and 5 examine the repetition of whole sections in novels: Section 4 considers the contribution that section repetitions make in the non-linguistic structure of the narratives, whilst Section 5 discusses the way in which non-verbatim repetition may provide evidence for inferred meanings and the role of repetition in the communication of non-propositional feelings. Section 6 discusses the extent to which re-reading a text is a form of repetition and Section 7 provides a concluding summary.

2 Lexical repetition

Toolan (2009) demonstrates how a corpus-based approach to lexical repetition, and what he terms 'para-repetition' (the repetition of a concept through different lexis), may contribute to the priming of the reader in short stories: the comparative frequency of salient names and words helps to prepare the reader for what is significant in the story. Caink (2012) notes such a role for the pattern of lexical repetitions in *Prime*: the schoolgirls in the Brodie set are distinguished by the reasons for which they are 'famous' within the school context, and the number of repetitions reflects the significance of each character.

Relevance theory proposes that an individual has a cognitive disposition to seek as many positive cognitive effects as possible with as little cognitive effort as possible. Any speech comes with a presumption of optimal relevance, in that the hearer can assume the speaker is making their utterance as relevant as possible in the context given the trade-off between the effort made and the positive effects derived. In a literary text, the reader can assume that their increased, non-spontaneous effort encouraged by the text will be worth the effort in terms of positive effects (Furlong 1996). Lexical repetition in relevance-theoretic terms can have a variety of effects depending on the context (Sperber and Wilson 1995: 219–222). In a literary text, repetition may involve the strengthening of assumptions and inferences constructed by the reader/hearer on the first occurrence of the word or phrase (Furlong 1996: 126–127; Pilkington 2000: ch. 5). That is, the reader may be encouraged to access their encyclopaedic knowledge of the words and concepts for a second time, thus strengthening these associations and meanings in terms of their presence in the reader's mind. The reader may also be encouraged to add to the original knowledge by accessing other associations of the word or phrase. Further cases of repetition will not similarly strengthen the same information. Rather, as the fact of the repetition itself becomes salient, initial assumptions may be modified: the fact that it becomes manifest that the writer is deliberately repeating a word or phrase becomes a new piece of information to be combined with the reader's current beliefs about the novel to give rise to new inferences. Informally, the reader begins to wonder why the author is repeating this word and what the relevance of it is to the wider meanings of the novel. For example, multiple references to Sandy's eyes may initially encourage multiple weak inferences ('poetic effects' in Sperber and Wilson 1995: 217–223) about Sandy's role as observer and judge of Brodie. Further repetitions later in the novel may encourage the accessing of wider associations for 'eyes' such as notions of 'seeing clearly', 'insight', which may throw light on Sandy's role. The repetition may therefore gradually encourage non-spontaneous inferences and these inferences will contribute to and may adapt a reader's 'global inferences' concerning the novel as the reading progresses (Clark 1996).

Sandy's eyes are referred to throughout *Prime*; it is possible that some readers may miss the repetition, or its extent. An example of repetition in a relatively small section of text can be seen in (1) with the lexeme *clutch*. This passage in Chapter 2 looks forward some 20 years to reveal that Sandy will enter a convent:

(1)

> Sandy, who was now some years Sister Helena of the Transfiguration, *clutched* the bars of the grille as was her way, and peered at him through her little faint eyes [...]

'What was your biggest influence, then, Sister Helena? Was it political, personal? Was it Calvanism?'

'Oh no, said Sandy. 'But there was a Miss Jean Brodie in her prime.' She *clutched* the bars of the grille as if she wanted to escape from the dim parlour beyond, for she was not composed like the other nuns who sat, when they received their rare visitors, well back in the darkness with folded hands. But Sandy always leaned forward and peered, *clutching* the bars with both hands, and the other sisters remarked it and said that Sister Helena had too much to bear from the world since she had published her psychological book which was so unexpectedly famed. But the dispensation was forced upon Sandy, and she *clutched* the bars and received the choice of visitors, the psychologists and the Catholic seekers, and the higher journalist ladies and the academics who wanted to question her about her odd psychological treatise....

The Prime of Miss Jean Brodie (Spark 1961: [34–35, my italics])[1]

The lexeme appears four times. In relevance-theoretic terms, the first use of 'clutched' triggers the accessing of the reader's knowledge about the lexical item and, given that this is the first reference to Sandy's later career as a nun, there may be a weak assumption of entrapment or spiritual anxiety. The possible weak inference that there is a sense of unease, if not desperation, in Sandy is strengthened when the word is repeated, this time with mention of 'both hands', an addition that is unnecessary if not to emphasise the sense of anxiety. The fact of the second and third repetitions may be sufficient in itself for the reader to infer an intended significance, if this was not the case at the second repetition. The reader may seek to derive some relevance from this fact, in association with the already accessed knowledge about the lexeme. The cognitive effort involved will give rise to further cognitive effects ('relevance'). The strengthened sense of associations with 'clutching' may encourage a link to Sandy's enforced 'dispensation' and at this stage of the novel, the repetition within the prolepsis ('looking forward') contributes to weak inferences about the focus of the novel as a whole.[2]

These repetitions also play a role in signalling the structure of the narrative to the reader (Caink 2012). The density of references in relation to text can be seen to fall away as the narrative progresses, but the relative density rises as the narrative reaches a climactic point of revelation (that Brodie intended one of her protégés, Rose, to become a colleague's lover whilst Sandy would report back, combined with the revelation that their roles are reversed and Sandy becomes the lover of the art master [109–110]). Section 4 below presents evidence that section repetition similarly contributes to foregrounding the same moment in *Prime*.

3 Sentence repetition

The verbatim repetition of whole phrases and sentences plays a similar role to lexical repetition cognitively, in that the reader is encouraged to re-access and strengthen the cognitive effects derived the first time around, and the fact of the repetition itself may encourage inferences about authorial intention. However, sentence repetition may hold over larger sections of text in an extended narrative such as a novel: in repeating a whole phrase or sentence, there is simply more material to be echoed and noticed by the reader than there is with individual lexical items, involving several lexical items, underlying structure and possibly a proposition, in addition to associated pragmatic inferences.

What may come to the fore to a greater extent with the repetition of whole phrases and sentences is a more conscious process of inferencing such as we have already suggested may appear in particularly marked cases of lexical repetition. Repetition of phrases and sentences within a conversation may give rise to any number of effects (suggesting, for example, emphasis, or exasperation, or irony[3]) depending on what is mutually manifest to the speaker and hearer. Within extended fiction, as the repetition signals increased salience, the reader becomes increasingly aware of the repetition and may increasingly indulge in non-spontaneous inferencing regarding the reason for the repetition and the possible significance of the repeated text. This is partly because the likelihood of whole sentences being repeated in language use is relatively low (setting aside aphorisms and quotations). A non-spontaneous response from the reader may therefore be encouraged by sentential repetition even more so than by lexical repetition.

For example, in *Loitering with Intent*, the phrase 'I went on my way rejoicing' appears with minor grammatical variations six times:

(2)

a. That I was a woman and living in the twentieth century were plain facts. That I was an artist was a conviction so strong that I never thought of doubting it then or since; and so, as I stood on the pathway in Hyde Park in that September of 1949, there were as good as three facts converging quite miraculously upon myself and I went on my way rejoicing. [15]

b.... I lit on another book I hadn't seen for years. It was the autobiography of Benvenuto Cellini. It was like meeting an old friend. I borrowed both books and went on my way rejoicing. [53]

c. When I got out at High Street Kensington it was raining and cold, and I went on my way rejoicing. [75]

d. Some pleasant happenings I recall, and, again, some unspeakable misfortunes which, when I remember, strike terror into me and wonder that I have, indeed, come to this age of fifty-eight, from which, by God's grace, I am now going on my way rejoicing. [94]

e. I straightened the covers on the revolting bed, let myself out of the flat and went on my way rejoicing. [129]

f. And so, having entered the fullness of my years, from there by the grace of God I go on my way rejoicing. [172]

The different immediate textual contexts in which each instance occurs promote different inferences for a reader. On the first occasion during an initial reading, the phrase can only be taken as a reflection of the narrator's positive feelings at the three 'facts' (2a). The first repetition some 38 pages later (2b) may be missed as a repetition by some readers, but may create a dim resonance in others. The spontaneous inference may regard it as a reflection of the narrator's frame of mind following her discovery of Cellini's autobiography in the library. It may also relate to warm feelings Fleur expressed towards Maisie Young a few lines earlier.

The second repetition (2c) is more likely to resonate as a repetition of significance, for three repetitions suggest a pattern rather than coincidence. There is no obvious explanation in the immediately preceding text for such celebration, other than a weak implicature that Fleur rejoices at her friendship with Gray Mauser having been in his company immediately before this example, but this remains a very weak inference. The lack of obvious relevance therefore encourages further cognitive effort by the reader. The reversal of expectation, in that rain and cold is generally associated with displeasure, may encourage the weak inference that the narrator's private thoughts are paramount and somehow unaffected by the vicissitudes around her. The reader may recall the equally unusual reversal of expectations at the outset of the novel when the budding novelist-narrator speaks of her delight in unattractive behaviour (for example, 'I was fascinated by his swinishness' [2]; Mrs Tims is 'an awful woman. But to me, beautifully awful'. [8]).

Three repetitions may imply that the sentence has particular import to the narrative because it is reappearing like a musical *leitmotif*. The inference is strengthened in (2d) because the sentence forms part of a quotation from Cellini's autobiography, thus simultaneously revealing its provenance. Weak inferences may be promoted at this point concerning the relation between the novel, the narrator and Cellini's somewhat infamous autobiography of murder and intrigue. The fact that the novel has a first person narrator opens up the possibility that this is in some sense a stock phrase for the narrator. Its repetition is therefore a form of mimesis – we all have our stock phrases that we knowingly or not repeat. The nature of the phrase and the nature of Fleur and the narrative may give rise to a host of weak inferences.

The fourth repetition (2e) appears in a context that requires only minimal cognitive effort to compute adequate relevance: Fleur rejoices because she has regained the stolen manuscript of her novel. But its status as a repeating figure is well-established, preparing the ground for the final, most prominent repetition (2f) as the final words of the novel. The repetition here acts like a musical cadence marking the closure of the narrative. Section 5 below returns to the significance of 'final words'.

These iterations give rise to different inferred meanings on each occasion because of their distinct contexts. The musical analogy is instructive. For example, the second rendition of the opening section in a *da capo* aria, regardless of the addition of florid decoration, is different as a result of the intervening section. The repetition of the final line(s) in verses in folk songs and ballads may promote distinct meanings according to what has occurred in the preceding verse, as do the structures of some jokes and comic songs.[4]

4 Section repetition

Verbatim section repetition necessarily occurs in *The Comforters* (Spark 1957) because the character Caroline Rose hears her own experience being recounted in a novel. Otherwise, verbatim repetition of more than one sentence is rare in a genuinely communicative context. The focus here is on sections that are *not* verbatim repetitions. The repetition of a scene, even if only minor lexical or syntactic repetition occurs, is here termed 'section repetition'.

In drawing a distinction between simple repetition and 'parallelism', Leech (1969: 77) maintains the latter involves some repetition that establishes a frame within which other elements may be changed. For example, Brutus's speech in Shakespeare's *Julius Caesar* includes the sentence 'Not that I loved Caesar less, but that I loved Rome more', Act 3, scene 2). The repetition-with-variation sets up significant semantic parallels between the items that have changed: *Caesar* ~ *Rome, less* ~ *more.* What becomes prominent is precisely what is changed in the context of repetition. Such parallelism however occurs with a close association between the iterations. The reason for this is clearly that the effect of parallelism will be lost if the original structure has passed out of the reader's short-term memory. This and the following section examine instances where Spark employs section repetition with often substantial variation. The repetition may occur with considerable text between the original passage and its repetition. We shall see that the section repetitions occur in three structural points in the narrative and thus contribute to highlighting the non-linguistic narrative structure.

4.1 Non-verbatim recounting by a character

The Ballad of Peckham Rye (Spark 1960) opens with a confrontation between Mavis and a man later revealed as Humphrey:

(3)

'Get away from here, you dirty swine,' she said.
'There's a dirty swine in every man,' he said.
'Showing your face round here again,' she said.
'Now Mavis, now, Mavis,' he said.
She was seen to slam the door in his face, and he to press the bell, and she to open the door again.
'I want a word with Dixie,' he said. 'Now Mavis, be reasonable.'
'My daughter,' Mavis said, 'is not in.' She slammed the door in his face.
Ballad of Peckham Rye (Spark 1960: [7])

There then follow further events of that night and a brief analeptic section ('flashback') to the wedding at which Humphrey refused to marry Mavis's daughter, Dixie, and which has given rise to this confrontation. Four pages after this opening scene, Mavis recounts the exchange to others:

> (4)
>
> ...So I went to the door, and lo and behold there he was on the doorstep. He said, 'Hallo, Mavis,' he said. I said, 'You just hop it, you.' He said, 'Can I see Dixie?' I said, 'You certainly can't,' I said. I said, 'You're a dirty swine. You remove yourself,' I said, 'and don't show your face again,' I said. He said, 'Come on, Mavis.' I said, 'Mrs Crewe to you,' and I shut the door in his face.
>
> *Ballad of Peckham Rye* (Spark 1960: [11])

This storytelling by a character clearly shares some aspects of the narrator's account, but Mavis leaves out Humphrey's rejoinder ('There's a dirty swine in every man'), the fact that she re-opened the door to him, and adds a final quip. Her account therefore suggests two aspects of being human. The first is the way in which our minds regularly improve our recollections in order to bolster our self-esteem (see, for example, Marcus 2008), which may be implied here. The second facet is one to do with language use, the fact that it is virtually impossible for us to reproduce verbatim our own speech after the event. What we may recall will be, at most, some specific lexical items and the gist of what was intended.

Mavis's account of this exchange reflects the fact that verbatim repetition very rarely occurs in spontaneous speech, at least as part of communicative language use. Verbatim repetition of more than a single sentence is possible in written language, but it is not characteristic of non-literary texts. It is the presence of repetition and parallelism that lies at the centre of Jakobson's definition of his 'poetic function', when the principle of equivalence applies to the contiguous text (Jakobson 1960: 358). The exchange is therefore an example of mimesis, the text enacting the reality.

There are several instances in Spark's oeuvre where section repetition is made by the narrator. The question such repetitions give rise to is, why are they used. But also, given that an author can give a narrator verbatim repetition in a literary text, the question might be turned around to consider why verbatim repetition is *not* employed.

4.2 Section repetition and narrative structure

One reason for section repetition in Spark's novels is the contribution it makes to the narrative structure. For example, in *Prime*, the novel opens with the 'Brodie set' standing with their bicycles at the school gates chatting to boys before they are joined by their former teacher. The boys are dispensed with and the girls walk to the tram stop with Brodie while the following conversation is held (the section is too long to be quoted in full here, partly because it is interpolated by sections detailing introductory information about the girls and the school context):

> (5)
>
> 'It has been suggested again that I should apply for a post at one of the progressive schools, where my methods would be more suited to the system than they are at Blaine. But I shall not apply for a post at a crank school. I shall remain at this education factory. There needs must be a leaven in the lump. Give me a girl at an impressionable age, and she is mine for life.'
>
> The Brodie set smiled in understanding of various kinds.
>
> [...]
>
> 'Who are the gang, this time?' said Rose, who was famous for sex-appeal.
>
> 'We shall discuss tomorrow night the persons who oppose me,' said Miss Brodie. 'But rest assured that they shall not succeed.'
>
> 'No,' said everyone. 'Of course they won't.'
>
> *The Prime of Miss Jean Brodie* (Spark 1961: [5–10])

The narrative then moves back six years to when these girls were first in Miss Brodie's class and, besides frequent brief proleptic moments (*annonces* in Genette's 1972 terms), the narrative moves chronologically through the 1930s towards the moment when it is revealed how Sandy 'betrays' Brodie to the headmistress. In Bridgeman's (2005) account of the novel using Genette's structuralist approach, it is the narrative at this point in 1936 through to the betrayal of Brodie that is termed 'First narrative' or the principal narrative sequence. Except for the opening scene and the proleptic *annonces*, the majority of the novel is therefore a 'completing analepsis', bringing the reader back to this opening scene in 1936 just before the final chapter. Bridgeman makes the point that the repetition of the opening scene (included in (8) below) signals to the reader the imminence of the final 'betrayal'.

Whether or not one sees the repetition as heralding the close of a completing analepsis and the return to the First narrative is questionable. Such a structuralist account is one that can only be constructed once the novel has been read in its entirety and even then may capture little of the experience of reading the novel (Toolan 2001; Caink 2012). But pragmatically, the repetition of the opening scene provides strong evidence for inferences derived about the structure of the narrative.

As noted above, lexical repetition signals the arrival of a climactic revelatory point in *Prime* [109–110]. It is significant that two pages after this narrative climax, the repetition of the opening scene occurs as the narrative resumes the playing out of the chronological account.

In *Loitering with Intent*, the opening scene (in (6a)) is retold at a similar point, the beginning of the final chapter (included here as (6b)):

(6) a.

One day in the middle of the twentieth century I sat in an old graveyard which had not yet been demolished, in the Kensington area of London, when a young policeman stepped off the path and came over to me. He was shy and smiling, he might have been coming over the grass to ask me for a game of tennis. He only wanted to know what I was doing but plainly he didn't like to ask. I told him I was writing a poem, and offered him a sandwich which he refused as he had just had his dinner himself. He stopped to talk awhile, then he said good-bye, the graves must be very old, and that he wished me good luck and that it was nice to speak to somebody.

This was the last day of a whole chunk of my life but I didn't know that at the time. I sat on the stone slab of some Victorian grave writing my poem as long as the sun lasted.

Loitering With Intent (Spark 1981: [1])

b.

It was in the middle of the twentieth century, the last day of June 1950, warm and sunny, a Friday, that I mark as a changing-point in my life. That goes back to the day I took my sandwiches to the old disused Kensington graveyard to write a poem with my lunch, when the young policeman sauntered over to see what I was up to. He was a clean-cut man, as on war memorials. I asked him: suppose I had been committing a crime sitting there on the gravestone, what crime would it be? 'Well, it could be desecrating and violating,' he said, 'it could be obstructing and hindering without due regard, it could be loitering with intent.' I offered him a sandwich but he refused; he had just had his dinner himself. 'The graves must be very old,' said the policeman. He wished me the best of luck and went on his way.

Loitering With Intent (Spark 1981: [155])

The penultimate chapter in *Loitering with Intent* ends with the first person narrator, Fleur, having achieved a sense of equilibrium following the vicious intrigues of the Autobiographical Association. She reads admiringly Newman's and Cellini's autobiographies that have been much cited throughout the preceding narrative, and notes how she feels she has 'escaped' from the Association. Crucially for her as an aspiring novelist, she realises that the characters of the Association were now 'objectified' for her and that she would be able to write about them one day, indeed 'I have written about them ever since, the straws from which I have made my bricks.' [154]

Smiley (2006) claims, on the basis of examining 100 novels, that most novels have some form of climax (whether a form of action or the revelation of key information) at approximately 85–90% of the way through a novel. The moment that Fleur reaches her sense of equilibrium is on page 154 of a 172-page novel, precisely the 90% point, and the readerly expectation of a climax around this point may in itself imply that this is a moment of 'climax' within the novel. The repetition of the opening scene immediately follows this moment.

In *Prime*, the repetition of the opening scene immediately follows the 85% point of the narrative, the revelations mentioned above (the 104th and 105th pages of a 123-page novel[5]). Both *Prime* and *Loitering with Intent*, therefore, employ the repetition of the opening scene to signal a form of completion of the 'rising action' and the move into the final stages of the narrative.

Spark also employs repetition at the other structurally significant moment in the narrative: the end. We can see examples of this in both *Ballad* and *Prime*. The wedding in which Humphrey appears to reject Dixie is first told on the second page of the novel, included here as (7a), and appears again on the final page (7b):

(7) a.

He was standing at the altar with Trevor, the best man, behind him. Dixie came up the aisle on the arm of Arthur Crewe, her stepfather. There must have been thirty-odd guests in the church. Arthur Crewe was reported in the papers next day as having said: 'I had a feeling the wedding wouldn't come off.' At the time he stepped up the aisle with Dixie, tall in her flounces, her eyes dark and open, and with a very little trace round the nose of a cold.

[... *brief analepsis* ...]

Here they were, kneeling at the altar. The vicar was reading from the prayer book. Dixie took a lacy handkerchief from her sleeve and gently patted her nose. Humphrey noticed the whiff of scent which came from the handkerchief.

The vicar said to Humphrey, 'Wilt thou have this woman to thy wedded wife?'

'No,' Humphrey said, 'to be quite frank I won't.'

He got to his feet and walked straight up the aisle. The guests in the pews rustled as if they were all women.

Ballad of Peckham Rye (Spark 1960: [8])

b.

There was Dixie come up to the altar with her wide flouncy dress and her nose, a little red from her cold, tilted up towards the minister.

'Wilt thou have this woman to thy wedded wife?'

'No, to be quite frank,' Humphrey said, 'I won't.'

Ballad of Peckham Rye (Spark 1960: [142])

The passage in (7b) is the beginning of the short two-page chapter at the end of the novel, hence may be pragmatically perceived as constituting 'the end'. This brief final chapter also includes the repetition not of a scene, but of the narrator's account of the rumours generated by the wedding [14, 143].

Finally, in *Prime*, the proleptic account of the inquiring young man in (1) returns in the very final words of the novel, with one of the repeated utterances becoming the final words of the novel (this is included in (9) below).

Of course, repetitions at the very end of a novel are relatively minor indicators of closing structure in comparison with the physical experience the reader has of the novel drawing to a close (or the equivalent indicator on an e-reader). The fact remains however that section repetition does not appear randomly in these novels; the sections involved in such repetition are associated with the beginning and the end of the narrative, and immediately following the climax and completion of the 'rising action'. The narrative structure comes with as much a guarantee of optimal relevance as does any gestural contribution in a conversation and Spark's use of repetition contributes to the inferred meanings promoted by what is climactic and what is allowed to resonate at the close of the narrative.

5 Repetition and the communication of meanings and feelings

This section examines the contribution that non-verbatim section repetitions may make to implied meanings on account of what has been changed. It then considers how repetition may promote affective communication.

5.1 The salience of changes

Given that verbatim repetition is available in a literary narrative, why does Spark use only partial repetition? For example, we saw in (6) how some linguistic material and content is identical, but much is not.

Human memory is not organised like a computer with a specific address for each item. On a computer, once a file is loaded onto the memory, a perfect copy of it may be accessed at any time. For reasons of evolution, human memory is based around context (we are often able to recall things by association with other things), frequency (the greater number of times we have accessed the memory, the easier it is to recall; hence rote learning) and 'recency' (more recent occurrences may be more salient).[6] These aspects of human cognition must be central to a pragmatic account of extended prose narrative and the reader's experience of them.

Given the nature of human memory, a reader is unlikely to recall much of earlier sections, depending on how recently they were read. To some extent, therefore, verbatim repetition in a novel is unnecessary: it would serve no purpose that cannot be achieved through partial repetition of the type that we see in (6) and (7) in evoking the recollection of an earlier section. In a sense, the partial repetitions of (6b) and (7b) are precisely what the human mind deals in: partial recall rather than verbatim recall. By including a few shared details, the earlier scene can be evoked for the alert reader, enough for the reader to observe that repetition is taking place. The shared elements included in the repetition need only be a few lexical items, or indeed, a shared lexeme (such as the noun 'flounces' in (7a) and adjective 'flouncy' in (7b)).

In a relevance-theoretic cognitive based account of communication, much of the processing is at a 'subpersonal' level (as in Dennett 1969); the interlocutor is not necessarily consciously aware of the process of inferencing that may lead to the calculation of fresh propositions or even consciously aware of what may be manifest (Sperber and Wilson 1995: 40–41). Similarly in the reading experience, an awareness of repetition need not be entirely conscious. The fact that the scene has been evoked previously may be adequate for the repetition to have some 'glow' of significance as a result of a dim familiarity; the accessed information from the reader's cognitive environment may be that much more easily accessed (with less cognitive effort) and the assumptions may become slightly more manifest.

The repetition of lexical items is used in *Prime* even before the section repetition occurs, suggesting that it is intended to prepare the reader for the repetition. For example, in the opening scene of the novel, the girls are described as 'loitering', and the lexeme appears again with 'loitered' on the same page [5] to describe the girls' behaviour. When the scene is repeated [112], the word appears again *before* it is apparent that the specific scene is being repeated:

(8)

> Then she would find them, perhaps, loitering with the bicycle boys after school, and the bicycles would rapidly bear the boys away, and they would be bidden to supper the following evening.
>
> They went to the tram stop with her. 'It has been suggested again that I should apply for a post at one of the progressive, that is to say, crank schools. I shall not apply for a post at a crank school. I shall remain at this education factory where my duty lies. There needs must be a leaven in the lump. Give me a girl at an impressionable age and she is mine for life. The gang who oppose me shall not succeed.'
>
> 'No,' said everyone. 'No, of course they won't.'
>
> The Prime of Miss Jean Brodie (Spark 1961: [112])

The word 'loitering' appears in the first paragraph of (8), before the repeated scene in the second paragraph. At this stage, the opening paragraph does not describe the specific scene, but rather the suggestion ('perhaps') of habitual behaviour, created by the three uses of the modal *would*. The repetition of 'loitering' is not therefore part of the repeated section itself, but may play a minor role in evoking the recollection for the reader.

In considering why verbatim repetition is not used, then, we can note that there is a purely practical reason: not everything *needs* to be recalled. If context is a key to our access to a memory, then some contextual clues – either as priming or in the repetition itself – may be adequate. But the effect of parallelism is to make what has changed more salient. The changes that the author has chosen to make in the repetition of a section may partly have significance in a literary work because of the expectation that a reader has of a literary work.

For example, consider the end of *Prime* in which Spark returns to the visit of the 'inquiring young man', the first rendition of which we saw above in (1). The passage is brief, but its appearance at the very end gives it prominence:

(9)

> And then there was that day when the inquiring young man came to see Sandy because of her strange book of psychology, 'The Transfiguration of the Commonplace', which had brought so many visitors that Sandy *clutched* the bars of her grille *more desperately than ever*.
>
> 'What were the main influences of your school days, Sister Helena? Were they literary or political or personal? Was it Calvinism?'
>
> Sandy said: 'There was a Miss Jean Brodie in her prime.'
>
> *The Prime of Miss Jean Brodie* (Spark 1961: [126, my italics])

We noticed in the original passage in (1) above that the lexeme 'clutch' appears four times to describe the way in which Sandy held the bars of her cell during the interviews. (9) uses essentially the same formulations and lexis as (1). However, it includes the addition of the adverbial phrase 'more desperately than ever'. The choice of repeated text and the new material carries some prominence. The reader may be encouraged to infer a host of weak implicatures regarding Sandy's choices in the preceding narrative in the light of such implied torment. If a literary reader, pursuing a consciously non-spontaneous response to the novel, chooses to compare the two passages, the difference can only strengthen such inferences.

Minor changes are not always so prominent and do not always encourage implicatures. In (7b), the only change that is made to

Humphrey's key utterance is in the positioning of the reporting phrase 'Humphrey said'. This minor change reflects the author's manipulation of prosody: the reader is very likely to recall this startling response in church and the variation is reminiscent of the repetition that one finds in ballads with minor reformulations for variety, hence it contributes to the aesthetic effect of the various allusions to balladry in the novel.

Finally, the foregrounding of narration is often cited as central to Spark's aesthetic (for example, see works in Gardiner and Maley 2010 and Herman 2010, particularly the editors' own contributions). As we saw with respect to Mavis's storytelling in (4), the partial account is a reflection of language use in spontaneous speech. Verbatim repetition is virtually impossible without rote learning and our memories are influenced by our own 'wishful thinking'; in other words, memories are created by our present needs, rather than being an accurate reproduction of past events and thoughts. Given that verbatim repetition *is* available to an author in written prose, it means that the author's decision to provide a narrator's partial repetition is itself strongly suggestive of the oral storytelling tradition. It contributes to the foregrounding of the act of narration found in language such as 'There was Dixie come up to the altar' in (7a) or 'And then there was that day when ... ' in (9). The partial repetition contextualises the very notion of narrative omniscience.

5.2 Shared experience and affective communication

When the narrator of *Prime* repeats the opening scene of the novel (8), the arrival of the scene is mediated by a paragraph that, as we have noted, primes the reader for the repetition. There is a sense in which the scene is gradually brought 'into focus', as we shift from the hypothetical ('perhaps') and habitual behaviour of the girls over a period of time ('would') to the specific scene in the second paragraph. The reader may sense a degree of reminiscence via this 'soft focus' and the shared experience that is being evoked.

This sense of shared experience that a section repetition brings to the fore is a strong element in the possible effects of extended narrative. Unlike most art forms, the novel is rarely experienced in one sitting; the reader experiences the novel in conjunction with experiencing their own existence over a period of time that includes eating and sleeping, mulling and forgetting and so on. When Spark employs repetition, it involves the invocation of shared experience that, in the context of the narrative, can encourage its own emotional response, one of those ineffable non-propositional elements of affective communication in literary texts (Sperber and Wilson 1995; Furlong 1996: 113ff; Pilkington 2000: ch. 6; Blakemore 2008).

Consider the final lines of *Prime* (9). The addition of 'more desperately than ever' may confirm the weak implicature in (1) that Sandy/Sister Helena is troubled and anxious. As we have seen, the weak implicature that existed before is strongly supported, throwing not a new light, but a stronger interpretive light on the events of the preceding narrative. The reader and Sandy are looking back together.

The novel then ends on the repetition of 'There was a Miss Jean Brodie in her prime'. This ending simultaneously alludes to the title of the novel and may for the reader bring the sense of reminiscence to the fore again: the repetition and the sense of musical cadence may encourage feelings associated with a shared emotional journey, one that includes something of the lack of clarity and uncertainty of lived experience. The fact that the experience is shared with fictional characters is irrelevant, for the characters and their experiences exist in the reader's cognitive environment alongside the reader's own (possibly less vivid!) experiences. Spark's use of repetition makes this shared experience strongly manifest. It is an example of one way in which an extended fictional text may promote affective communication.

6 Re-reading as a form of repetition?

It is possible that a 'literary reader' may deliberately seek out the original section that is being repeated to compare it with the repetition. Such an act moves the reading experience away from the spontaneous response towards the non-spontaneous response of re-reading (Furlong 1996, 2008).

Jucker (1994, cited in Furlong 2008: 288) notes a paradox for a relevance-theoretic account of re-reading: if there is a trade-off between effort and effect, processing a repeated text would appear to yield roughly the same set of assumptions for additional effort, making the experience therefore technically 'irrelevant'. However, if a literary text is, as Nabokov suggests, a text that is intended to be re-read, one might suggest that the perceived literary nature of the text does itself provide a presumption of optimal relevance if re-read. Section repetition is one of many textual features that present an array of additional contextual effects when, as we have observed, the repetition is partial. In Furlong's terms, the reader is a cumulative re-reader, adding to the 'global inferences' concerning the novel as a whole (Clark 1996).

However, given the vagaries of human memory, literary re-reading, at least on the first few re-readings, cannot be an exact repetition. Even with principal elements of the narrative and character roles already known, much of a literary text may be available for discovery for the first time and much that was previously distantly manifest may become strongly manifest. Some cognitive effort may be reduced owing to the repetition (Furlong 2008: 289), but much will not. The observation of new patterns and significances may promote additional cognitive effort which will yield new effects for the reader. Theoretically, this process might be likened to the non-spontaneous search for optimal relevance when we mull over an earlier conversation and only belatedly realise an implicature.

It is also an inevitability that a reader's individual cognitive environment will have changed between readings. If cognitive effects are computed out of a combination of the reader's cognitive environment in conjunction with the ostensive communication, in relevance-theoretic terms, the change in cognitive environment alone may give rise to distinct effects from the same text, even if the reader is blessed with 'perfect' recall. Re-reading here is reminiscent of the repetitions examined in Section 3: the inferences change because the context has changed. The only difference is that the re-reading process draws on a changed cognitive environment rather than a changed text.

Finally, in addition to strengthening and enriching the reader's inferences about the novel's meanings, a re-reading places the skill of the author centre stage. Re-reading may give rise to a much stronger sense of the work as performance (Bauman 1975; Fabb 2002). With the broad outlines of the plot already known, it is the artistry used that becomes part of the interest and hence evaluation comes to the fore.

7 Conclusion and summary

This chapter has examined aspects of the role played by lexical repetition, sentential repetition and section repetition in Spark's three novels. All three types of repetition may play a role in foregrounding the structure of the narrative that in turn might promote inferences about the relative significance of events. We saw how section repetitions may appear in relation to the beginning and close of a narrative, and immediately following the climactic moment 85–90% of the way through the narrative.

Verbatim repetition of more than a sentence rarely occurs in conversation, but it is available in writing, and repetitions-with-variation ('parallelism') are hallmarks of the literary text. The changes in a repeated section may encourage inferences on the part of the reader with respect to the elements that are new and provide strong evidence for a sense of the oral storytelling tradition, with the concomitant foregrounding and contextualisation of the act of narration.

Repetition over an extended piece of fiction makes demands on the reader's memory. If the reader is not aware of the repetition, the repetition may still provide a re-accessing and a strengthening of some contextual assumptions at the 'sub-personal' level (in the sense of Dennett 1969). Some recognition of a section may be enabled by the repetition of specific lexemes and linguistic structures. In cases where a reader is aware of the repetition, there may be a more robust strengthening of contextual assumptions and the reader may infer meanings from the fact of the repetition itself.

In the final section I argued that re-reading cannot result in an identical experience because even with a (rare) perfect recall, a reader's cognitive environment will have changed between readings.

One of the attractions of approaching an extended narrative within a relevance-theoretic framework is that the theory is a general cognitive theory and thus provides ways of understanding the global reading experience. That is, we are able to examine the linguistic together with the non-linguistic, the real-world experience of living and experiencing one's own life at the same time as reading the extended fiction. It is a platitude about a novel, that it is rarely experienced in one 'sitting', but this fact distinguishes it from most forms of art and entertainment. A theory that is able to treat with the changing cognitive environment of the reader, both 'outside' the novel and 'within' it, affords an opportunity to better understand the act of reading and the artistry of the novelist in exploiting the possibilities of that act of reading.

Notes

1. All page references in square brackets are to the Penguin editions of *Prime* and *Ballad*, and the Virago Modern Classics edition of *Loitering with Intent*.
2. The word is later repeated in a passage from the narrator's point of view describing the reasons why people visit a nun: '... it provides a spiritual sensation, a catharsis to go home with, especially if the nun clutches the bars of the grille.' [121]
3. See, for example, Sperber and Wilson (1995: section 4.9) on echoic irony.
4. Examples of *da capo* arias in 18th century operas may be found in, say, Handel's *Julius Caesar* or Mozart's *Idomeneo*; a typical example of repetition in folk songs would be 'Frankie and Johnny', alternatively known as 'Frankie and Albert' by Bob Dylan on *Good as I Been to you* (1992).
5. The novel begins on page 5 in the Penguin edition, hence the apparent discrepancy between these facts and the page references.
6. See, for example, Marcus (2008: ch. 2), Anderson (1990) and Anderson and Schooler (2000).

3

'Oh, do let's talk about something else-': What Is Not Said and What Is Implicated in Elizabeth Bowen's *The Last September*

Siobhan Chapman

1 Introduction

Elizabeth Bowen described *The Last September* (*TLS*) as 'the only one of my novels to be set back deliberately, in a former time'.* The reader, she explained 'must look, be conscious of looking, backward' (Bowen 1952: 124). Bowen's first readers did not need to look backward very far – the book was published in 1929 and set in 1920 – but the historical setting is of supreme importance. *TLS* is set during what, as Bowen acknowledged, became commonly known as 'the Troubled Times': the period leading up to the establishment in 1922 of the Irish Free State, a period that was marked by 'roving armed conflict between the Irish Republican Army and British forces still garrisoning Ireland' (Bowen 1952: 125). This period of transition in Irish history, and in particular the end of the era of the Anglo-Irish ascendancy, is a major theme of *TLS*, but is rarely addressed explicitly. The characters in the novel, whose lives are increasingly affected by the fighting going on around them, generally avoid discussing the armed conflict directly and when they do discuss it, do so in vague and nonspecific terms. In *TLS*, what is not talked about is what is most significant.

*I presented earlier versions of this paper at the 'Colloquium on pragma-stylistics: recent research and open questions' at the University of Sussex in May 2012, at the International PALA conference at the University of Malta in July 2012 and at the Irish Literary Society in London in October 2012. I am grateful to the audiences on these occasions for very helpful discussions.

In this chapter I offer a reading of *TLS* that explores the question of how a topic that is generally either apparently ignored or explicitly eschewed can nevertheless be of central importance in the novel. I follow some recent critics in suggesting that attitudes to the armed conflict and its implications are communicated in the novel, but communicated implicitly rather than explicitly. However, unlike these recent critics I support this claim with formal analysis using pragmatic theory in the Gricean tradition, including recent 'neo-Gricean' developments. Such pragmatic theory is directly concerned with explaining the differences between 'what is said' on any particular occasion, or by extension what is not said and 'what is implicated', or what the speaker intends to communicate. The class of Quantity implicatures, introduced by Grice and developed in neo-Gricean pragmatics, is of particular interest in this context, because Quantity implicatures are implicit meanings that can be explained with reference to what a speaker might have said on a particular occasion but chose not to. Drawing on recent work that distinguishes between the classes of 'closed' and 'open' Quantity implicatures (Geurts 2010) I will consider examples of Quantity implicatures that arise when characters choose ways of talking that implicitly deny the severity or downplay the pertinence of 'the Troubled Times' and also examples of those that arise when the narrator describes occasions when characters do not speak.

2 *The Last September* and 'the Troubled Times'

The central location in *TLS*, and the setting for most of its events, is Danielstown, a country house in rural Ireland. Danielstown is a fictionalised 'Big House': the home for generations of a land-owning Anglo-Irish family of the Protestant ascendancy, landlords to typically Catholic smallholders and farmers. Danielstown is home to Sir Richard and Lady Naylor, who in September 1920 have staying with them Lady Naylor's nephew Laurence, an undergraduate on vacation from Oxford, and Sir Richard's niece Lois, who has recently finished school. The novel begins with the arrival of the Montmorencys as house guests. Francie Montmorency is a perpetual invalid and is married to Hugo, who is ten years her junior. During the course of the novel Danielstown is also visited by an accident-prone young woman called Marda Norton who is engaged to be married to a man in Kent. The occupants of Danielstown are confronted with increasingly strong intimations of the presence of IRA activity on and around the estate. For instance, Lois glimpses an unknown man in a trenchcoat in the shrubbery, Laurence is held up at gunpoint and Lois and Marda, exploring a ruined mill, disturb a sleeping gunman who discharges his pistol, wounding Marda's hand. By the end of the month the visitors have departed, Laurence has returned to Oxford and Lois has gone to stay with a family in Tours to improve her French. On the very last page of the novel the reader is informed that the following February Danielstown, along with two neighbouring Big Houses, is burnt to a ruin by nationalist insurgents.

For much of the novel the armed conflict going on around them appears less important to the residents of Danielstown than their own social and emotional relationships. These develop in the context of a range of tennis parties, dinners and dances that together constitute what elsewhere Bowen recalled as the 'dashing and sentimental intercourse...between officers and the country house family' (Bowen 1942: 10). Before his marriage to Francie, Hugo had been in love with Laura, who was Sir Richard's sister and Lois's mother. During the course of the novel he conspicuously falls in love with Marda. Lois is courted by Gerald, a handsome young officer in the British Army, and she tries to convince herself that she is in love with him. As the visitors arrive, Lois expects that she may fall in love with Hugo, but in fact finds herself drawn to Marda. When Marda leaves Danielstown, apparently to marry the man in Kent, Lois agrees to marry Gerald. However, they are both forced to recognise the fact that she does not love him and have separated before Gerald is killed when his patrol is ambushed.

A recurrent observation made by critics of *TLS* is that, although the political and the personal stories are kept largely separate, with the personal appearing to dominate, the two are intimately connected. Corcoran notes that the book has many of the tropes of a country house novel but, 'Where typically in such novels characters are brought together so that they may interrelate in plots of social and erotic intrigue, in Bowen the relations never get very far' (Corcoran 2004: 40). Interpersonal relationships do not work out as expected and prove to have no future, just as more generally the Anglo-Irish ascendancy status and lifestyle will not survive. Lassner and Derdiger identify as a major theme of the novel the 'threat to self-proclaimed civilized order' (Lassner and Derdiger 2009: 197). Brown describes *TLS* as 'a novel of transition', capturing Ireland's movement from colonial to postcolonial (Brown 2012: 20). Bowen herself commented that in writing the novel she wanted the reader to understand that 'all this...is done with and over' (Bowen 1952: 124).

For many of the novel's critics, then, the parties and other social occasions that apparently dominate it, and the personal relationships to which these provide context, are not its main theme; 'the social comedy is not the point of *The Last September*' (Reynolds 1992: 153). The end of British rule in Ireland and its implications for Anglo-Irish families such as the Naylors is what Wells-Lassagne calls 'the central story', despite the fact that it 'remains in the margins of the actual novel' (Wells-Lassagne 2007: 459). For such critics, the personal relationships between characters, far from being 'the point' of the novel, serve to illustrate or to exemplify the more general themes of loss and change. Wessels explains that Bowen is in the business of 'establishing a close conjunction between the politico-historical and the personal, of rendering the wider context in terms of the crisis of the individual' (Wessels 1995: 89), and McElhattan Williams comments that she uses characters 'to reinforce physically what she is depicting thematically' (McElhattan Williams 1995: 231).

Critics have further noted that the armed conflict and the concomitant issues of colonialism, violence and change are obscured in *TLS* not only because of the superficially more focal interpersonal issues, but also because of the repeated failures of the characters to engage with and to talk about the political and military state of Ireland. It is not that the characters are not aware of this state, or do not have views on it, but rather that they are prepared to express these views only indirectly. Corcoran comments that the characters interact using 'edgy insinuation' (Corcoran 2004: 45) and Esty explains that they communicate with 'indirect language' (Esty 2007: 258). Brown draws attention to the extensive use of 'exclusion' in *TLS*, which he sees as characterised by 'language that evades' (Brown 2012: 4, 6). For Glendinning, the central themes of the novel remain 'implicit' (Glendinning 1988: 1). The reason for this form of communication may be the ambiguous position in which the Anglo-Irish of the time found themselves, which, Bowen claimed, was 'more nearly heart-breaking than they cared to show'. She explained: 'Inherited loyalty (or at least, adherence) to Britain – where their sons were schooled, in whose wars their sons had for generations fought, and to which they owed their "Ascendancy" lands and power – pulled them one way; their own temperamental Irishness the other' (Bowen 1952: 125). What is communicated implicitly is central to *TLS*. In analysing the novel it would be beneficial to have access to a formal and principled account of implicit meaning. The next section will outline one aspect of such an account, namely the pragmatic theoretical notion of Quantity implicatures. The following two sections will consider how this aspect of pragmatic theory might be employed in analysing implicit meaning in *TLS*.

3 Quantity implicatures

The term 'neo-Gricean' is applied to a range of present day pragmatic theories that share a general impetus, rather than to one specific theoretical framework. These theories are essentially Gricean in nature because of their commitment to establishing a distinction between 'what is said' and 'what is implicated' and to delineating principles of language use that explain the differences between these two types of meaning. Neo-Gricean theories differ both in how they distinguish between the said and the implicated and in the number and nature of the principles they posit.

Quantity implicatures were initially introduced into pragmatics as part of Grice's theory of conversation. One of the four 'categories' of maxims he proposes to account for the specific workings of his 'cooperative principle' is the category of 'Quantity', which in turn contains two maxims: 'Make your contribution as informative as is required (for the current purposes of the exchange)' and 'Do not make your contribution more informative than is required'. Grice immediately adds a lengthy and characteristic caveat about the second of these maxims, which is worth noting:

> The second maxim is disputable; it may be said that to be overinformative is not a transgression of the Cooperative Principle but merely a waste of time. However, it might be answered that such overinformativeness may be confusing in that it is liable to raise side issues; and there may also be an indirect effect, in that the hearers may be misled as a result of thinking that there is some particular *point* in the provision of the excess information. However this may be, there is perhaps a different reason for doubt about the admission of his second maxim, namely, that its effect will be secured by a later maxim, which concerns relevance.
>
> (Grice 1975: 26–27)

Grice offers two different types of examples of implicature based on the maxims of Quantity. A particularised conversational implicature will typically arise if one of the maxims is deliberately flouted. The first maxim of Quantity presents Grice with one of his most striking and frequently cited examples of implicature. The writer of a reference for a candidate applying for a philosophy job who offers no more than 'Dear Sir, Mr. X's command of English is excellent, and his attendance at tutorials has been regular. Yours, etc.' is blatantly not offering information sufficient to the purposes of his communication and is therefore taken to be implicating that Mr. X is no good at philosophy. Again, Grice is more cagey about his second maxim of Quantity, suggesting that a speaker who is overinformative, offering not just a required piece of information but assurances that the information is certain, may be taken to be implicating that the information is in fact controversial. Again, he suggests that this maxim may need to give way to the more explanatory maxim of Relation.

Grice's initial discussion of generalised conversational implicatures, which were to become so central and so controversial in the subsequent development of pragmatic theory (see, for example, Horn 1972; Levinson 2000; Geurts 2010), is limited to a sketchy account of the operation of the first maxim of Quantity. Generalised conversational implicatures are normally conveyed by the use of specific words, in the absence of particular circumstances that might prevent them from arising. Someone who says 'X is meeting a woman this evening' is generally taken to be implicating that the person being met is not X's mother, wife, sister or close platonic friend. Similarly, if someone says 'X went to a house yesterday and found a tortoise inside the front door', we will generally assume that the house was not the speaker's own. Grice offers the following explanation:

> When someone, by using the form of expression *an X*, implicates that the X does not belong to or is not otherwise closely connected with some identifiable person, the implicature is present because the speaker has failed to be specific in a way in which he might have been expected to be specific, with the consequence that it is likely to be assumed that he is not in a position to be specific. This is a familiar implicature situation and is classifiable as a failure, for one reason or another, to fulfil the first maxim of Quantity.
>
> (Grice 1975: 38)

The motivation behind much work in neo-Gricean pragmatics over the past few decades has been to curtail the number of separate pragmatic principles necessary for the generation of implicatures. Grice's framework of four categories containing between them nine maxims, together with his throw-away comment that more maxims might prove necessary, has been seen as just too unwieldy and *ad hoc* to offer a defensible account of speaker meaning in context. Neo-Gricean frameworks operate with fewer principles, but all retain some notion of quantity. Levinson (2000), for instance, posits a Q-Principle, an I-Principle and an M-Principle. Of these, the Q-Principle is explicitly concerned with quantity of information and incorporates the speaker's maxim 'do not say less than is required' and the recipient's corollary 'what is not said is not the case'. Horn (1972, 2006, 2007) also identifies a Q-Principle, but in his framework this is complemented and balanced by just one other principle, the R-Principle.

Grice's hesitantly distinguished maxims of Quantity are distributed between Horn's two pragmatic principles. The first maxim of Quantity provides the foundations for Horn's Q-Principle, which enjoins speakers to 'make your contribution sufficient' or 'say as much as you can'. The Q-Principle licenses hearers to understand that if there is something that the speaker has not said, or has avoided in favour of a less informative statement, this is because, as far as the speaker knows, it is not the case. Grice's second maxim of Quantity forms the basis of Horn's R-Principle where, as Grice suspected, it joins forces with the requirements of relevance. The R-Principle places an onus on the speaker to 'make your contribution necessary' or to 'say no more than you must'. It licenses the hearer to infer more precise or more informative meanings than have literally been communicated to him, on the assumption that the speaker has given a bare minimum of information. Horn's two potentially competing sets of demands on speaker and hearer hold each other in check, assuring a balance between the amount of information a speaker is compelled explicitly to offer and the amount of information a hearer is empowered to infer.

Following the R-Principle, a hearer will fill out what was said to reach a more informative interpretation and he will typically do so in a way that relates to general expectations or stereotypical situations. The assumption underpinning such interpretations is that, in saying no more than she must, the speaker has not stated explicitly what can reasonably be assumed from background knowledge. So for instance if a speaker says (1) a hearer will probably fill out what she has said to reach the additional, implicated meaning (2):

1. Mary won a new contract for her firm and received a handsome bonus.
2. Mary won the handsome bonus after and as a result of winning the new contract.

The Q-Principle encourages hearers to understand that if an alternative statement would have been more informative than what was said, the speaker is implicitly denying the validity of that alternative statement.

If she had been in a position truthfully to make the stronger statement it would have been more informative to do so. So for instance to say that something is 'excellent' is stronger and more informative than to say that something is 'good'. Choosing 'good' will generally be taken to implicate that 'excellent' is not applicable; for instance, (3) will be taken to implicate (4).

3. Mary's work in the preceding year had been good.
4. Mary's work in the preceding year had not been excellent.

Examples such as the pair (3) and (4) above provided the basis for Horn's account of 'scalar implicature', one of the most productive but also one of the most controversial developments of neo-Gricean pragmatics (e.g. Horn 1972, 2007). Scalar implicatures owe a debt to Grice's notion of generalised conversational implicatures attached to the use of certain words unless blocked for some reason by context. Horn posited a range of scales in which semantically related words were arranged in descending strength; <excellent, good> would form a fragment of one such scale. The use of an item from such a scale typically implicates the negation of any item to its left, that is of any semantically similar but stronger or more informative item. The many other scales posited by Horn include connectives such as <and, or>, verbs such as <love, like> and, following Grice's original observations about implicatures associated with indefinite noun phrases, articles such as <the, a>.

Recent work in neo-Gricean pragmatics has treated semantic scales with some caution. Where scalar implicatures have been retained, they have generally been understood as less rigid, more fluid and, crucially, more context dependent phenomena. Sauerland, defending the notion of scalar implicatures, argues that 'in specific discourse contexts sometimes further scalar implicatures become available' (Sauerland 2004: 368). Israel, who posits a closer link between pragmatics and grammar than is licensed in traditional Gricean pragmatics, suggests that 'scalar reasoning' seems to be a basic cognitive ability. He argues that he is following recent work by Horn in suggesting that the original conception of scalar implicature may be too narrow: 'Scalar inferences are often not logically valid, but rather depend on general and contingent pragmatic knowledge about how the world normally seems to work' (Israel 2011: 53). This opens up the possibility that the relevant scales against which items are interpreted pragmatically may vary from context to context and may in fact be locally created in different contexts.

Geurts (2010) is dedicated to the rejuvenation of Gricean pragmatics and more specifically of Quantity implicature. Geurts argues that it is possible to work with many aspects of Grice's original conception of pragmatics without being rigidly wedded to his framework of categories and maxims, which were in any case proposed tentatively. Quantity implicatures, he argues, are based on the simple and obvious fact that 'speakers convey information not only by what they say, but also by what they *don't* say' (Geurts 2010: 1). The almost exclusive attention to scalar implicatures in recent neo-Gricean literature has led to the relative neglect of other types of Quantity implicature and has caused Quantity implicatures to be seen as chiefly triggered by individual lexical items, rather than by whole utterances. The following exchange, for instance, does not involve a scalar implicature because there is no single word which can be singled out as inducing an implicature of the denial of a stronger alternative. Nevertheless the implicature that arises is undoubtedly determined by expectations of Quantity. The speaker is taken as implicating that it is her belief that the potential and more informative alternative answer ('Yes') does not apply (Geurts 2010: 31).

5. X: Has A's book come out?
   Y: He has corrected the proofs.

Geurts argues that there are two distinct types of Quantity implicatures, which he labels 'closed' and 'open', and that both are always dependent on context. In the case of closed Quantity implicatures, what is implicated is determined by the existence of a closed set of stronger alternatives that might have been uttered but were not. The set of alternatives is constrained by considerations of relevance; what counts as a relevant alternative is determined in context by the accepted common goals of the conversation, by what is taken to be the hearer's interest and by general interest. Some of these factors 'will be fairly constant across contexts; others will be more dependent on specific contextual features' (Geurts 2010: 53). So for instance, (6) implicates (7):

6. Many of the nurses were drunk.
7. Not all the nurses were drunk.

It is usually accepted in any context in which (6) is uttered that the stronger alternative 'All of the nurses were drunk' would be relevant to the purposes of the conversation and of interest to the hearer if it were true. Closed Quantity implicatures, then, include the traditional class of scalar implicatures, although Geurts himself is wary of the term 'scale' and prefers to describe alternatives as being arranged in an unordered 'set'. They also include examples such as the following, where C's answer is likely to implicate that C has no firm belief about what type of furniture Bonnie has gone to buy:

8. A: Where is Bonnie?
   C: She went out to buy a piece of furniture.

Here it would not be possible to posit scales on which 'piece of furniture' is related to the more informative but lexically simpler alternatives such as 'chair', 'table', 'bed' etc. But what might be considered to be 'general interest' makes these all possible alternatives that C might have uttered but has not. Geurts generalises, suggesting that: 'there are general expectations to the effect that, when introducing a new discourse entity, speakers should employ expressions of at least a minimum level of specificity' (Geurts 2010: 46). Failing to do so introduces the implicature that the speaker is not in a position to offer the more specific alternative, either because she does not know or because she does not care. Closed Quantity implicatures, then, depend on comparing what the speaker has said with available alternatives that she might have said but has not. What counts as 'availability' in relation to these alternatives is determined not by the existence of fixed lexical scales, but by context relative factors such as economy, previous use, frequency of use and general or particular expectations of specificity.

Open Quantity implicatures are exemplified for instance by the following:

9. Mildred: What did you do when you got home?
   George: I fell asleep in front of the television.

Geurts explains:

> It is rather unlikely that falling asleep in front of the television is the only thing George did when he got home. He may have taken off his coat and shoes, made himself a cup of tea, and so on. What George's answer is meant to convey is that falling asleep in front of the television was the only noteworthy thing he did. But clearly, noteworthiness is a matter of degree, and therefore the [open Quantity] implicature prompted by George's answer is much less determinate than your average [closed Quantity] implicature.
>
> (Geurts 2010: 128)

The next two sections apply recent developments in the theory of Quantity implicatures to the analysis of implicit meaning in *TLS*. In particular, they consider the possibility of using of Geurts's distinction between 'closed' and 'open' Quantity implicatures in explaining two different ways in which meaning is implicated in the novel. Section 4 considers some of the sets of alternatives that may be established in *TLS* and the closed Quantity implicatures that choices from these sets may introduce. Section 5 considers some of the less determinate open Quantity implicatures that may be introduced on occasions when characters do not speak and the narrator makes it apparent that the act of not speaking is itself significant.

4 'One so easily says too much': Avoiding the issue in *The Last September*

In this section I consider some examples of characters' selection of the vocabulary with which to discuss the contemporary situation in *TLS*, which indirectly reveals characters' attitudes to 'the Troubled Times'. I suggest that within the context of the novel a set of alternative vocabulary items for referring to the situation is established, such that a choice of one item from the set implicates that alternative items are not applicable or in some way not appropriate.

The business of naming the state of affairs in Ireland in 1920 was a fraught one. Insurgent forces were making increasingly bold attacks on the British troops garrisoned throughout Ireland and, in turn, those suspected of involvement with the IRA were being pursued and punished with increasing violence, but there was no official state of war between Britain and Ireland. Bowen's own use of the phrase 'the Troubled Times' reflects this. Elsewhere in autobiographical writings she described them as 'the bad times' or as a series of 'reprisals and counter-reprisals' (Bowen 1942: 439 and 1986: 260). Characters in *TLS*, when they refer to the armed conflict at all, often do so by means of vague or general noun phrases. Soon after the arrival of the house guests the Montmorencys, Francie Montmorency discusses their hosts Sir Richard and Lady Naylor with her husband Hugo, commenting: 'Times have been worse down here. Yes, I thought, you know, she had a rather strained look. What does Richard think of the situation?... Oh, and had you any idea that Lois was so grown up?' (*TLS*: 18). Strikingly, Hugo's reply responds only to the question about Lois. But later at dinner he attempts to make conversation with Lady Naylor's nephew Laurence:

> He said at one to Laurence: 'And what do you think of things?'
> 'Things? Over here?'
> 'Yes – yes.'
> 'Seem to be closing in,' said Laurence, crumbling his bread detachedly; 'rolling up, rather.'
> 'Ssh!' exclaimed Lady Naylor, running out a hand at both of them over the cloth.
>
> (*TLS*: 24–25)

Terms such as 'times', 'the situation' and 'things' have, in the terminology used by Geurts, a very low 'level of specificity' and might be taken to be the characters' way of implicating that a stronger alternative term is not appropriate. The set to which these terms belong is established by general interest but also, in the context provided by the novel itself, by 'frequency of use'. As the novel progresses, the stronger alternative term 'war' is offered on a number of occasions. For instance the visitor Marda, a relative outsider to the conversational mores of Danielstown, says to Hugo 'How far do you think this war is going to go?' (*TLS*: 82). A little later Laurence, who is more *au fait* with Anglo-Irish conventions but who delights in breaking taboos and challenging the social *status quo*, asks the army officer Gerald 'How is this war of yours really going?' (*TLS*: 92). The applicability of terms at times becomes a matter of controversy in itself. At a tennis party at Danielstown shortly after the arrival of the Montmorencys, Gerald is in conversation with the Hartigans, a group of unmarried sisters from a nearby house. The sisters have just apologised for telling an anecdote about how unpleasant English accents sound:

> 'It was splendid of you to forget I was English. Well, we shall all be leaving you soon, I dare say; all we jolly old army of occupation.'
> 'Oh, one wouldn't like to call you *that*,' said Miss Hartigan, deprecatingly.
> '-as soon as we've lost this jolly old war.'
> 'Oh, but one wouldn't call it a *war*.'
> 'If anyone would, we could clean these beggars out in a week.'
> 'We think it would be a great pity to have a war,' said the Hartigans firmly. 'There's been enough unpleasantness

> already, hasn't there?... And it would be a shame for you all to go,' added Doreen warmly, but not too warmly because they were all men.
>
> (*TLS*: 37–38)

Gerald offers 'war' as a much stronger alternative to phrases such as 'the situation' or 'things' and it is explicitly rejected by the Hartigans, who in this conversation are representatives of the Anglo-Irish community. The use of weaker expressions takes on a pragmatic meaning specific to the context established within the novel. It is possible to posit a set of alternatives that includes both the explicit term 'war' and weaker terms such as 'the situation', 'things' and perhaps even 'unpleasantness', such that the choice of a weaker term is an implicated denial of the applicability of the stronger term and hence a refusal to allow that the fighting constitutes anything as severe and as potentially transformative as war.

The controversy over terms extends not just to naming 'the Troubled Times' themselves, but also to identifying the main protagonists, specifically the members of the Irish Republican Army. Soon after Marda's arrival, the local postman brings news to Danielstown of a nearby raid: 'It had been a great raid, the postman said; if the boys had not fled it would have been almost a battle' (*TLS*: 78). This piece of reported speech is interesting because of the scalar relationship that the postman suggests between 'raid' and 'battle', but also because of his choice of the term 'the boys' to refer to the armed insurgents. The term suggests some degree of sympathy, identification and perhaps familiarity on the postman's part, but it also avoids any more specific identification of what type of people he is talking about. Although the British troops are widely discussed throughout *TLS*, in terms both of specific ranks and regiments and also of named individuals, there are strikingly few references to their opponents. When such references are made, non-specific vocabulary such as that chosen by the postman is often used. At dinner on the night of the Montmorencys' arrival, Lois reports a rumour that 'men' have buried guns on estate land (*TLS*: 25). The Naylors' fiercely loyalist acquaintance Mrs Fogarty has a drawing-room filled with 'cushions with Union Jacks that she wouldn't, she said, put away – not if They came at night and stood in her room with pistols' (*TLS*: 71). It is again left to Laurence to identify the more specific term when he says provocatively to Gerald: 'I sometimes rather wish that I were a gunman' (*TLS*: 92). The term 'gunman' could be seen as belonging to the same set as the less specific alternatives and as being implicitly rejected whenever one of these less specific terms is used.

A particularly striking example of the deliberate use of a term that is less specific than 'gunman', is Marda's use of 'someone' on the occasion when she and Lois disturb an armed man in the abandoned mill. This episode is significant in terms of both the interpersonal and the political themes of the novel. Entering the mill has brought Marda and Lois both physically and emotionally close to each other. Disturbing the gunman has brought them face to face with the realities of the armed conflict. But afterwards both are keen to downplay the significance of the event and they try to prevent Hugo from entering the mill. Marda speaks first in this extract:

> 'Someone went upstairs backward, not very sensibly, not having eaten much for four days. There was some plaster – the pistol went off, naturally. It was silly, really. Look at my beastly hand – I was holding on to the door.'
> 'Let me get past-'
> 'But we *swore*, Mr Montmorency-'
> '*You* deserve to be shot!' He turned in a manner terrifying to all of them – most of all to himself – on this interruption. 'You don't seem to see, you seem to have no conception-'
> 'Then why sit there and smoke?' said Lois, trembling. 'I saw you – you and your old conceptions.'
> 'Shut up,' said Marda, 'Oh, do shut up!'
> 'Don't stand there, let me go past; I'll-'
> 'Oh, do let's talk about something else-'
> 'We swore,' went on Lois priggishly. 'There never was anybody, we never saw anybody, *you* never heard-'
> But nobody listened. Vaguely, he waved her silent.
>
> (*TLS*: 126–127)

Marda describes the shooting as 'silly', which in the context of what has happened serves as a rejection of any more informative evaluation in terms of danger or culpability. She uses the unspecific term 'someone', implicating that to use a more informative term such as 'gunman' would be inappropriate. She also attempts to prohibit speech on the subject with her 'shut up!' and her pleading to change the subject. This preoccupation with not talking about what might appear to be most relevant is another salient characteristic of *TLS* and is the topic of the next section.

5 'No one spoke': The narration of silence in *The Last September*

The last section was concerned with examples in which characters in *TLS* talk about the situation in Ireland so as implicitly to deny its severity and possible consequences. Characters in the novel are also preoccupied with the importance of simply not talking about 'the Troubled Times', or indeed about their own troubled relationships which in some ways mirror these; Lady Naylor's 'shh' when Hugo and Laurence began to discuss 'things' at dinner and the comments from Marda and Lois in the extract above are examples of this. This section is concerned with instances of not talking in the novel, specifically with occasions on which the narrator comments that speech did not take place. In doing so she implicates that something might have been said but was not. This implicature from narrator to reader can be explained as deriving from a flouting of Grice's second maxim of Quantity; a statement that something did not take place is apparently unnecessary and uninformative, so the reader seeks an implicated meaning which makes it cooperative. In Horn's neo-Gricean framework the narrator introduces an R-implicature that the negative statement is necessary and informative, and therefore that the absence of speech was significant.

On each occasion when the narrator comments that speech has not taken place, then, she implicates that something might have been said but was not; that is, she implicitly draws attention to a potential utterance that might have been expected but was not produced. There is also a further implicature that the specific content of the potential utterance was not applicable or not appropriate. On each occasion, this further implicature depends on a flouting of Grice's first maxim of Quantity. A failure to speak when an utterance might be expected is apparently not sufficiently informative, so the reader and perhaps the other characters may understand the character who is significantly not speaking to be denying that something specific can appropriately be said. In neo-Gricean frameworks such as those used by both Horn and Geurts, this is a Q-implicature; in Geurts's terms characters may be taken to be conveying information by what they 'don't say'. Quite what it was that might have been said but, by not being said, is implicitly being denied is more difficult to establish. Geurts has described how 'open' Quantity implicatures are much less determinate than 'closed' ones, deriving from the assumption that if there was something more informative to say the speaker would have done so. Silence in a context where speech might have been expected might be argued to produce the most 'open' implicatures of all. There can be no clue from what was said to what could have been said but was not. The implicature must be driven entirely by context and by a knowledge of what would be most noteworthy or relevant in the situation.

First, here are some examples in which the narrator comments on occasions of not saying:

> Mrs Montmorency and Laurence sit in embarrassed silence before dinner: 'Now there were no voices'.
>
> (*TLS*: 20)

> Lois having glimpsed the man in the trenchcoat, initially plans to tell the others. On returning to the house she discovers: 'But it was impossible to speak of this'
>
> (*TLS*: 34–35)

> Mrs Montmorency and Laurence sit together again, this time after a tennis party: 'There was nothing to say'
>
> (*TLS*: 53)

> Driving in the trap with Hugo, Lois reflects on: 'what had remained unsaid'
>
> (*TLS*: 62)

> Lois reflects on the aftermath of Marda's wounding by the gunman: 'one had not spoken again of it'
>
> (*TLS*: 132)

> Hugo is miserable at Marda's departure: 'There was to be no opportunity for what he must not say to be rather painfully not said'
>
> (*TLS*: 138)

> At the very end of the novel, Sir Richard and Lady Naylor witness the burning of Danielstown: 'not saying anything'
>
> (*TLS*: 206)

Examples such as these build up a context in which the very act of not speaking itself becomes significant. In the account of Marda's departure, for instance, what is annoying Hugo is not that there will not be time for him to say something but that there will not be time for him to say nothing. Exactly what is not said, and might be taken to be implicitly denied, cannot be predicted by the form of words used precisely because no words are used. The wider context in which each example occurs, however, suggests what is not said and this is generally pertinent to one of the two main, related preoccupations of the novel: the escalating armed conflict surrounding the characters and the parallel turmoil of their own interpersonal relationships. In concluding this section I will consider in a little more detail two of the above examples. First, here is a slightly longer quotation from the scene in which Lois returns from the shrubbery:

> But as Lois went up the steps breathlessly, her adventure began to diminish. It held ground for a minute as she saw the rug dropped in the hall by Mrs Montmorency sprawl like a body across the polish. Then confidence disappeared, in a waver of shadow, among the furniture. Conceivably, she had just surprised life at a significant angle in the shrubbery. But it was impossible to speak of this. At a touch from Aunt Myra adventure became literary, to Uncle Richard it suggested an inconvenience; a glance from Mr Montmorency or Laurence would make her encounter sterile.
>
> But what seemed most probable was that they would not listen . . . She lighted her candle and went up to bed – uncivilly, without saying good night to anyone.
>
> (*TLS*: 34–35)

By not speaking Lois does not implicate that she did not see a gunman; such a very specific implicature would not be available to the other inhabitants of the house. But by not speaking she does implicate that nothing noteworthy or potentially significant has happened to her since she left the house. She has learnt the lesson of Danielstown that anything that draws attention to the ongoing armed conflict, or anything that suggests it might be important or relevant to the lives of those in the house, must not be said.

Lois's later trap ride with Hugo is significant largely in terms of the relationship between the two and what that relationship will not be. As we have seen, aspects of relationships between characters in *TLS* are often indicative of the more general theme of a social and political establishment that is unviable and has no future.

> They were silent in a mutual criticism. As they came down and the mountains, drawn behind, were once more scenic, as hedges ran up at the sides of the road, the illusion of distance between them faded; they obtruded upon each other; a time when they could have talked was gone. They might have said, she felt now, anything; but what had remained unsaid, never conceived in thought, would exercise now a stronger compulsion on their attitude.
>
> (*TLS*: 62–63)

This passage in itself does not offer the reader enough context to know what they have not said and therefore what, by not saying it in a context in which it might have been said, they have implicitly denied. For that the reader must look to the context provided by what has preceded this passage in the novel, particularly Lois's expectation that she will fall in love with Hugo, and Hugo's expectation that seeing Lois will revive painful memories of his own love for her dead mother Laura. The act of not speaking in this extract implicitly denies both Lois's potential love for Hugo and Hugo's past love for Laura.

6 Conclusions

Critics of *TLS* have generally noted a tension between the central importance of 'the Troubled Times' and its implications on the one hand, and the characters' reluctance or refusal to discuss it on the other. They have further noticed that potential relationships between characters, ostensibly a major concern of the novel, in fact function largely as reflections on the major themes of change, transition and finality. In this chapter I have explored the possibility of using pragmatic theory in the Gricean tradition to explain how characters and narrator implicate more than they say and therefore how they address the central themes implicitly. The analysis has been based on the theory of Quantity implicatures, particularly recent developments in which such implicatures are viewed as localised and contextual, including Geurts's distinction between 'open' and 'closed' Quantity implicatures. The theory of Quantity implicatures, and Geurts's development of it in particular, has proved particularly useful in explaining the significance of the terminology used to describe 'the Troubled

Times', and also of occasions when the narrator draws attention to characters' failure to speak. Neo-Gricean pragmatics has offered a useful framework for analysing Bowen's indirect handling of her themes. At the same time, the problem posed by the central tension in *TLS* has offered an intriguing new type of data for neo-Gricean pragmatic analysis.

4
Before and After Chekhov: Inference, Interpretation and Evaluation

Billy Clark

1 Introduction

This chapter considers some of the inferential processes involved in reading, understanding and evaluating Anton Chekhov's story *The Lady with the Little Dog* (Chekhov 2002, originally 1899/1903).[1] This story has been very highly valued over the years but many readers report thinking it unimportant or even banal on first reading. The discussion here aims to account for some of the specific inferences involved in understanding the story and also to consider two things which have not been much discussed in previous pragmatic stylistic work: differences between inferences made after first and subsequent readings of a text and the role inferential processes play in evaluating texts. It also aims to consider to what extent an account of reader inferences can account for the fact that many readers report being puzzled by the story on first reading and then go on to value it very highly.

This chapter begins by summarising the plot of the story and describing some responses and partial interpretations, based partly on my own intuitions and partly on remarks made by critics and commentators. It then describes some initial conclusions developed partly from classroom work, including the conclusion that the approach developed here can go some way towards explaining not only how readers respond to the text but also why it has been valued by individual readers. The next section develops discussion of how the story has come to be valued by individual readers, both formally and informally, and considers how a focus on inferential processes might contribute to a fuller account of how works come to be culturally valued. A key aspect of this is the assumption that individual readers will value work more highly if they find themselves spontaneously thinking about that work again after they have read it. The section also suggests that an account of how a text is culturally represented and valued can make use of Dan Sperber's (1996) work on how cultural assumptions are (meta)represented and his notion of an 'epidemiology of representations' which aims to explain how cultural assumptions develop and spread among populations. A general conclusion is that work which focuses on inferential processes can make a significant contribution in understanding how works come to be valued formally and informally, by individuals and by cultural groups more widely.

2 *The Lady with the Little Dog*

The Lady with the Little Dog has appeared in many anthologies and translations in English as well as other languages. It has been described as one of Chekhov's greatest stories and, of course, Chekhov has been described as one of the greatest short story writers, influencing many more recent writers, including Isaac Babel, Ernest Hemingway, Eudora Welty and Raymond Carver. This story has properties common to many of Chekhov's stories, including skilful and condensed characterisation and, for many readers, a perceived contrast between deceptive simplicity on first reading and continuing resonance after reading and on rereading the story. Here is a very brief summary of the plot of the story. The discussion here is based on the English text in the 2002 Penguin edition translated by Ronald Wilks (Chekhov 2002).

The Lady with the Little Dog tells (part of) the story of a relationship between an older ('not yet forty') man, Gurov, and a younger woman, Anna Sergeyevna. Gurov is an unfaithful husband who has had a series of short-lived affairs. Anna is more innocent and has not had an affair before. Their relationship begins in Yalta, at a time when this was a popular holiday destination and health resort. Their time together in Yalta begins when Gurov wags a finger at Anna's dog and ends when Anna is called home by her husband. Both Anna and Gurov assume that this means the affair is over and Gurov returns to Moscow. Gurov is surprised, however, to find that he cannot stop thinking about Anna. He lies to his wife, visits Anna's home town and they meet again. They establish a new routine where Anna visits Moscow regularly and sends word when she has checked in to her hotel. The story ends with the couple trying to think of a solution so that they no longer need to deceive. The last paragraph suggests that they think they will succeed and that they are at the beginning of something:

> And it seemed – given a little more time – a solution would be found and then a new and beautiful life would begin. And both of them clearly realised that the end was far, far away and that the most complicated and difficult part was only just beginning.
>
> (Chekhov 2002: 240)

3 Responses

In some ways, this is a simple story of a jaded man who discovers love late in life. But the story has had a significant impact on a wide range of readers. Richard Ford (2007: xi) describes the story as 'the all-time short story gold standard' and 'as good as any of us will ever read'. In an earlier discussion (Ford 1998: viii–ix), he reports his own experience as beginning with bafflement:

> My own college experience was to read the great anthology standard 'The Lady with the Dog' ... and basically to be baffled by it, although the story's fundamental directness and authority made me highly respectful of something I can only describe as a profound-feeling gray light emanating from the story's austere interior.
>
> (Ford 1998: viii)

Ford goes on to describe how he puzzled over the significance of the story, later began to announce he liked the story, although 'only because I thought I should' (Ford 1998: ix) and eventually to consider it a masterpiece.

Ford suggests his own reasons for appreciating the story now. One is that Chekhov made an imaginative leap in choosing something seemingly mundane as subject matter for a story. Ford also suggests that the story '... is full of fine, nuanced, writerly precisions, skewering verbal and dramatic ironies, great if concisely set emphases, and the pathos of human frailty half-enlivened by sex.' (Ford 2007: xii). Janet Malcolm (2001) makes suggestive comments about Chekhov in general. She quotes the playwright Ivan Scheglov writing to Chekhov to criticise an earlier story ('Lights' 1888) as saying 'I was not entirely satisfied with your latest story. Of course, I swallowed it in one gulp, there is no question about that, because everything you write is so appetising and real that it can be easily swallowed.' (Malcolm 2001: 20). She goes on to suggest that 'We swallow a Chekhov story as if it were an ice, and we cannot account for our feeling of repletion' (Malcolm 2001: 22).

Clearly, there is a lot to say in exploring how Chekhov's writing combines the properties of being 'easily swallowed' and leading to a 'feeling of repletion'. With a view to contributing to an explanation of this, the next section considers some of the inferential processes involved in reading and responding to the story.

4 Exploring inferences

There is, of course, not enough space here to discuss all of the inferential processes readers might go through in reading this story. Instead, this section describes inferences around some key passages of the story. This discussion was initially inspired by classroom work with final year undergraduate students working on a module called 'Writing Techniques' at Middlesex University between 2008 and 2011. Only a small proportion of these students were taking programmes which involved studying literature. The programmes which they were studying included programmes in English Language, Advertising, Media, PR and Publishing. While the discussion was then, and is here, largely based on relevance theory (Sperber and Wilson 1986/1995), the discussion does not depend on this specific theoretical approach.

Our first way into the story was to consider different translations of the title of the story. As there are no articles in Russian, Chekhov's original title *Dama s sobachkoy* (Дама с собачкой) translates as *lady with dog* where *dog* contains a diminutive morpheme. Since Chekhov did not have the option of choosing whether or not to include a definite or indefinite article, translators have to decide whether or not to include one of these forms in English. They also choose whether to translate *sobachkoy* as simply *dog* or as *little dog* or conceivably even as *doggie*, although this has not been suggested as far as I am aware. *Little dog* has been suggested, as has *lapdog*. The possibilities we discussed in class included: *The lady with the little dog*; *The lady with the dog*; *Lady with dog*; *The lady with a little dog*; *A lady with a little dog*; *The lady with the lapdog*; *Lady with lapdog*.

How should translators choose between these and other options? There are two overlapping kinds of inferential process which the title will support: inferences made before reading the story (about what kind of story to expect) and inferences made while and after reading the story (about specific parts of the text or about its overall significance). In class, we discussed these different possibilities before students had read the story and then discussed them further after reading.

Without developing a detailed semantic analysis of *a* or *the*, the choice between these two can be understood as being to do with how the author/narrator thinks of the lady and dog. *A* would suggest little more than that the story is about a specific lady and dog (whether or not anyone thinks of them as special in any particular way). *The* would suggest that someone definitely is thinking of this lady and this dog as significant and salient in some way. A key point, then, is that the choice of *the* suggests a point of view from which the lady and the dog are being represented. We can understand *a lady with a dog* as representing the author's or narrator's point of view, or of one of the characters in the story, but *the* suggests that this is likely to be how one or more characters in the story think of the lady. When students discussed the story in class, it seemed clear that this would be taken to reflect how Gurov thought of Anna.

Absence of articles is a fairly marked choice in English and students recognised that this is fairly typical of titles of paintings or artworks, a suggestion reinforced by some of the choices made for covers of collections containing the story, including some versions of the 2002 collection we used in class, which feature Toulouse-Lautrec's 1891 oil painting *Lady with a Dog*. This suggests inferential paths which consider the story as a portrait. This might lead to conclusions about the story being seen as portrait-like in presenting a particular person or kind of person, or about how the writer presents something more universal by showing us something specific (as we will see below, there is a passage where Anna is described as resembling a painting). This would, however, detract from the sense that the story is about Anna Sergeyevna and the details of Gurov's relationship with her.

Arguments for particular decisions will, of course, be affected by how the story as a whole is understood. In class, we reached a consensus in favour of use of the definite article. This was partly because we did not think the story as a whole was portrait-like or suggesting something general about a particular kind of person, even though it could be understood as mainly about Anna in some ways. The key consideration, though, was that this story was mainly about Anna as perceived and responded to by Gurov. Key evidence came from the opening two paragraphs of the story in the translation we used:

> People said that there was a new arrival on the Promenade: a lady with a little dog. Dmitry Dmitrich Gurov, who had already spent a fortnight in Yalta, and who was by now used to the life there, had also begun to take an interest in new arrivals. As he sat on the terrace

> of Vernet's restaurant he saw a young, fair-haired woman walking along the Promenade, not very tall and wearing a beret. A white Pomeranian trotted after her.
>
> And then he came across her several times a day in the municipal park, and the square. She was always alone, always wearing that beret, always with the white Pomeranian. No one knew who she was and people simply called her 'The lady with the little dog'.
>
> (Chekhov 2002: 223)

The translator begins by referring to Anna as *a lady with a little dog* and moves on to describe her as *the lady with the little dog*. In both places, this is represented as how 'people' talk about her. The choice of *a* is appropriate at first as people are spotting her (and talking about her) for the first time. As they refer to her on subsequent occasions it is appropriate to assume that they would describe her using *the* (a choice not available to the people of Yalta, of course). Students were fairly unanimous in considering that the title should reflect how Gurov would think of Anna after he had seen her several times around town and perhaps later as he thinks back to their time together in Yalta. This suggested that the choice should be *the lady with the little dog*.

The choice of translation for *sobachkoy* follows fairly straightforwardly from current pragmatic theories. We would expect translators to reflect the fact that Chekhov used a diminutive form and the phrase used to describe Anna needs to be able to pick her out from other people around town. If there are no or very few other people around with dogs, then *the lady with the dog* should be enough to pick her out. If there are other people, and other ladies, with dogs, then a more specific description will be needed. A 'neo-Gricean' approach to pragmatics such as that developed by Horn (1984, 2004) might account for this with reference to a Q-Principle and an R-Principle, which jointly stipulate that speakers should say as much as they need to and no more than they must (for discussion, see Chapman 2012 and this volume). A relevance-theoretic approach would say that the effort involved in processing the word *little* should lead to enough effects to justify this effort. Since the word *little* helps to describe and identify the dog, this is enough to justify the effort involved. There is no risk of unintended implicatures from the use of *little* here, so it seems reasonable to include this word in the translation.

This discussion leads naturally into consideration of how Chekhov's writing reflects particular points of view. The opening sentence (in the passage above) reflects the point of view of people in Yalta in general.

The second sentence moves on to tell us about Gurov and we follow his point of view until the end of paragraph two. Paragraph three begins with a representation of Gurov's thinking: 'If she's here without husband or friends,' Gurov reasoned, 'then it wouldn't be a bad idea if I got to know her.' (Chekhov 2002: 223). From now on, the story tells us about Gurov and his thoughts. Everything which unfolds reflects Gurov's point of view.

As the story unfolds, we see that Gurov is cynical and jaded. He has had a series of affairs and plans to begin one with Anna in a fairly calculated way and without much excitement. As he goes to bed after their first day together, he thinks about her, deciding that she is awkward and unaccustomed to male attention. He remembers her 'slender, frail neck, her beautiful grey eyes' and goes to sleep thinking 'Still, there's something pathetic about her' (Chekhov 2002: 226).

Perhaps the most striking passage providing evidence of Gurov's initial attitude towards Anna is the passage where Gurov responds to Anna after their first sexual encounter in her room. The sexual activity is, of course, strongly implicated but not explicitly mentioned. The lack of explicitness is easily explained pragmatically given social attitudes at the time of writing. Anna is clearly upset about 'what had happened' and the description of her reflects Gurov's less than sympathetic attitude:

> ... In her own particular, very serious way, Anna Sergeyevna, that lady with the little dog, regarded what had happened just as if it were her downfall. So it seemed – and it was all very weird and out of place. Her features sank and faded, and her long hair hung sadly on each side of her face. She struck a pensive, dejected pose, like the woman taken in adultery in an old-fashioned painting.
>
> 'This is wrong,' she said. 'You'll be the first to lose respect for me now.'
> (Chekhov 2002: 227)

As mentioned above, this description compares her to a painting. One effect of this is to indicate how Gurov thinks of her as he looks at her, considering how she resembles a painting and so implicating that he is fairly detached and not really empathising with her.

Gurov's response to her utterance is to slowly and silently cut and eat a slice of water-melon: 'On the table was a water-melon. Gurov cut himself a slice and slowly started eating it. Half an hour, at least, passed in silence.' (Chekhov 2002: 227)

This clearly strikes readers as inconsiderate at best and probably heartless. The inferences readers make here depend partly on inferences made when reading the description of Anna and Gurov's previous behaviour. It is clear that Anna is innocent and unsure of herself while Gurov is cynical and self-confident. Readers are likely to wonder how Gurov will react to Anna in this vulnerable state. Some of the implicatures of Anna's last utterance include:

(1) (a) People will not respect me if they discover I have committed adultery.
(b) I am ashamed of myself.
(c) I care about your opinion of me.
(d) I would like to hear you disconfirm my suggestion that you will lose respect for me now.

Readers anticipating Gurov's response might expect him to reassure Anna and to deny the suggestion that he will lose respect for her. If he does not do this, he will surely implicate that he does not disagree with her and that he will indeed lose respect for her. In fact, even if he did deny it, she might not believe him. The fact that he does not bother to speak at all gives rise to strong implicatures not only confirming what Anna has suggested by non-denial but even reinforcing this by not considering that her utterance is worthy of a reply. As well as the strong implicatures here about his attitude to Anna's expressed feelings, Gurov suggests that he is not even interested in conveying phatic implications about his willingness to communicate with Anna (for discussion of phatic communication within a relevance-theoretic framework, see Nicolle and Clark 1998; Zegarac 1998; Zegarac and Clark 1999; Padilla Cruz 2007).

Another key passage in the story comes later when Gurov has been surprised by his inability to stop thinking about Anna. He anticipates his memory of her fading but is surprised that he keeps thinking of her. He finds himself desperate to speak about her but not able to. Finally, he bursts: 'One night, as he left the Doctors' Club with his partner – a civil servant – he was unable to hold back any longer and said: "If you only knew what an enchanting woman I met in Yalta!" ' (Chekhov 2002: 233). The civil servant's response is disappointing in ways which parallel Gurov's earlier response to Anna:

> The civil servant climbed into his sledge and drove off.
> But then he suddenly turned round and called out:

'Dmitry Dmitrich!'
'What?'
'You were right the other day – the sturgeon was off!'

(Chekhov 2002: 233)

Echoing Gurov's behaviour with the watermelon in Yalta, the civil servant does not respond straight away, although a shorter time passes before he speaks. His response does not connect with Gurov's comment at all. Both responses involve food: eating watermelon in Gurov's case; talking about sturgeon for the civil servant. Gurov's response to this is dramatic: 'This trite remark for some reason suddenly nettled Gurov, striking him as degrading and dirty.' (Chekhov 2002: 233). Gurov is unable to sleep that night, has a headache the next day and continues to have trouble sleeping until he decides to pack up (lying to his wife about where he is going) and head to Anna's home town.

This is clearly a turning point in the narrative. It is important in changing Gurov but also in encouraging inferences about how he has changed. It is even possible that his dramatic response is partly inspired by an awareness at some level that the civil servant's comment echoes his own behaviour earlier. It sets in motion all of the rest of the story, leading to Gurov finding Anna at the theatre, to a new arrangement where she regularly visits Moscow to see him and to the final inconclusive ending where Gurov and Anna are looking for a solution to their problem.

Another area we explored in class was the relationship between local inferences and more global ones. Local inferences are relatively specific ones which follow on from specific, local parts of the story. An extremely local example might be the inference that *her* at the end of the first paragraph of the story refers to the lady with the little dog. Global inferences are ones which follow on from the story as a whole. (For discussion of the contrast between local and global inferences, see Clark 1996, 2009, in press). In class, we arrived at these by identifying particular inferences and connecting them with inferences about the story as a whole and its significance. A number of the more global conclusions we discussed were about how Gurov changes during the story. The two passages above contribute to these conclusions about how a jaded, cynical man is changed when he unexpectedly falls in love. Others concern the nature of human relationships and desires and how we can be seen as weak and 'pathetic' (echoing Gurov's description of Anna mentioned above).

While there is no space to discuss them fully here, it is clear that the story provides evidence for a wide range of conclusions and interpretations. This can be seen as contributing to the 'feeling of repletion' mentioned by Malcolm (2001) above. The sense that the story is 'easily swallowed' follows partly from details of how it is written and constructed and the straightforward, fairly recognisable, characters and plot developments involved. The story as a whole is also 'easily swallowed' in that the story as a whole can be represented shortly and straightforwardly, for example as a story in which a cynical older man has an affair with an innocent younger woman and unexpectedly falls in love. The next section speculates on other aspects of the story which might contribute to its having been highly valued.

5 Exploring evaluations

Post-Gricean work on pragmatic inference and literary stylistics has mainly focused on inferential processes made while reading texts (for an early example, see Leech and Short 1981: 231–254; for more recent discussion, see Black 2006). There has also been discussion of how contextual assumptions create expectations prior to reading. These include assumptions about the author, attitudes to the text expressed by others and assumptions about the physical presentation of the text, including its cover design (see, for example, discussion in Clark 2009). There has been little discussion of how formal interpretations are developed (Furlong 1996 is a notable exception) and very little work on evaluation (although Fabb 1995 and Pilkington 2000 explore the nature of 'aesthetic' and affective responses). Work in stylistics in general has also said little about evaluation. There has been a recent increase in interest in this area (see, for example, papers in van Peer 2008) as well as on feeling and embodied experience (see, for example, Stockwell 2009). However, this work has not focused much on inferential processes.

The discussion above has explored some of the inferential processes involved in reading and responding to *The Lady with the Little Dog*. This suggested that the story is 'easily swallowed' because the writing is clear, precise and easy to follow, and because the characters and events are fairly recognisable and not challenging. The 'feeling of repletion' which this writing gives rise to can be seen as following on from the rich range of inferential conclusions which it provides evidence for, the possibility of exploring further inferential paths and the complexity of some of these, particularly those based on recognising a parallel between

Gurov's changing attitude to his affair and our changing attitude to the story.

This section makes a number of speculative suggestions about factors which might contribute to positive evaluations of this work and possibly to other literary works (although I would not claim that these can be generalised widely or taken to be strongly correlated with positive evaluations). These are partly based on ideas developed in the discussion above and partly on Sperber's (1996, 2000) work on metarepresentation and the spread of cultural assumptions. Some of these have been discussed above: the ease with which particular passages and the story as a whole can be recalled and the nature of effects which can be derived from them. The new factors discussed in this section which might play a role are awareness of positive responses from others and the metarepresentational nature of representations of other people's responses. A final possible factor only mentioned here is positive evaluation of particular features such as linguistic dexterity, sound patterning and so on. This section considers each of these factors briefly.

5.1 Ease of recalling particular parts of the text

It seems likely that readers will continue to derive inferences after reading texts if they are able to represent particular parts of the text and continue to derive inferences from them. Clear examples here are the watermelon and the sturgeon episodes. Readers can easily represent these and can carry on thinking about their significance, how they connect with their own experiences, and so on, after finishing the story.

5.2 Ease of representing the work as a whole

As mentioned above, the story as a whole can easily be represented and readers can carry on deriving inferences from this after reading.

These first two factors clearly connect with the notion of the text being 'easily swallowed' as well as with relevance-theoretic assumptions about processing effort, i.e. the assumption that (other things being equal) the less effort involved in processing a stimulus, the more relevant it is. This point goes beyond that, though, since it also suggests that readers are more likely to revisit an interpretation if they can entertain a representation of what they have read fairly easily.

The next two points relate to the notion that the text provides a sense of 'repletion' and to the other key notion in determining the relevance of stimuli, according to relevance theory: the derivation of cognitive effects.

5.3 The relevance of the outputs of particular inferential processes derived

Alongside ease of processing and recalling passages of the text, and the text itself, the text will need to give rise to significant effects if it is to be valued. The more that readers can continue to derive effects on thinking about the story, the more likely they are to continue to think about it and feel positively about it. These effects might follow on from individual parts of the text or from the text as a whole.

5.4 The extent to which relatively complex inferential processes reward extra effort with extra effects

Relevance theory predicts that more complex inferential processes will need to lead to more significant cognitive effects if readers are to continue making inferences and to develop positive evaluations of the text.

One aspect of the story which we discussed in class and which also seems to contribute to positive evaluations is a parallel between Gurov and readers of the story. Gurov believes at first that he is involved in something relatively mundane which is transient and whose memory will soon fade. He is surprised to find that he keeps thinking of Anna and that his relationship with her is very important to him. Like Gurov, many readers report thinking that the story is relatively unimportant at first. The characters do not seem special and their relationship seems relatively mundane. Some readers are also disappointed that the ending is unresolved. However, many readers then go on to find themselves thinking about the story again after they have read it, reanalysing what has happened and its significance. We resemble Gurov in our developing response to the story. This adds a layer of complexity to the global inferences we can derive from the story and is arguably one factor which contributes to positive evaluations of the story and to the sense of 'repletion' mentioned above.

5.5 Awareness of positive responses of other people and the metarepresentational nature of representations of other people's responses

The factors discussed so far are fairly straightforward and follow on from relevance-theoretic assumptions and the discussion above. There are two factors we have not discussed above which also seem relevant, both of which relate to Sperber's (1996, 2000) work on metarepresentation and the spread of cultural assumptions.

Sperber (1996) proposes an 'epidemiology of representations' to study how cultural assumptions spread among populations in ways which are similar to the study of the spread of diseases. A question Sperber asks concerns how ideas become 'contagious' or easy to 'catch' and how they spread among populations. A key notion in Sperber's discussion is that ideas are not 'replicated' when they spread from one individual to another, as suggested by Dawkins (1976), but that instead they are modified and that this involves ideas which resemble each other passing from one individual to another. Another key notion in Sperber's account is metarepresentation (for discussion of metarepresentation more generally, see Sperber 2000). Metarepresentation plays a key role in the spread of cultural assumptions since some ideas are represented by individuals as being shared by other individuals. It is also possible for an individual to entertain a representation which they do not fully understand if they can represent it as entertained by another. I might, for example, believe (2) even though I do not know what exactly a Higgs boson particle is:

(2) The notion of a Higgs boson particle is hugely important in contemporary science.

I can entertain this assumption embedded under more complex representations such as (3):

(3) [Dan says that] the notion of a Higgs boson particle is hugely important in contemporary science.

If I trust Dan well enough, I might even entertain something like (4) and consider it true:

(4) The notion of a Higgs boson particle (whatever that is exactly) is hugely important in contemporary science.

Assumptions like this might well play a role in how we approach literary texts. Many readers will know in advance that *The Lady with the Little Dog* is considered a masterpiece and some will approach it already believing that it is a great work. This is bound to affect some of the inferences they make as they read the work. Perhaps some readers even entertain assumptions such as (5):

(5) [Given what other people say about it] *The Lady with the Little Dog* is one of the greatest stories ever written (even though I can't see why yet).

This will not only affect how readers make inferences as they read but also how they return to it afterwards. They might puzzle, as Ford reports doing, about why this seemingly unimportant story is considered so great. He says, 'What I didn't understand, back in 1964, when I was 20, was what made this drab set of non-events a great short story – reputedly one of the greatest ever written.' (Ford 1998: ix).

Ford's puzzlement is shared by many readers. There is clearly a metarepresentational aspect involved and this might also be described as a 'salient inference' in the sense suggested by Clark (2009), i.e. a case where readers are more aware than they are in general of the nature of some of their inferential processes. In fact, this awareness might lead them to move towards the kind of non-spontaneous interpretation which Furlong (1996) sees as typically literary, i.e. as one in which readers make conscious efforts to consider as much evidence as possible for particular interpretations and carry on looking for new interpretations in the expectation that this work will be rewarded with extra effects.

Before closing, there is one final factor which I will briefly mention but not discuss further here.

5.6 The extent to which formal and other factors are valued

As suggested by Ford's discussion, it is clear that some readers value the work because of Chekhov's particular skill with words. This point may go beyond the scope of a linguistic pragmatic approach since it is not (or not only) about how writers and other communicators manipulate their texts in order to give rise to particular inferential conclusions. Note, though, that a representation such as 'Chekhov has an amazing ability to communicate with words' is a conclusion inferred from evidence in the text and that some assumptions about Chekhov's skill concern the way he manipulates reader inferences, for example by presenting relatively little information explicitly and encouraging readers to infer much more. Assumptions about Chekhov's skill as a writer might also be metarepresented and it is clear that assumptions like this are both widely held and recognised to be widely held.

6 Conclusions

While it is too soon to draw strong conclusions, the discussion above suggests some factors associated with particular kinds of inference which are likely to affect the degree to which literary works are valued. Some of these can be seen as related to key assumptions of relevance theory about processing effort, the ease of deriving inferences from (particular parts or the whole of) the text and how relevant these conclusions are. Others build not on specifically relevance-theoretic assumptions but on the notion of metarepresentation in general and Sperber's proposed epidemiology of cultural representations in particular.

It is not clear, of course, that we will be able to point to general properties of texts which make a work more likely to be positively valued. One reader might be interested in formally or conceptually simple texts. Another might value more obscure or challenging writing. There are clearly many factors involved in determining how positively a work is valued. These will include assumptions about how particular works fit into a range of cultural assumptions, including assumptions about what makes a work categorisable as 'popular' or as 'literary'. Nevertheless, it is surely worth attempting to categorise some of the processes involved in developing individual and collective evaluations of literary works. This discussion aims to begin a process of more formal and fully developed investigation.

This chapter aimed to develop only a very brief exploration of some of the inferential processes involved in reading and responding to *The Lady with the Little Dog*, to consider why it has been highly valued and to consider why many readers begin by underestimating the significance it will eventually have for them. The discussion above identified some specific inferential processes and argued that the text is easy to understand, is easy to represent as a whole and provides evidence for a wide range of conclusions, some of them complex in a way which rewards further thought. The speculative discussion of what gives rise to positive evaluations suggested some ways in which the evaluative process can be understood with reference to inferential processes inspired by texts, including by developing Sperber's (1996) ideas about representation and the spread of cultural assumptions. I argued that one aspect of the story which contributes to positive evaluations is a parallel between Gurov's developing attitude to Anna and readers' developing attitudes to the story. Given this, I can't resist ending by echoing the last words of the story and suggesting that 'the most complicated and difficult part' of pragmatic stylistic work on evaluation is 'only just beginning.'

Note

1. I am grateful for helpful comments on this work from audiences at the Poetics and Linguistics Association conference at the University of Sheffield in 2008 and at EPICS V, the 5th International Symposium on Intercultural, Cognitive and Social Pragmatics, Pablo de Olavide University, Seville in 2012.

5

Outsourcing: A Relevance-Theoretic Account of the Interpretation of Theatrical Texts

Anne Furlong

> The only thing that all forms of theatre have in common is the need for an audience. This is more than a truism: in the theatre the audience completes the steps of creation... In the theatre this is modified by the fact that the last lonely look at the completed object is not possible – until an audience is present the object is not complete... I think any director will agree that his own view of his own work changes completely when he is sitting surrounded by people.
>
> (Brook 1990: 142)

> The drama is not for the library, but for the theatre; and it is not for the joy of the little group of dilettantes, but for the stimulation of the public as a whole.
>
> (Matthews 1908: 223)

1 Introduction

Plays are interpretive events. However, it is not clear what ought to constitute the basis for the interpretation: the play text, or performance. I contend that performance provides critical evidence in ways that the playwright foresaw and intended. However, the teaching of drama rarely (or at least inadequately) incorporates performance elements; instead, students are taught to treat plays identically with non-dramatic texts such as novels. I believe this oversight profoundly impoverishes the student experience of theatre. In this chapter, I want to lay the basis for a principled argument for treating performance as an essential part of the interpretation of dramatic texts, using the framework of relevance theory. To support my arguments I will draw on the problems raised by two plays – Strindberg's *Miss Julie* and Ibsen's *A Doll's House* – and demonstrate that interpretive difficulties raised by reading are best (perhaps only) resolved through decisions made in and communicated by performance.

There is at present no theory of drama, criticism, or interpretation which adequately accounts for the interpretation of plays, including whose interpretation a production is communicating or providing. Connor (1999) wonders whether a play's 'meaning' is to be found in the dramatist's comments, the close readings of scholars and students, or the playgoers' experience. She overlooks actors and directors, yet surely a defining feature of a play is that it is written to be performed. Hamilton notes that we 'evaluate plays differently when considering them as texts for reading' rather than as 'scripts' (Hamilton 2001: 307). Sauer (1995) argues that performance is central to the teaching of drama and Barish calls 'stage and study' 'inextricably linked' (Barish 1994: 47). So we have two incompatible approaches to the interpretation of drama: on the one hand, 'everyone knows' that Shakespeare's plays, for example, must be performed to be 'understood'. On the other hand, few students of literature – in my experience – include or consider performance in their course. This is not far removed from teaching Mozart, for instance, from his scores alone, without listening to the music being played.

So, for example, Meyer (1971) carries out the kind of close reading that Heilman (1956: 13 quoted in Nardin 1965: 594) advocates:

> The printed play is somewhat like the symphonic score which the music critic, *imagining the performance,* may study rigorously to see how it is 'composed'.
>
> (Meyer 1971: 473, italics added)

Yet Meyer checks his conclusions against 'the only recording of [Mozart's Sonata in A Major]' (Meyer 1971: 476): performance, not analysis, is the ultimate test of interpretation. By contrast, scripts for television or film are rarely studied, except in specialist film courses. A glance at the text of the published shooting script for *Little Miss Sunshine,* an award winning film, suggests why. The first page reads in part:

> 1 ECU – VIDEO PIXELS
>
> Five young women stand side by side, waiting to be judged – breathless, hopeful. A name is announced, and four hearts break.

> The camera ZOOMS across the smiles of the losers to find a winner. She breaks into tears, hugs the nearest runner up.
>
> Begin CREDITS. MUSIC – quiet, melancholy – plays over all the opening scenes, leading to the Title Card.
>
> ...
>
> 2 This is OLIVE. She is big for her age and slightly plump.
>
> She studies the show very earnestly.
>
> (Arndt et al. 2007)

Compare this text with a script used in production. Photographs of the text used by Ridley Scott in the making of the 1979 film *Alien* are viewable online (e.g. at propbay.com) While the text of published and working scripts may be the same, actual shooting scripts are typically heavily marked and altered. Neither, I suggest, would repay the effort required for a non-spontaneous *literary* interpretation.

Non-dramatic fiction may exploit play form, as McCarthy (2006) has done in *The Sunset Limited: A Novel in Dramatic Form*. Conversely, some plays (the 'closet dramas') are not only not intended for performance, but may in fact be impossible to stage as written (as with Byron's *Manfred*). Nevertheless, the writer of non-dramatic fiction (novels, for example) aims at a reader. A playwright does not. Instead, she[1] writes for a director, actors and an audience. It is not the *text* of the play but the *performance* that communicates the interpretation and the effects the writer intended. The general practice of teaching plays through reading alone – without incorporating elements of performance – is thus deeply flawed.

Scholars have focused on practice (Chapple and Davis 1988), pedagogy (Long 1977), or theory (McConachie 2007), but have not satisfactorily addressed the question of *how* a performance communicates the intended interpretation.[2] In this paper I will sketch out an answer by applying the relevance-theoretic model of communication to the interpretation of dramatic texts in performance. The playwright manifestly intends the audience to form their interpretation on the basis not of the text, but of the production of the script in performance. Drawing on the notion of non-spontaneous interpretation, I will account for 'extra' effort invested by the director and actors, arguing that it is ultimately their reading that forms the basis for a production. Though a playgoer need not construct a literary interpretation of the play, clearly the people who produce the play must do so, strongly suggesting that they are the playwright's first addressees.

My argument is that it is performance, not reading, that provides the evidence for the director's interpretation of the writer's informative intention. I propose also that the notion of evidence requires significant adjustment. Evidence consists not only of the text of the play, but also of the paralinguistic and extralinguistic clues provided by the actors' relationships to their character, their fellow actors and the playgoer. A relevance theoretic approach can illuminate some of the interpretive challenges presented by the protagonists of Strindberg's *Miss Julie* and Ibsen's *A Doll's House*, suggesting that they are both elucidated to some extent and (potentially) resolved on stage.

For the purposes of this discussion, this chapter is limited to texts written for performance. I assume that the director and actors will work with the text as given, not redacting or engaging in resistant readings. Finally, I assume that the plays are performed theatrically (though not necessarily professionally). Within these constraints I am proposing a principled account of how the interpretation of plays works. T. S. Eliot regarded most performances as 'interruptions' of the relationship between writer and viewer; in 'a true acting play', the actor added nothing (Eliot 1924: 96). On the contrary, every dramatist 'outsources' part of her communicative function to the director and his actors, and while many plays can produce rich cognitive effects through reading alone, the intended interpretation is most faithfully, *albeit* partially, communicated through performance. Thom (2009: 69) remarks that '[s]pectators at a performance are often able to distinguish, at least to some extent, between the performance and what is performed'. While the ultimate audience of the script is the playgoer, the contributions of directors and actors mean that the communication of the intended interpretation is not limited to the text and is to some extent inaccessible through reading alone.

2 Critical perspectives

> ...one of the most important things that experimental performance has taught us is that even though you can treat the text as texture and material, ultimately it is impossible to liquidate it.
>
> (Sidiropoulou 2011: 156)

Text, performance and interpretation are inseparably connected, as, indeed, are playwright, director, performer and viewer. Theatre and drama specialists routinely assert that plays are meant to be played, not read. Essif (1998) points out that '[b]y nature, the dramatic text is explicitly designed to generate another (performance) text' (Essif 1998: 26). Yet 'the continuum between text and performance' 'has often divided these two fields', Henderson (2009: 111) writes. 'Too often', Essif remarks, 'teachers do not exploit the creative potential of the performance project for teaching textuality' (Essif 1998: 26); indeed he urges that '[s]ince dramatic texts have a greater potential to make students aware of their role as readers in the production and process of textual meaning, we would do well to introduce drama and performance at the earliest stages of literary studies' (Essif 1998: 26).

Meyer suggests that a performer makes 'the relationships and patterns potential in the [text] clear to the mind and ear of the experienced listener' (Meyer 1971: 461). He notes that 'every critical analysis is a more or less precise indication of how the work being analysed should be performed' (Meyer 1971: 461). Beckerman rejects the notion that 'artistic effect is independent of artistic form'; rather, the 'basis for a sound dramatic analysis is significantly different from the practice of literary interpretation' (Beckerman 1971: 399). He adds that 'what distinguishes dramatic analysis from literary interpretation is not any single aspect of textual examination'; instead, 'the difference is a factor of the contexts of literary and dramatic works' (Beckerman 1971: 404). He concludes that the 'purpose of dramatic analysis is not to arrive at definitive interpretations of the work, but to discover and test dramatic possibilities' (Beckerman 1971: 405).

Snuggs asserts 'the axiomatic principle that no passage can be safely interpreted out of its context' (Snuggs 1947: 115). But context in literature courses and teaching is usually regarded as largely literary-historical – that is, the writer's social and historical context, or the context provided by the history of literature more generally – and not as the context provided and created by performance. In theory-oriented courses, 'context' may mean specific critical positions and premises, as Martin's strongly Freudian reading of *The Jew of Malta* demonstrates. He argues that where *Hamlet* serves 'the reality principle, whose key instantiating moment is the threat of castration' (Martin 2008: 367), 'Marlowe's tragic mimesis...acts out and perpetuates the psychopathology it dramatises' (Martin 2008: 368). Nardin correctly identifies such teaching and critical practices as 'fundamentally the approach to the poem, an approach to a piece of literature designed to be read by one person alone, to be analysed closely in terms of imagery and...content'. They turn 'all plays into closet drama', which is 'disastrous both critically and pedagogically' (Nardin 1965: 591–592).

Not all theatrical practitioners and theorists take this position. The Shakespearean scholar Weimann approvingly quotes playwright Heiner

Müller's praise of his collaborator Robert Wilson's abstention from interpreting and judging a text:

> ...a good text does not need interpretation by either a director or an actor. What the text says is said in the text.... Interpretation is the work of the spectator. This must not happen on stage (153).
>
> (Weimann 1992: 958)

His admiration is misplaced, as there is no 'neutral' way to utter a line and all performance is interpretation. But even Weimann, assuming as he does that performance ideally involves a minimum of interpretation, notes that we need more than 'traditional Shakespearean criticism with its privileging of one predominantly scriptural type of meaning' (Weimann 1994: 790), on the basis that (quoting Pavis 1992) '[these practices] open the dramatic text up to theatrical experimentation without separating the reading of the text, the discovery of its meaning and the stage translation that would explain the pre-existent textual meaning' (Weimann 1994: 790). He goes on to argue that far from 'privileging the authority of performance over that residing in the text', he 'consider[s] it imperative to start from a concept of dramatic discourse in which the premises and conditions of theatrical communication themselves are inscribed' (Weimann 1994: 793), rejecting the spurious distinction 'between text-centred and stage-centred approaches' (Weimann 1994: 794). This 'spurious distinction', as I will now explain, has dominated many of the approaches to the teaching of dramatic texts.

3 The problem

> The emphasis on 'reading' a play...suggests that a reading and a viewing are the same thing. They are not.
>
> (Nardin 1965: 592)

The problem is that too often students of literature are taught to interpret plays as they would novels, poems and short fiction. I think plays are quite distinct in a number of crucial ways, most especially in the relationship between context and addressee. A number of critics have got here ahead of me.

Kermode (Kermode 2000: 4) notes the 'commonplace that only in performance can the sense of Shakespeare's plays be fully apprehended'. Grotowski argues that 'the text *per se* is not the theatre, only through the actor's use of it' (Grotowski 2002: 21). Nevertheless, in typical literature courses the *reader* is assumed to be the intended addressee. A survey of the syllabi of English literature courses in several large Canadian universities, at introductory and upper levels, supports my claim. Courses that cover a range of genres rarely if ever mention performing as part of the study of drama, nor do they include screenings of filmed performances or movie adaptations. More tellingly, evaluation is by way of writing (writing for credit, unedited work, formal and informal essays, written exams) and undefined 'participation'. No indication is given that students might be expected to participate in performance. More specialised courses (Topics in Shakespeare, for example) often include screenings of filmed performances or movie adaptations, but again, evaluation is typically by means of written submissions and 'participation', with no indication that the classes will include or explore performance. Those courses that do explicitly include a performance component – warning students that they will be expected to attend at least one theatrical performance during the semester or participate in performances themselves – turn up usually in English departments that are affiliated with theatre or drama programmes (such as University of Toronto Mississauga, which has an institutional relationship with a professional theatre). I provide URLs for a number of departmental offerings at University of Toronto Mississauga in the Appendix.

Teachers and instructors behave as if the following were obviously true:

(a) There is no difference, in principle or interpretive practice, between a play and a non-dramatic prose text.
(b) Language is the primary vehicle of drama: thus the interpretation arrived at by the *reader* is sufficient.
(c) The reader can arrive at the intended interpretation of a play by means of a 'literary interpretation' independent of performance.

I will argue that (a–c) are basically wrong-headed. They ignore the role of non-linguistic and non-propositional evidence; they limit context to the cognitive resources of the (individual) reader; and they misjudge the intended audience(s).

It is not, however, self-evident that (a–c) are false, or, if so, why. The answer lies in the disputed, underdeveloped and misguided conception of evidence, context and audience. It is true that the addressee of the play is the *theatre audience*, as the addressee of the novel is the *reader*. But while the reader develops his interpretation on the basis of the evidence supplied by the novelist in her text, the viewer of the play does not. Instead, he relies on the evidence supplied by a performance of the play: that is, the interpretations of the director and actors. Through performance, the viewer experiences the effects the playwright intended and constructs the interpretation she intended him to recognise and entertain.

However, it is one thing to make this claim and another to support it. The relevance-theoretic model of interpretation elucidates the relationship between writer and audience. Extending it to include 'intermediaries' – directors and actors – can tease out the subtle negotiation of responsibilities that occurs in the interpretation of plays through performance. Below I provide an overview of the relevance-theoretic model of non-spontaneous interpretation that I work with. I touch on the connection between performance and communication and develop some implications of this approach.

4 Non-spontaneous interpretation

Sperber and Wilson (1986/1995) developed relevance theory to account for the interpretation of utterances. The theory makes two fundamental claims about cognition and communication: that 'human cognition tends to be organised so as to maximise relevance'; and that 'every act of ostensive communication communicates a presumption of its own optimal relevance' (Sperber and Wilson 1995: 260). These claims mean that there is a single exceptionless criterion guiding the interpretation process, both generating and evaluating interpretations. 'Relevance' is a property (Sperber and Wilson 1995: 261) and is quantifiable: something is *relevant* to the extent that the positive cognitive *effects* it produces are large and to the extent that the cognitive *effort* needed to achieve these effects is small. The greater the positive cognitive effects an utterance produces, the more relevant it is; and the more effort it takes to achieve these effects, the less relevant it is (Sperber and Wilson 1995: 264–266). Relevance involves a dynamic relationship between effort and effect; when there are no longer adequate effects for the effort expended, we stop processing the utterance (Sperber and Wilson 1995: 271–272).

Plays present something of a challenge for relevance theory. Surely the performance of a play yields roughly the same interpretation as the reading of it and, generally, audiences do not expect a radically different interpretation from reading a play than from seeing it. That expectation may be confounded: an underrated effect of performance is to change our understanding of any aspect of a play, from a line reading to characterisation to global inferences. In such cases, performance yields effects *not* available through reading. There are three ways in which this might occur: the performance may achieve relevance through poetic effects; or the viewer may aim at a non-spontaneous interpretation; or the evidence provided by performance may go well beyond the textual.

4.1 Poetic effects

'Interpretation' in relevance theory has generally meant what I call 'spontaneous interpretation' in communicative situations where the threshold of adequate relevance is low. Social interactions, work-place relations, family dealings and casual reading are typical of the communicative events which most work in relevance theory has focused on. The cognitive relevance of much of this communication is achieved by the satisfaction of social, personal, or other goals. But there are utterances whose relevance is achieved through 'poetic effects' – a wide array of weakly implicated assumptions made barely more manifest. Relevance is achieved, not through making a subset of these assumptions more salient or manifest, but by the effect of the whole range. They may produce 'impressions',[3] stimulate sensory responses, or call up memories, images and other non-propositional assumptions. Perhaps for a viewer engaged in the spontaneous interpretation of a play in performance, relevance is achieved in part through these poetic effects.[4] Billington's remarks below on Kelly Reilly's performance in the Donmar 2003 production rely on precisely such impressions, gleaned from the smallest of gestures on the actor's part. We might also consider the vital role played by the stage designers, sound and light people; they create the conditions on stage which reinforce or supplement the work of the actors.

4.2 Non-spontaneous interpretation

It is my view that we also engage in *non-spontaneous* interpretation, aiming not at *optimal* but at *maximum* relevance. The addressee invests 'extra' cognitive effort in order to achieve an interpretation which is *exhaustive* – that is, one which accounts for all the evidence of the text; *plausible* – one which is warranted by the evidence of the text and the intended context and any other evidence he can find; and *unified* – one which contributes to the construction of a core set of global inferences which is strongly manifest in the context in which any part of the text is processed. Non-spontaneous interpretation can be undertaken of any text; but not all texts can support such treatment without, on the one hand, slipping into eisegetical interpretation (in which the reader supplies virtually all the crucial contextual assumptions, *un*warranted by the evidence of the text) or, on the other hand, degenerating into irrelevance (as the process fails to yield effects which are even adequate for the effort invested). In the case of works aimed at readers (novels, stories, newspaper articles, essays and so on), readers can perform non-spontaneous interpretations, generating rich complex readings on the basis of the evidence supplied by the text. Perhaps they do the same with plays in performance.

4.3 Context and evidence

When a work is written to be performed, it is not entirely clear what constitutes 'evidence', for either spontaneous or non-spontaneous interpretation.

In verbal communication, utterances provide evidence for the set of assumptions the communicator intends her addressee to entertain, that is, represent mentally. These assumptions may be explicatures or implicatures. The difference between these concerns whether the assumption is

> a 'development of... a linguistically encoded logical form of the utterance, or of... a sentential subpart of a logical form'
>
> (Carston 2002: 124)

> or

> 'a subset of the contextual implications used in processing the utterance' [implicated premises] or 'a subset of its contextual implications' [implicated conclusions]
>
> (Carston 2002: 135)

My point is that the linguistic evidence is only part of the intended context for the interpretation. Playgoing is a complex and intensely somatic experience. A performance includes language, both spoken (dialogue) and written (as part of the set). But the playwright also ostensively communicates through the actors' movements and interactions; the lighting and sound (such as music or effects); the visual components (colour, texture, depth, dimension); cultural materials (costumes, furnishings, props): in short, the *mise en scène*.

The nature of these stimuli is such that imagination alone cannot replace them. No matter how experienced and sophisticated, a reader has access only to his own cognitive environment (that is, the set of assumptions manifest to an individual at a given time (Sperber and Wilson 1995: 39)). When his cognitive environment does not include the assumptions made manifest by performance, clearly the context is impoverished. Non-trivially, this impoverishment concerns precisely those assumptions which will likely give rise to poetic effects. As a result, the interpretation based on reading alone, though it may be rich, non-spontaneous and literary, is not the one foreseen and intended by the playwright.

The concerns raised by the problem of teaching plays without performance can therefore be addressed through a relevance theoretic model of communication. Is the language of the play enough? Can the imagination replace the experience of performance? Is the playwright communicating *in*directly to her audience, not through the language alone (or even primarily, in many cases) but through the performance? And if so, then are directors and actors vehicles or critics, artists or interpreters? I will answer these in part through a reconsideration of the multiple audiences of the play text.

5 Playwright, director, actor, playgoer

From a relevance-theoretic perspective, the relationship between writer, director, actor and playgoer can be represented in terms of the role each plays in producing or interpreting the evidence on which the playgoer will base his interpretation. Note that directors and actors *must* aim at non-spontaneous interpretation, since they are aiming at maximal rather than optimal relevance: they are aiming at an interpretation which is exhaustive, plausible and unified, since they must have very rich interpretations on which to draw in order to perform. I have already noted other possible participants, such as the designers and crew. The complexity and diversity of the relationships among these individuals mean that performances vary in terms of how 'unified' the work of everyone involved is, and the degree to which the elements of the production support or detract from the others.

5.1 Playwright

The writer supplies the words of the play; she may include directions (which the viewer does not hear); a preface (or similar commentary, also unheard by the viewer); exploit stylistic and 'poetic' elements, including imagery, figures of thought and speech, allusions, irony and so on. From this text, the first reader constructs the interpretation intended for him. I suggest that the director is the first audience the writer has in mind for two reasons. For one thing, since the writer depends on a director to produce her play, she must ensure that her work is sufficiently compelling to warrant the time and effort not only to read it, but also to bring it to the stage. For another, and more fundamentally, the writer depends on the director to communicate her intended interpretation to the audience. She will reach her audience through the director and so has him in mind as her first (though not final) addressee.

5.2 Director

The director arrives at an interpretation (partly provisional: rehearsal and performance and production will confirm or disconfirm, add to or alter it), aiming at a non-spontaneous interpretation. Clearly the words he reads will be the ones the viewer hears; but, critically, the director is reading in order to arrive at a view of the intended 'realisation' on stage, including non-textual elements (design, theatrical space, light, sound, costume) and performance elements (actors). Having established his (provisional) interpretation, he enlists the second readers: the actors, the second audience envisioned by the playwright.

5.3 Actor

The actor arrives at an interpretation (partly provisional, like the director's). He – preferably but not necessarily – aims at exhaustiveness and unity, investing significant cognitive effort in processing the utterances and testing line readings; in making decisions about his relationship to other actors (and characters), to the space and to the viewer. He will take into account non-textual elements decided on or provided by the director or producer. In performance, he fuses all these elements in a (re)presentation that functions at the same time as communication: his own, the director's and – crucially – the writer's. Part of what he communicates is evidence for the director's interpretation of the text, part is evidence for his own interpretation of the text, or at least of his role/character. To the extent that he is communicating his own interpretation the actor is a literary critic in Malarcher's sense (Malarcher 1994); but to the extent that his acting communicates the director's understanding of the intended interpretation, he is representing or generating the evidence for that interpretation and realising the writer's aims for her ultimate addressees: the playgoers.

5.4 Playgoer

A sophisticated viewer (that is, a playgoer with the experience, intelligence and skill to produce a robust non-spontaneous interpretation) recognises that he is dealing with distinct (though intimately related) interpretations of the play. He must process the text of the play; the behaviour of the actors; the stage environment; other audience members and the theatrical space. He must discriminate between those elements he can ascribe to the writer with confidence – for example, the dialogue and some of the actions. As Thom (2009: 69) notes, he will treat the actors' and director's contributions differently from the writer's. Their contributions greatly enrich and complicate both the context and the resulting interpretation. The playwright thus communicates to the viewer, not directly through the text of the play, but through the interpretive and representational decisions made by all those involved in the production of the play: director, actors, stage hands, costumers, lighting designers and so forth. Irvin (2009: 37) calls these 'the unique ingredients introduced by a particular company' and notes they 'are always of tremendous aesthetic significance'. These interventions, as well as the highly variable behaviour of audiences, make the production of performed texts an especially fraught interpretive enterprise.

6 Performance and/as communication

Plays therefore differ from non-dramatic texts in two important ways: first, some of the most important evidence for the intended interpretation is not available from reading alone; and second, the kind of cognitive effort involved differs significantly from that involved in reading because of the different cognitive load involved in processing written as opposed to spoken language. Playgoers do not read dialogue: they hear it. Therefore, one kind of processing effort is significantly reduced. Instead, increased effort is invested in paying attention to other elements of performance, especially sensory ones such as sound and physical behaviour. The viewers must also expend effort in constructing hypotheses which are confirmed, disconfirmed or altered in the course of the performance. Consequently, what is gained in reduced processing effort with respect to language is offset by increased effort as the result of the amplification and introduction of evidence, and kinds of evidence, and the need to discriminate between the contributions of the director and actors, and the writer's intentions.

An interpretation constructed solely on the basis of reading a play is necessarily insufficient, because reading alone will not provide the addressee with the evidence for the intended interpretation: only performance can do so. While treating a play as literature will doubtless lead to satisfying interpretations (spontaneous or otherwise), the reader does not and cannot experience what the writer produced her text for. He may focus on the language of the text, its beauty or poetic qualities; he may study its structure; he may use it as evidence of the culture in which it was produced, or to reflect on his own time; he may delight in the events or sympathise with the characters. But the experience – no matter how rich it may be in other respects, is impoverished because crucial evidence is not available to him. As Irvin (2009: 37) notes, 'the nature of a theatrical performance is always vastly underdetermined by appeal to a text or originary performance on which it draws'. That is, any particular production is not identical to 'the play', but each production communicates evidence which helps the audience form an understanding of the interpretation the playwright intended.

To test this general approach, I will consider two plays – *A Doll's House* and *Miss Julie* – which present complementary challenges to the reader, critic, actor and director. Over the course of these plays, a 'new' Nora emerges apparently out of nowhere, while Julie disintegrates into a suicidal dissociative state in the space of a few hours. While the characters travel in opposite directions, the dramatic or interpretive problem they present is the same: how to reconcile these right-angle turns with unity of character (assuming, of course, that the playwright values or is aiming at unity of character).

However, these shifts are problematic only if we assume that the playwright intended the playgoer to construct a plausible, unified, exhaustive – that is, non-spontaneous – interpretation. Other explanations suggest themselves: the playwrights might have made remarks to the effect that women are frivolous, inconsistent, irrational (and thus lacking unity of character), though the evidence of the play suggests otherwise; the playwrights were limited by cultural constraints along the same lines, or were pandering to their audience's prejudices; the playwrights deliberately introduced these discrepancies in order to challenge prevailing views of women (or theatre); the playwrights were just not very good. None of these is persuasive, however, given the responses of playgoers and critics from the first performances to the present day. Moreover, actors and directors have struggled to represent Nora and Julie's 'alterations' either as revelations of their true (hitherto concealed) nature, or as breaks caused by the intolerable pressures they are subject to.

If Nora and Julie were characters in fiction, we could resolve the difficulties raised by their actions by considering the evidence provided by the writer in the text. We might widen the context to include assumptions about the writers and their times, their political or social views;

we might invest 'extra' effort to raise some of the wide array of very weak contextual effects (poetic effects) to greater manifestness; we might interpret the characterisation ironically and consider the kinds of people who might think such behaviour normal or expected and see how their views are treated by the text. In short, we might engage in 'literary criticism', non-spontaneous interpretation generated by cognitive and communicative relevance, by eisegetical and exegetical interpretation, commentary, personal response, description, evaluation and so on. Despite the contributions made by any and all of these ways of treating the text, it is in performance and only in performance that these dilemmas can be resolved.

7 Nora and Julie

Miss Julie is the product of the union of a wealthy aristocrat and a woman of much lower status. Her attitudes and conduct reveal deep internal rifts in her character: a strong-willed woman raised to dominate men, she is crawlingly servile; a passionate physical and sexual being, she is undone by a single intimate encounter. The arc of her development is irresistibly downhill, ending with her begging her lover for a way out and accepting the straight razor he offers her as an invitation to destroy herself.

The inconsistencies in her character 'as written' have drawn critical attention. Lamm notes 'the objections which contemporary critics made to the deficient motivation', finding Julie's suicide 'improbable' (Lamm 1924, 1971: 111). Templeton remarks that '[t]he ending of *Miss Julie* is the most troublesome part of the play for readers *and playgoers* of Strindberg's drama. Critics offer various, often conflicting interpretations of the manner and significance of Julie's turn toward suicide' (Templeton 1990: 478, italics added). Frye faults one production for diminishing 'the sense of causality in the action that Julie requires to elicit our sympathy' (Frye 1997: 534). Lane, in his critique of Bergman's 1981 production, writes that Julie engages in 'a deliberate self-degradation through which [she] might destroy herself in order to find herself...with Jean merely an instrument of Julie's self-determination' (Lane 1982: 434). Brustein describes Jean '[s]lobbering with uncontrollable fear' as 'he hypnotizes Julie into going into the barn with his razor' (Brustein 1962: 160) – an improbable combination.

If the play presents a problem, performance offers a solution. Chaudhuri treats performance as both interpretation *and* communication: 'Although the stage directions do not specify what Julie's reaction to Jean's choice is, I would think that this would be an important moment of choice for the actress playing the role' (Chaudhuri 1993: 329). Nestruck's review of a recent Canadian production declares that 'Jillard *gets* Miss Julie right from her first tipsy entrance' (Nestruck 2011, italics added). Michael Billington, in his review of a Donmar production of Marber's variation on *Miss Julie*, remarks that '*For once* the heroine's suicide seems inevitable rather than willed' (Billington 2003, italics added). Importantly, Billington attributes this singular result to the actor playing Julie, calling her performance 'astonishing' and picking out, not her words, but her 'splayed fingers and inturned toes', indicating Julie is 'a woman ill at ease not only in her own body but in her current social limbo' (Billington 2003). These productions depend on the actor's success in forging a single woman out of the multiple identities Strindberg has provided.

Similarly, critics, reviewers and playgoers are universally made uneasy by the apparent revolution in Nora's character in Ibsen's *A Doll's House*. As Weckwerth puts it, '[a] common criticism of *A Doll's House* holds that the role of Nora is ill constructed, an argument hinging on the impossibility of [her] transition from domestic squirrel to intellectual Valkyrie' (Weckwerth 2004: 137). And as with *Miss Julie*, productions of *A Doll's House* are almost universally judged on the degree to which they can make this transition credible.

Contemporaries of the Finnish actress Ida Aalberg, one of Nora's earliest interpreters, remarked on her 'peculiar ability to communicate the contradictions of human nature... merged with her original view of Nora's personality' (Byckling 2006). Spencer's equivocal review of the 2009 Donmar production focuses on Gillian Anderson's 'superb Nora, by turns sexy, neurotic, manipulative, terrified and in the last great act absolutely merciless' (Spencer 2009). Loney says of Claire Bloom that 'she discovers a quiet firmness, even a nobility, which make her decision and action believeable' (Loney 1971: 206). And Bergman's 1974 production in Oslo is faulted for the actor's performance, but blame is put on the director's decisions: '[a]s a result of [Nora's] forceful personality throughout the play, the ending comes as no shock and the final scenes... were surprisingly unmoving' (Young 1974: 410). Here, too, the viewer's difficulty with Nora's dramatic metamorphosis is resolved, not through the character's words but through the *performance* of character in the production.

My point is that no amount of analysis and discussion can resolve the difficulties presented by Nora and Miss Julie in these texts, so long as we insist on treating the plays like novels. Only performance provides the rich context, the additions to the playgoer's cognitive environment, in which the varied, subtle forces at work on these women in these situations can be developed, resolved, or held in creative tension. The critics' emphasis on the actors' decisions suggests the central role of the director's and performer's non-spontaneous interpretation. Productions succeed or fail on the strength or weakness, the plausibility or improbability of their interpretations.

To some extent, each production (and performance of a production) presents a specific version of a play. Not all will be equally valid – which is to say, not all will convince the audience to the same extent that the interpretation of the text which is communicated by a given production is what the playwright manifestly intended her play to convey. That audiences can make such judgments, even when they have not read the script, strongly supports Thom's contention (2009: 67) that viewers can distinguish between 'performance' and 'what is performed'. That is, playgoers can tell the difference between the play and its realisation. The theatre critics' opinions I have discussed trace and articulate those discrepancies.

The actor's ability operates as the limiting factor to the communication of the director's interpretation; where the actors are weak or incompetent, his interpretation of the text will be weakened as well. Where the actors' talents and abilities exceed those of the director, the interpretation will be enriched (perhaps by correction, alteration, additions). In any case, *every* aspect of performance can contribute to the playgoer's construction of a non-spontaneous interpretation of the text. That is, in the cases I outlined at the beginning – where the plays are performed as written (in the most naïve sense) – the viewer will regard performance as both the representation of an interpretation and as the communication of the writer's intended interpretation and judge the felicity of both. That is, the viewer can evaluate the performance, the director's interpretation and the play, *on the basis of performance alone* – and not on their interpretation of the text of the play derived from their reading of it.

8 Implications, prospects and conclusions

Relevance theory provides a single, exceptionless criterion – the principle of relevance – which both drives the process *and* constrains the production of interpretation. A relevance-theoretic approach allows us to grant the actor's critical and evaluative potential, regarding his performance as providing the evidence for the director's interpretation while communicating his own. To the extent that these distinct interpretations support and reinforce one another, the performance can produce a rich array of poetic effects which are the outcome of assumptions made barely more manifest, not just by the text, but by prosody, physical movement, spatial relations and the communication of emotional states through the actor's art and techniques.

Let me return to the assumptions I identified at the outset:

(a) There is no difference, in principle or interpretive practice, between a play and a non-dramatic prose text.

While the *process* of interpretation is the same, dramatic texts *as such* are addressed *not* to the viewers, but to the director and actors who enrich the plays through performance.

(b) Language is the primary vehicle of drama: thus the interpretation arrived at by the *reader* is sufficient.

I have argued that performance contributes an extraordinarily wide range of new, additional, or complementary evidence. A great deal of this is non-propositional (let alone non-linguistic) and the imagination of the *reader* cannot replace or supply the effects produced by performance.

(c) The reader can arrive at the intended interpretation of a play by means of a 'literary interpretation' independent of performance.

I am not contesting the vital contributions of literary readings or scholarly views. And of course, it is also true that novel reading produces equally partial, variable and incomplete interpretations. But where the novelist communicates directly with her reader, the playwright aims at the playgoer, the theatre audience. While it is possible and acceptable to treat a play as literature – see Mahaffey's meditation on Nora as an emblem of Christian forgiveness (Mahaffey 2010) – these readings are impoverished interpretations *in comparison with* those made on the basis of performance.

No single production exhausts or even conveys a full interpretation. The inevitably partial[5] and unpredictable nature of performance may thus seem to make the case for reading. But apart entirely from the exhilaration of live performance, the fact that any one production can communicate only a fraction of the potential means that they invite, perhaps even demand, non-spontaneous interpretation, in retrospect, and especially in new productions and adaptations. Plays may consist only of 'words, words, words', but they can 'drown the stage with tears/And cleave the general ear with horrid speech/Make mad the guilty and appall the free,/Confound the ignorant, and amaze indeed/The very faculties of eyes and ears'.[6] In the case of performance, outsourcing *enriches* rather than impoverishes.

Appendix: Course descriptions and syllabi

University of Toronto, Department of English. ENG140Y1Y: Literature for our time, http://www.english.utoronto.ca/undergrad/2012-13courses/courses/eng140y1yl0101.htm

University of Toronto, Department of English. ENG150Y1Y: The literary tradition, http://www.english.utoronto.ca/undergrad/2012-13courses/courses/eng150y1yl0101.htm

University of Toronto, Department of English & Drama. English ENG220Y1Y: Shakespeare, http://www.english.utoronto.ca/undergrad/2012-13courses/courses/eng220y1yl0201.htm

University of Toronto, Department of English & Drama. English ENG336Y1Y: Topics in Shakespeare, http://www.english.utoronto.ca/undergrad/2012-13courses/courses/eng336h1fl5101.htm

University of Toronto Mississauga, Department of English & Drama. English ENG140Y5Y: Literature for our time, http://www.utm.utoronto.ca/english-drama/sites/files/english-drama/public/shared/course-descriptions/english/L-ENG140Y5Y-2012-13FW.pdf

University of Toronto Mississauga, Department of English & Drama. English ENG220Y5Y: Shakespeare, http://www.utm.utoronto.ca/english-drama/sites/files/english-drama/public/shared/course-descriptions/english/L-ENG220Y5YL0201-2012-13FW.pdf

University of Toronto Mississauga, Department of English & Drama. English ENG336H5F: Topics in Shakespeare, http://www.utm.utoronto.ca/english-drama/sites/files/english-drama/public/shared/course-descriptions/english/L-ENG336H5F-2012Sum.pdf

University of Toronto Mississauga, Department of English & Drama. English ENG352H5S: Canadian drama, http://www.utm.utoronto.ca/english-drama/sites/files/english-drama/public/shared/course-descriptions/english/2012ENG352H5S-Sum.pdf

Notes

1. Throughout the paper, unless discussing a specific writer, I refer to the playwright as 'she' and any other participant in the communication as 'he'.
2. Texts concerned with how a performance communicates interpretation are generally limited to practical handbooks aimed at trainee actors and directors, or to philosophical or semiotic discussions concerned with the ontological

status of interpretation. See Rabkin (1985), Nemiro (1997), Zangwill (1999), McAuley (1998), Walker (2003), Davies (2009), Irvin (2009) and Thom (2009).

3. 'poetic effects . . . do not add entirely new assumptions which are strongly manifest in' the mutual cognitive environment, 'Instead, they marginally increase the manifestness of a great many weakly manifest assumptions'. They 'create common impressions rather than common knowledge, . . . this sense of apparently affective rather than cognitive mutuality' (Sperber and Wilson 1995: 224).
4. Poetic effects consist of a very wide array of very weakly communicated assumptions, which are made barely more manifest. Relevance is achieved, not through raising a subset of these assumptions to full manifestness, but by the cumulative effect of the whole. The addressee takes the primary responsibility for representing any individual one. Poetic effects are not restricted to texts with ostensively 'poetic' aims; they operate in spontaneous interpretation of vague and indirect communication as well as of works with literary ambition. For an extended discussion of poetic effects, see Pilkington (2000).
5. As Hollander puts it, '[p]erformance implies a temporal act, a following of a text upon a particular occasion' (Hollander 1971: 477).
6. *Hamlet*, 2, 2, 568–571.

6
Relevance Theory, Syntax and Literary Narrative

Barbara MacMahon

1 Introduction

In this chapter I explore an aspect of linguistic form, syntax, and examine its role in the construction of character and voice within the various levels of narrative in an extract from *The Children's Book* by A. S. Byatt. I start with the assumption that it is necessary to have a pragmatics of communication and interpretation. Without such a theory, stylistic approaches, which pay attention only to form, inevitably fall into difficulties in trying to account for why a particular form should have certain effects in a given context. Here I take a relevance theory view, which prioritises the interaction of decoded linguistic form with context. Context here is defined widely to include the cognitive environment of communicative participants. I focus particularly on the literary context in which there are various embedded levels of narrative. I show that relevance theory notions of interpretive use and the related notion of metarepresentation from cognitive psychology can account for this type of 'nested' narrative. I also argue that within nested narratives, linguistic form can be exploited for its communicative value. This potential is also available in non-literary utterances, but is developed in particularly elaborate and subtle ways in the literary text.

The chapter begins with an outline of relevant theoretical frameworks, followed by discussion of how these approaches might help us to understand the nature of literary narrative in general, as well as dealing with particular problems of interpretation in stylistics. The subtleties and complexities of the use of syntax in the literary extract are discussed using the theoretical approaches in Section 5. My analysis of the text culminates in Section 5.4 in an explanation of how syntactic structure within a metarepresentative narrative contributes to the communication of a central character's mind style. I argue that the overlap between the syntactic styles of character and narrator is key to establishing narrative alignment with the character and creating a sense of empathetic fusion between narrator and character perspectives.

2 Interpretive use and metarepresentation

The related concepts of interpretive use from relevance theory (Sperber and Wilson 1995: 224–232) and metarepesentation from cognitive psychology (Cosmides and Tooby 2000; Sperber 2000) have proved useful in accounting for the nature of literary communication, particularly the kind of communication at work in narrative fiction (MacMahon 2001, 2009a, 2009b, 2012). Interpretive use sits alongside descriptive use in the relevance theory model. These are two modes of communication which differ in terms of the relationship the speaker has to the proposition expressed. In descriptive use the speaker uses the proposition derived from the logical form of decoded linguistic material as a representation of a state of affairs in the world.[1] In interpretive use, the speaker uses the proposition as interpretive of a thought or utterance. This could mean that the thought directly 'quotes' a previous utterance, loosely or closely resembles an imagined utterance or thought (both cases of actual interpretive use), or simply presents the proposition as a possible thought worth considering (desirable interpretive use). Interpretive use involves presenting a proposition along with an attitude towards that proposition. In irony, for example, the speaker dissociates herself in some way from the proposition expressed and therefore from the person or kind of person who might use the same proposition descriptively. Imagine two people being shown around a house by an estate agent. One whispers to the other 'Nice wallpaper!' If this is an ironic utterance, the speaker is presenting the proposition as something someone might believe (perhaps the owner of the house/the designer of the wallpaper/people who like that kind of thing) and at the same time distancing herself from it. The attitude towards the proposition expressed in interpretive use may alternatively be associative, as for example in an approving quote, and indeed may be more or less associative or dissociative along a continuum. In 'desirable' rather than 'actual' interpretive use, the attitude towards the proposition expressed is simply one of attending to the proposition as 'worth considering' or interesting in some way. Sperber and Wilson include all types of speculation as desirable interpretive use, arguing that a speculation is a desirable in that it is a 'temporary representation of better hypotheses to come' (1995: 230).

Desirable interpretive use need not aim at the truth however; it may simply present propositions which are interesting and worth entertaining. As an example, Sperber and Wilson invite their readers to consider the statement:

> There is a prime number greater than 8,364,357 and smaller than 8,366,445

without knowing whether it is true or even plausible (1995: 229). This is desirable interpretive use which may, in the right context, simply be worth thinking about for any number of reasons.

Interpretive use, whether actual or desirable, is a public and linguistic case of metarepresentation. Metarepresentation is the act of representing a representation, for example holding a mental representation of a thought (a thought about a thought), uttering a verbal representation of a thought (an utterance about a thought), holding a mental representation of an utterance or uttering a verbal representation of another utterance (Sperber 2000: 3). As well as verbal metarepresentations (cases of interpretive use) the concept of metarepresentation includes non-verbal processes, such as some aspects of representing other minds, for example understanding that another person is experiencing pleasure or fear. Metarepresentation has received considerable attention in cognitive and evolutionary psychology and is considered by Cosmides and Tooby (2000) as one of a number of related, evolved and probably innate cognitive capacities which are decoupled from an individual's set of architectural truths and interactions with the real world. These capacities include being able to mentally simulate a physical event, participate in pretend play and create and understand fiction. In terms of providing an explanatory pragmatic account of this type of verbal communication, including its manifestation in literary communication, the concept of interpretive use is enough. The notion of metarepresentation as part of a set of decoupled cognitive activities, however, enhances the account in providing a theoretical explanation for the widespread, probably universal existence of oral or written literary cultures. It also connects the literary version of interpretive use with the other, clearly related activity types such as pretend play and mental simulation.

3 Communication in narrative

Literary stylistics provides models of narrative which illustrate the possibility for multiple layers of voice in narrative. In addition to actual authors, stylisticians have proposed the idea of implied authors, external (heterodiegetic) and detached third person narrators, omniscient third person narrators, unreliable narrators, narrative focalisation through the minds of characters, first person (homodiegetic) narrators and character reflectors.[2] Building on the stylistic approaches from a pragmatic perspective, the relevance theory notion of interpretive use allows us to explain these narrative possibilities as communicative strategies which are not entirely different from other, non-literary instances of communication. In addition, using the concept of offline capacities such as metarepresentation enhances the picture further by relating the possibilities for multiple embedded narrative voices to the fundamental cognitive capacity to think about thoughts (one's own thoughts, others' thoughts, possible thoughts) and also by relating the literary invention of fictional worlds to the related cognitive capacities for offline pretend play and simulation. The use of implied authors, implied narrators, psychological and spatio-temporal focalisations and character narrators can be seen as options within a metarepresentational framework which can result in relatively simple, 'flat' narratives, or multiply embedded metarepresentations in which, for example, an author represents an implied narrator who in turn represents a character who in turn represents another character. In this way, both the pragmatic model (relevance theory) and the overarching model of decoupled cognition can be used in an attempt to explain or theorise narrative, both as a cognitive process and a communicative act.

To show how non-literary and literary cases of interpretive use might be related, take another example of irony. When a speaker ironically refers to her friend's bungled and messy attempt to open a packet of crisps as 'smooth', she is expressing a proposition something like 'Your action is smooth' along with an attitude communicating something like 'This proposition is ridiculous'.[3] This resembles the structure involved in an author's representations of the thoughts and utterances of an unreliable third or first person narrator. Similarly but perhaps less obviously, an author's representation of a reliable narrator's representation of events and characters' thoughts and utterances might equally involve an attitude of association or endorsement of the narrator's utterances, along the lines 'this would be a fair way of representing these, albeit fictional, events'. In fact these models provide us with a way of understanding what is interesting about many fictional narratives: the reader's exploration of how she is to understand the events and representations described often takes priority over the content of those propositions. Indeed, many works of fiction seem to direct the reader's attention to this process by misleading, giving one impression about the narrator and gradually revealing information which leads to a reformulation of attitude towards the narrator's representations.

To sum up before moving on to the discussion of what is communicated by syntactic structures in literary texts, my theoretical starting position is to assume that literary fiction is metarepresentational in two related and perhaps collapsing ways. First, fiction itself is a cognitive activity which is related to the capacity to represent other representations, that is to metarepresent. Both are decoupled: they run 'offline' and are separated from what Cosmides and Tooby term 'the architecturally true' set of representations held by an individual at a given moment. Within fiction we have narrative layers which are instances of interpretive use, verbal metarepresentations which can be multiply embedded and involve a real author, a fictional narrator, or at least narrative voice, and fictional characters.

4 The interpretation of syntax in stylistics: A contested example

Syntax is central to much of stylistics and there has been plenty of attention given to the role of syntax in the construction of what Fowler (1977) called mind style.[4] Many introductory stylistics textbooks invite students to identify and 'analyse' syntactic structures such as phrase types and sentence types and consider their effects in literary passages (see, for example, Wright and Hope 1996: chs. 1–3, Thornborrow and Wareing 1998: ch. 3). While I believe that such attention to form is important in raising awareness of how the literary text works, without reference to a theory of interpretation, and crucially to a theory of how we access and use context in conjunction with linguistic material, it is difficult to sustain such analyses. Halliday's much discussed (1971) work on Golding's *The Inheritors* provides insights into the way particular syntactic forms play a part in the construction of mind style. He shows that third person narrative representations of the thoughts of the central Neanderthal character, Lok, are typically intransitive constructions, such as 'he rushed to the edge of the water', or constructions in which the human agency behind the events is otherwise diminished, for example 'the bushes twitched again' (when in fact a man is twitching the bushes) and 'the stick rose upright' (when in fact a man is raising the stick). Halliday's argument is persuasive: the sentence structures reflect a simple, undeveloped worldview in which actions are not seen as relating to their consequences and inanimate objects appear to move independently. Though there is attention to context, Halliday does not examine the mechanism by which a third person narrative can appear to take on the mind style of the character and what kinds of significance the character's thoughts take on as a result, which is in my view the most interesting question. Simpson, with reference to Fish's contention that stylisticians indulge in 'interpretive positivism' (Fish 1981; Simpson 1993: 103–105), revisits Halliday's work, showing that similar syntactic patterns – intransitive verbs, body part actors, inanimate actors – dominate in passages from *Pincher Martin*, another novel by Golding. Simpson's claim is that the sentence structures cannot be interpreted in the same way in the later novel. The clauses Simpson cites are taken from a passage in which Martin, the lead character, is drowning in the sea. Some examples are: 'He crouched', 'His hand let the knife go', 'sea water would burst out over his tongue'. Simpson's analysis shows that the syntactic structures do not have a stable meaning; in this text they cannot be taken to represent an undeveloped primitive mind style like Lok's. Simpson settles for the notion of a 'lowest common denominator' (105), arguing that the similarity between the two styles reflects similar loss or lack of control in the minds of the two very different fictional characters they represent. What is nevertheless still lacking for me in these analyses is, first, an account of the relationship between the general narrative and the representation of character, and second, an account of the way that the linguistic form appears to be used to communicate something about character. The metarepresentative nature of the narrative is what allows syntactic structures to reflect characters' (rather than narrators') thinking patterns, even in a third person narrative. At the same time, the different contextualisations of character and event allow the same syntactic patterns to be interpreted differently and context is central to most pragmatic accounts of interpretation, particularly relevance theory. Clark (2009) raises the problem of the lack of attention to pragmatics in these analyses. Using relevance theory, he also examines Halliday's and other stylisticians' interpretations of Golding. He argues that because inferencing is central to literary (as other) forms of interpretation it should also be central to discussions of the effects of literary style. More generally, Semino (2007) attempts to ground the relationship between linguistic form and mind style using a range of theoretical approaches including schema theory and cognitive stylistics, but pays only fleeting attention to pragmatics. In the following analysis I show how relevance theory and the cognitive theory discussed in sections 2 and 3 can explain the interpretation of aspects of syntactic structure within a metarepresentational third person literary narrative. In Section 5.3 the discussion includes different interpretations of similar structures associated with the speech of two different characters.

5 Narrative and syntax in the opening of *The Children's Book*

The following analysis refers to the first three pages of *The Children's Book* by A. S. Byatt.

5.1 The syntax of a narrative voice

The first two sentences of this novel are straightforward enough:

> Two boys stood in the Prince Consort Gallery, and looked down on a third. It was June 1895.

In an obvious way, the first sentence is unlikely to represent a descriptive statement by actual author A. S. Byatt. This is a third person narrator, or at least an imaginary voice. The novel, like many others, is already interpretive and metarepresentational in terms of the relationship between the actual communicator and the logical and propositional form of the thoughts expressed. These utterances describe a possible rather than actual world, a world 'worth considering' (Sperber and Wilson 1995: 229–230). There is some resemblance between the fiction and some facts we may know about England in the 19th century and indeed some of the characters are based on the family and associates of the writer E. Nesbit, though this is not clear from the opening pages. This is not descriptive use. Fiction uses a different mode of communication, a mode which seems to be special to literature but which at the same time is also frequently used in decoupled cognitive activities outside the domain of the literary text.

The narrative voice is unobtrusive, giving the feeling of 'no narrator' posited by Blakemore (2010), and yet already in the first few sentences of the novel, the language establishes something of a mind style and personality for this voice:

> Two boys stood in the Prince Consort Gallery, and looked down on a third. It was June 1895. The Prince had died in 1861, and had seen only the beginnings of his ambitious project for a gathering of museums in which the British craftsmen could study the best examples of design. His portrait, modest and medalled, was done in mosaic in the tympanum of a decorative arch at one end of the narrow gallery

> which ran above the space of the South Court. The South Court was decorated with further mosaics, portraits of painters, sculptors, potters, the 'Kensington Valhalla'. The third boy was squatting beside one of a series of imposing glass cases, displaying gold and silver treasures. Tom, the younger of the two looking down, thought of Snow White in her glass coffin.

Various features contribute to this impression, among them the focus, the subject matter, the historical references, the vocabulary and presuppositions. I will focus mainly on the syntax. The simple statements of the first two sentences convey a certain matter-of-factness, but the narrative soon moves into utterances of greater formal complexity, as in the third sentence.

> The Prince had died in 1861, and had seen only the beginnings of his ambitious project for a gathering of museums in which the British craftsmen could study the best examples of design.

Here we have a compound sentence, the second of which includes a very full and complex noun phrase (NP) as object. The complexity of the noun phrase is shown in Figure 6.1.

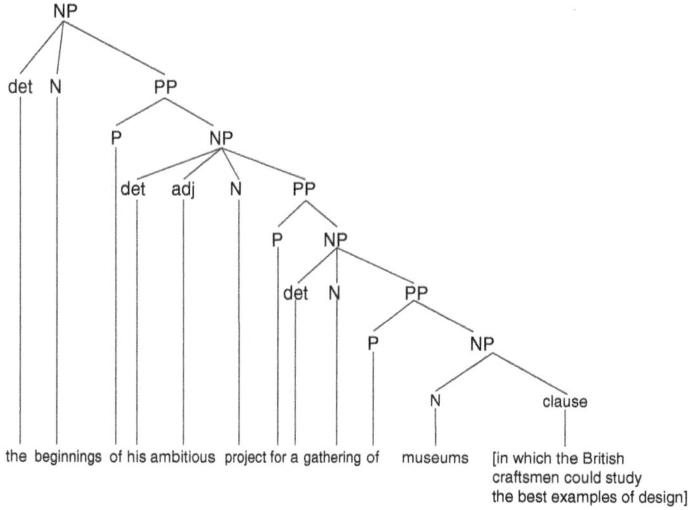

Figure 6.1 Tree diagram of the object noun phrase

The tree diagram is used in many approaches to syntax and is useful here in giving a visual representation of embedded phrases and clauses and showing their hierarchies. The structure of this noun phrase is enabled by recursive rules of English which allow a noun phrase to contain a prepositional phrase, allow a prepositional phrase to contain a noun phrase and so on. In the final noun phrase the head noun 'museums' is post-modified by a clause, which brings further complexity not shown here for reasons of space. The complexity, though unremarkable in a spontaneous reading, starts to characterise the narrative voice. Much the same propositional information could have been communicated in a set of simpler sentences and phrases, for example as follows:

> The prince had died in 1861. He had seen only the beginnings
> of his ambitious project. This project was for a gathering
> of museums. British craftsmen would be able to study
> the best examples of design in these museums.

The loading of the noun phrase in the original allows for the compacting of a good deal of interrelated information. Heavy and complex noun phrases are a feature of many texts and are a particular focus in critical discourse analysis, where they are described as nominalisations. In journalistic and political texts they are claimed typically to hide ideologies as presupposed facts, more difficult to challenge or respond to within the noun phrase than when they are separated out into their own clauses (see Fairclough 2003: 13). In Byatt's text the effect seems to be one which is quite common at the opening of novels, in which material presented as presupposed draws the reader into affecting a position of knowledge of the fictional world. Though we may not know that the prince had an ambitious project and that this ambitious project was for a gathering of museums and so on, we are addressed as if we do. The nominalisation works by presenting information in a way which does not make it salient enough for the reader to do more than register and accept it. It functions as a 'processing unit' (Blakemore and Carston 2005: 574–576), to be considered as a whole rather than broken down into its parts.

So much would also be true if we were to encounter this sentence in a non-literary text, say for example a book on the history of British museums. In such a text, we would be likely to interpret the propositional form of the utterance as what the author intended to communicate to us, as a descriptive utterance about a state of affairs involving British museums in the late 19th century. We may also derive implicatures which go beyond the propositional form, for example 'the prince's project was laudable' and 'it is a pity he died before it was completed'. At the same time the complexity and fullness of the noun phrase might convey an impression of a relatively scholarly, knowledgeable, educated and intelligent author. While the author might be hopeful of giving such an impression, such an impression from a non-fiction text is likely to be an implication rather than an implicature. Sperber and Wilson (1995: 30–31) discuss the non-verbal example of someone leaving out her broken hairdryer in the hope that another person in her house will notice and mend it. Even if the author deliberately chooses his words and syntactic structures to impress, as long as he does not intend his readers to recognise his intention, he is not communicating ostensively.

Because the fictional text is, as I have argued, a case of interpretive use (and therefore of metarepresentation), we might read more into the intended effects of the syntactic choices than we would in a history book. As discussed in Section 3 and at the beginning of this analysis, the nature of metarepresentation at this level (author metarepresenting narrator/narrative voice) is subtle and the demarcation between author and narrator is effaced – there are no quote marks or reporting clauses and no clearly dissociative attitude is communicated towards the propositions expressed, at least at this stage. In spite of this it is still possible to argue that Byatt's use of syntactic complexity in her metarepresentation gives an impression of a sophisticated, intellectual tone which is not incidental, but is part of an implicature, albeit perhaps a weak implicature, about the nature of the narrative voice. Sperber and Wilson (1995: 227–228) discuss the following example:

Peter: And what did the inn-keeper say?
Mary: Je l'ai cherché partout!

In Mary's utterance the choice of language may be intended to convey certain implicatures about the French hotel owner's manner of delivering the original statement and perhaps something about the French hotel owner's manner of thinking/worldview/way of dealing with customers. Similarly, the metarepresentative framework central to the novel makes it possible to use syntactic form to communicate implicatures about its narrative voice.

5.2 Narrative voice and character alignment

While the presence of the narrator is barely discernible as more than a voice in this and many other works of fiction, further on in the narrative we have more clearly demarcated metarepresentations in the form of interpretive uses explicitly attributed or implicitly attributable to more tangible, though still fictional, characters. There are places from quite early on in the extract where the external narrative can be read as moving into the perspective of the character Tom. In narratological terms, the narrative is frequently focalised in a number of ways typical of the genre, including the indirect and free indirect representation of Tom's thoughts. Following the external narrative opening, Tom's thoughts are explicitly reported:

> Tom, the younger of the two looking down, thought of Snow White in her glass coffin. He thought also, looking up at Albert, that the vessels and spoons and caskets, gleaming in the liquid light under the glass, were like a resurrected burial hoard. (Which, indeed, some of them were.)

The reporting clauses in 'Tom,...thought of Snow White' and 'He thought also', make these straightforwardly signalled metarepresentations, but we also get what I think we would probably read as narratorial interventions in 'looking up at Albert' – an observation Tom is unlikely to make about himself – and '(Which, indeed, some of them were.)' Unlike the thoughts introduced with reporting clauses, it is not possible to pinpoint with certainty the source of these representations as the narrator or Tom and this is where the literary text can exhibit quite a fluid movement between metarepresentational levels which must be negotiated by the reader and may be negotiated differently in different readings. The statement in parentheses could be read as Tom's own realisation. I see it as more likely being the narrator's reflection on Tom's thought. It can be read as a knowing adult comment on the boy's conjecture and its use and positioning of the word 'indeed' seem to me to characterise it as slightly more worldly and linguistically confident than is suggested by the brief glimpse of Tom's mind which precedes it.

Following this there are two sentences which could be read either as simple external narrative or as a free indirect representation of Tom's thoughts:

> They could not see the other boy clearly, because he was
> on the far side of a case. He appeared to be sketching
> its contents.

Free indirect thought generally lacks reporting clauses and quote marks and involves a fusion of narrator's and character's perspectives (see, for example, Traugott and Pratt 1980: 299–302). Here, as we would expect in the external narrator's perspective, we have distal deixis in the simple past tense and the third person pronouns, but we have a spatial positioning centred on Tom (and Julian). The other boy they are watching is 'on the far side of a case'. Perhaps more tellingly, in conjunction with the preceding report of Tom's thoughts, the way the boy is described as 'appearing' to be sketching could suggest that this is Tom making a deduction about what the boy is doing, without being sure of it. Where there is negative modality like this, the uncertainty and deduction is often a marker of a character's perceptions (Simpson 1993). The syntax is not my focus here. I refer to these sentences just to show that the narrative establishes an alignment with the consciousness of Tom early on. By this point in the novel then, we already have Byatt's metarepresentation of a narrator/narrative voice at least partly characterised by a capacity to express considerable cultural knowledge in complex noun phrases, a characterisation communicated within this metarepresentational level as a relatively weak implicature. There is no sense of dissociation from the propositions expressed in the narrative, which further blurs the distinction between actual author and narrative voice. In addition we have a metarepresentation of the character Tom's thoughts embedded within the narrative and, with the use of the word 'indeed', a slight distinction which alerts us to a movement from Tom's consciousness back to the encompassing narrative.

5.3 Syntax in the representation of speech

Following the brief reports of Tom's thoughts discussed in the last section, the narrative becomes readable as purely external again, with just the last sentence of this paragraph using the word 'appeared' again in what might be read as a return to Tom's perceptions, trying to make sense of the character Julian's behaviour:

> Julian Cain was at home in the South Kensington Museum. His father, Major Prosper Cain, was Special Keeper of Precious Metals. Julian was just 15, and a boarder at Marlowe School, but was home recovering from a nasty bout of jaundice. He was neither tall nor short, slightly built, with a sharp face and a sallow complexion, even without the jaundice. He wore his straight black hair parted in the centre, and was dressed in a school suit. Tom Wellwood, boyish in Norfolk jacket and breeches, was about two years younger, and looked younger than he was, with large dark eyes, a soft mouth, and a smooth head of dark gold hair. The two had not met before. Tom's mother was visiting Julian's father, to ask for help with her

> research. She was a successful authoress of magical tales. Julian had been deputed to show Tom the treasures. He appeared to be more interested in showing him the squatting boy.

After this, the reports of the boys' speech are interspersed with short paragraphs of narrative which we might well read as continuing to align with Tom's consciousness.

> 'I said I'd show you a mystery.'
>
> 'I thought you meant one of the treasures.'
>
> 'No, I meant him. There's something shifty about him. I've been keeping an eye on him. He's up to something.'
>
> Tom was not sure whether this was the sort of make-believe his own family practised, tracking complete strangers and inventing stories about them. He wasn't sure if Julian was, so to speak, playing at being responsible.
>
> 'What does he do?'
>
> 'He does the Indian rope-trick. He disappears. Now you see him, now you don't. He's here every day. All by himself. But you can't see where or when he goes.'
>
> They sidled along the wrought-iron gallery, which was hung with thick red velvet curtains. The third boy stayed where he was, drawing intently. Then he moved his position, to see from another angle. He was hay-haired, shaggy and filthy. He had cut-down workmen's trousers, with braces, over a flannel shirt the colour of smoke, stained with soot. Julian said
>
> 'We could go down and stalk him. There are all sorts of odd things about him. He looks very rough. He never seems to go anywhere but here. I've waited at the exit to see him leave, and follow him, and he doesn't seem to leave. He seems to be a permanent fixture.'
>
> The boy looked up, briefly, his grimy face creased in a frown. Tom said
>
> 'He concentrates.'
>
> 'He never talks to anyone that I can see. Now and then the art students look at his drawings. But he doesn't chat to them. He just creeps about the place. It's sinister.'

> 'Do you get many robberies?'
>
> 'My father always says the keepers are criminally casual with the keys to the cases. And there are heaps and heaps of stuff lying around waiting to be catalogued, or sent to Bethnal Green. It would be terribly easy to sneak off with things. I don't even know if anyone would notice if you did, not with some of the things, though they'd notice quickly enough if anyone made an attempt on the Candlestick.'
>
> 'Candlestick?'
>
> 'The Gloucester Candlestick. What he seems to be drawing, a lot of the time. The lump of gold, in the centre of that case. It's ancient and unique. I'll show it to you. We could go down, and go up to it, and disturb him.'

The speech itself is direct and is distinguished from the narrative voice by quote marks, though not (except in one utterance) by reporting clauses, so while it is not strictly *free* direct speech, it is not as overtly framed and demarcated as it might be. The narrator directly represents the words used by the characters (in the fictional world), and this linguistic form constructs aspects of each boy's fictional personality. Again, while we might derive such information from someone's speech in a non-fictional context, here these aspects of personality can be said to be communicated because of the embedding of the speech within the literary metarepresentation. Different things may be communicated by the syntax to different readers in different contexts, so here I just offer some possibilities. Neither boy uses much syntactic complexity. There are contexts in which a degree of complexity might be expected in spoken language, but the relatively simple sentences and phrases do not seem out of place in a conversation between two teenage boys who have only just met.

Julian's sentences are mostly complete, but many of them contain only one clause:

> 'No, I meant *him*. There's something shifty about him. I've been keeping an eye on him. He's up to something.'

Where there is more than one clause in these representations of Julian's speech, there is a tendency towards compound sentences such as:

> 'We could go down and stalk him.'

There is some limited complexity, as in the following sentence, where my brackets indicate a subordinate compound clause:

> 'I've waited at the exit [to [see him leave] and [follow him]].'

The simplicity of Julian's utterances seems to me to communicate a bluntness of delivery and also possibly a slightly enigmatic, elliptical style designed to excite Tom's curiosity. Tom's utterances are also minimal and simple, perhaps even more simple and minimal than Julian's. For example:

> 'What does he do?'
>
> 'He concentrates.'
>
> 'Candlestick?'

We already have enough context to interpret the style of Tom's utterances differently, though they bear some syntactic similarities to Julian's. As the younger of the two boys, and the one who is not in a familiar environment, Tom's utterances seem to me to convey an impression of someone lacking in confidence, bemused by the situation and not keen to enter into lengthy conversational exchanges for fear of getting out of his depth. While the boys' syntactic structures bear some similarity, the interpretations I have suggested here are very different. Furthermore, if we were to meet Tom and Julian as real people, these impressions might strike us as incidental pieces of information, that is as simple implications about them. Here instead the author is able to use syntactic structures to give rise to implicatures about the characters. Within the metarepresentational framework of the novel the very form of the language is used communicatively.

5.4 Syntax in free indirect thought

The simple syntax in the speech of both boys may communicate an impression of a straightforward and fairly simplistic mind style, but, for the character Tom at least, this is problematized by the juxtaposition of the speech with the aligned narrative which often surrounds it. The contrast is particularly evident in the narrative passages following the main part of the spoken exchange.

> Tom was dubious about this. There was something tense about the third boy, a tough prepared energy he didn't even realise he'd noticed. However, he agreed. He usually agreed to things. They

> moved, sleuth-like, from ambush to ambush behind the swags of velvet. They went under Prince Albert, out onto the turning stone stairs, down to the South Court. When they reached the Candlestick, the dirty boy was not there.
>
> 'He wasn't on the stairs,' said Julian, obsessed.
>
> Tom stopped to stare at the candlestick. It was dully gold. It seemed heavy. It stood on three feet, each of which was a long-eared dragon, grasping a bone with grim claws, gnawing with sharp teeth. The rim of the spiked cup that held the handle was also supported by open-jawed dragons with wings and snaking tails. The whole of its thick stem was wrought of fantastic foliage, amongst which men and monsters, centaurs and monkeys, writhed, grinned, grimaced, grasped and stabbed at each other. A helmeted, gnome-like being, with huge eyes, grappled the sinuous tail of a reptile. There were other human or kobold figures, one in particular with long draggling hair and a mournful gaze. Tom thought immediately that his mother would need to see it. He tried, and failed, to memorise the shapes. Julian explained. It had an interesting history, he said. No one knew exactly what it was made of. It was some kind of gilt alloy. It was probable that it had been made in Canterbury – modelled in wax and cast – but apart from the symbols of the evangelists on the knop, it appeared not to be made for religious use. It had turned up in the cathedral in Le Mans, from where it had disappeared at the French Revolution. A French antiquary had sold it to the Russian Prince Soltikoff. The South Kensington Museum had acquired it from his collection in 1861. There was nothing, anywhere, like it.
>
> Tom did not know what a knop was, and did not know what the symbols of the evangelists were. But he saw that the thing was a whole world of secret stories. He said his mother would like to see it. It might be just what she was looking for. He would have liked to touch the heads of the dragons.

All of the paragraphs in this section start with a sentence referring explicitly to Tom:

> Tom was dubious about this.
>
> Tom stopped to stare at the candlestick.
>
> Tom did not know what a knop was, and did not know what the symbols of the evangelists were.

These clearly external narrative reflections, in my view, direct attention to the character and so make us more likely to read what follows as metarepresentative of his thoughts. As the subsequent sentences use no explicit markers of reporting, they could in theory be read either as pure external narrative or as free indirect representations of Tom's thoughts. It is the opening references to Tom which signal to the reader a narrative movement towards Tom's perspective. We might, as readers, be more attuned to such signals if we have encountered them before; direct reference to a character immediately before a free indirect representation of her thoughts is a feature of many aligned narratives by writers as diverse as Jane Austen and Enid Blyton. If, as I think is likely, we do read what follows as a representation of Tom's thoughts, we might get a sense of a much more developed and elaborate mind style than is conveyed by his speech. Take for example this sentence:

> There was something tense about the third boy, a tough prepared energy he didn't even realise he'd noticed.

This, somewhat adult reflection on his own perceptions is accompanied by an appositional noun phrase structure: 'something tense about the third boy' is rephrased and redefined as 'a tough prepared energy he didn't even realise he'd noticed', and this second noun phrase is considerably more complex than any noun phrase Tom has uttered in his reported conversation with Julian. It includes two pre-modifiers of the head noun 'energy', one of them, 'prepared', quite a novel word choice in this position. It also includes the relative clause 'he didn't even realise he'd noticed' as a post-modifier for the noun. This noun phrase comes closer to the complexity of the narrator's noun phrase analysed in Section 5.1. The sense, as is usual in free indirect thought, is of a fusion of narrator and character perspectives. I think that the fusion here includes a mix of the forms of language we might attribute to the narrative voice and the character. The complexity of the noun phrase arguably resembles the complexity of Tom's thoughts, while at the same time the syntactic structure is also typical of what has already been established as the external narrative style and we are unlikely to attribute some of the particular word choices, such as 'prepared', to the character Tom as we have constructed him at this stage. In terms of the metarepresentation and interpretive use here, the attitude communicated towards the propositions expressed is associative – the opposite of the dissociation communicated in cases of verbal irony. The structure of the interpretive use is the same, but the associative attitude is less discernible. Just as there is some blurring between author and narrator, there is a similar merging of narrative and character dispositions and resulting mind styles.

Further complexity is evident in the next paragraph, particularly in the development of the description of the candlestick Tom stares at.

> It stood on three feet, each of which was a long-eared dragon, grasping a bone with grim claws, gnawing with sharp teeth.

The sentence is simple in terms of consisting of only one clause, headed by the verb 'stood', but the prepositional phrase following it, beginning with 'on', is quite complex. It contains a noun phrase headed by 'feet' and this noun phrase contains a relative clause running from 'each' to 'teeth'. This relative clause contains a verb, 'was', followed by another noun phrase headed by 'dragon'. 'Dragon' is post-modified within its phrase by the two further non-finite clauses: 'grasping a bone with grim claws' and 'gnawing with sharp teeth', and within each of these two clauses there are further phrases. Alongside the complexity of the full phrasal constituents and the phrasal and clausal embedding, the two non-finite clauses at the end display a repetition of structure which constitutes parallelism, a feature of poetic language. Similar features can be found in later sentences in the same paragraph. If we read these sentences as the narrator's implicit representation of Tom's thoughts, as I believe we are encouraged to do, the complexity may give rise to implicatures about a sophistication in Tom's observations of the candlestick, as well, of course, as communicating the intricacy of the candlestick via Tom's perspective. The narrator–character fusion again might suggest a meeting between two similar ways of seeing and understanding the world. My claim here is that repeated associative fusions of this kind give rise to a sense of empathy between narrator and character, which, in the absence of any evidence of narratorial unreliability, we as readers are invited to share.[5] What is also interesting is that the narrator–character alignment is established so quickly and so unobtrusively.

Halfway through the paragraph, the narrative voice appears to step outside of Tom's consciousness and report his thoughts explicitly:

> Tom thought immediately that his mother would like to see it.

Shortly after this there is a reporting clause (probably Tom's) announcing Julian's explanation of the candlestick:

> Julian explained.

This is followed by what is arguably Tom's free indirect representation of Julian's speech.

> He tried, and failed, to memorise the shapes. Julian explained. It had an interesting history, he said. No one knew exactly what it was made of. It was some kind of gilt alloy. It was probable that it had been made in Canterbury – modelled in wax and cast – but apart from the symbols of the evangelists on the knop, it appeared not to be made for religious use. It had turned up in the cathedral in Le Mans, from where it had disappeared at the French Revolution. A French antiquary had sold it to the Russian Prince Soltikoff. The South Kensington Museum had acquired it from his collection in 1861. There was nothing, anywhere, like it.

Read this way, this part of the passage is metarepresentationally at its most complex. Byatt represents a narrator/narrative voice representing Tom's thoughts in free indirect style representing Julian's speech, first in indirect style (for instance in the use of the reporting clause 'he said') and then in free indirect style for the rest of the paragraph. Implicatures and attitudes towards the propositional material can be communicated at each level. Interestingly, the syntactic structures in the representations of Julian's speech are generally simpler than many of those in the preceding representations of Tom's thoughts:

> It was some kind of gilt alloy.

This is a simple, single-clause sentence with relatively undeveloped phrases. However, there is more evidence of complexity than in Julian's earlier speech, for example:

> It had turned up in the cathedral in Le Mans, from where it had disappeared at the French revolution.

While this is also a simple sentence, it has a more complex noun phrase headed by 'Le Mans', containing a post-modifying relative clause in some ways similar to, though not as complex as, the narrator's NP post-modification already discussed. There is a sense that Julian's metarepresented utterances here also add depth to his character, but this new information is filtered through Tom's consciousness and we are likely to read it as such. Perhaps Julian is getting into his stride at this point, confidently displaying to Tom his superior knowledge of the museum's holdings by using a more developed and controlled syntax. At the same time, because of the metarepresentational structure, we are likely to make guesses at Tom's internal response to Julian's display – awe, resentment, bafflement? Any of these and others are possible. We have just been made aware that Tom himself is capable of elaborate and complex thoughts and so we might derive a further narrative implicature to the effect that Tom's intellectual sophistication is paradoxically hidden by a lack of confidence in his interactions with the other boy; he does not appear to respond to Julian during (his representation of) Julian's speech and there is explicit reference to Tom's difficulty understanding Julian at the beginning of the next paragraph:

> Tom did not know what a knop was, and did not know what the symbols of the evangelists were.

The effect of filtering Julian's speech through a narrative aligned with Tom is, I believe, to encourage the reader to feel a little like Tom, or at least like people like Tom – he is after all a fictional character. We might also feel a little bewildered at the information Julian is giving and the confident manner in which it appears to be delivered might make us experience, to an extent, a suspicion of Julian that we could attribute to Tom. At the same time as experiencing *with*, we have experience *of* Tom mediated through the narrator. The third person aligned narrative offers us at the same time a close, empathetic and a distanced, observational understanding of character.

To sum up, following the simplicity of both boys' explicitly reported conversational exchanges, the complexity of the syntax in Tom's free indirect thought allows us to construct a sense of a more complex and sophisticated mind style. In context, this might make available implicatures that he is an intelligent boy, sensitive to the artworks he is observing, but wary of his new acquaintance and unwilling to display his own control of a sentence. The narrative alignment, characterised in part by a fusion of linguistic forms, evokes a sense of empathy in which the reader may share. This is not to say that all readers will experience such a reading. A reader may not respond well to the sentence structures, or other aspects of context may constitute obstacles to an empathetic reading for any number of idiosyncratic reasons. At the same time, I think it is fair to say that the empathetic reading is at least invited by the character-aligned text.

6 Conclusion

I have used the opening pages of *The Children's Book* to illustrate the kind of third person narrative which moves frequently and unobtrusively into alignment with a character's perspective. My analysis shows how the theoretical frameworks outlined in the opening sections can explain how this kind of literary text communicates. A work of fiction such as this can involve multiple metarepresentations, the linguistic forms of which are explained as interpretive use of one kind or another in the relevance theory account. At each level of representation, syntax, among other things, plays a role in the construction of narrative or character voice. At each level the implications we can derive from the form of the language become available, in combination with other aspects of context, as weaker or stronger implicatures. In non-fictional contexts we can and do also use language interpretively to give rise to such implicatures, but the fictional text, with its tendency to use multiply embedded metarepresentations, offers especially rich opportunities to communicate more than might be expected via syntactic choices. This analysis can be related more generally to work on relevance theory and literature in which linguistic form is considered to be exploited for its communicative potential more than would be expected in the non-literary text (Pilkington 2000: ch. 5; Fabb 2002: chs. 3 and 4; MacMahon 2007). In my view, the relevance theory approach here and elsewhere offers a view of literary texts as acts of communication, providing a more persuasive explanatory account of exactly how we might move from form to interpretation than is in evidence in other, stylistic approaches.

Notes

1. Strictly speaking, the utterance represents a speaker's thought which is descriptive of a state of affairs in the world. In this chapter, for the sake of succinctness, I omit this detail in the discussion of both descriptive and interpretive use.
2. See Booth (1983), Chatman (1980) and Genette (1980) for the source of most of these terms and see Simpson (1993) and Fludernik (2009) for comprehensive overviews of the field.
3. At various stages of discussion in this chapter I feel it is important for illustrative purposes to spell out possible attitudes and implicatures communicated by examples of utterances. However, the very act of making these explicit inevitably risks overstating them and suggesting they are stronger and more determinate than they might actually be in any given communicative situation.
4. See Semino (2007) for a survey of work in this area.
5. For discussion of the history of empathetic narrative see Adamson (2001).

7

Negation, Expectation and Characterisation: Analysing the Role of Negation in Character Construction in *To Kill a Mockingbird* (Lee 1960) and *Stark* (Elton 1989)

Lisa Nahajec

1 Introduction

At the heart of the stylistic endeavour is the aim to illuminate the relationship between language choice and textual effect and meaning. This chapter examines how one element of language choice, linguistic negation, can contribute to stylistic effects. Simpson suggests readers can derive 'complex inferences from absences in the story' (2010: 299), whilst Nørgaard (2007) and Sweetser (2006) suggest that negation has significant stylistic and rhetorical potential. This study focuses on what inferences readers can derive from the possible presences that underlie the absences evoked through the use of negation and how this can contribute to the textual construction of fictional characters.

Take, for example, an utterance such as 'our hero was not tall, dark and handsome'; here the qualities of being 'tall', 'dark' and 'handsome' are absent from the entity designated a 'hero'. Such an assertion would appear to be less informative than a positive construction; it does not tell us what the hero is, only what he is not. Such an assertion raises questions about how readers infer meaning from utterances containing negation. Further, when characters are described via negation, how does noting an absence of attributes or actions contribute to the textual realisation of those characters?

This chapter takes a pragmatic stylistic approach to negation in tackling these questions. It takes as a starting point the notion that the story world, created in the interaction between writer, text and reader, can be fruitfully explored with the tools offered by a pragmatics based approach to language analysis. The following sections outline an approach to linguistic negation which draws on pragmatic, psycholinguistic, cognitive and linguistic aspects of the phenomenon. This approach proceeds on the premise that negation is a conceptual practice (Jeffries 2010), that is, the recognition and expression of a significant absence. Further, it is presuppositional in nature (Givón 2001) and constitutes an indirect form of communication open to a broadly Gricean (Grice 1975) account of the implicatures it generates.

The chapter goes on to explore the relationship between negation and characterisation in prose fiction, specifically looking at instances of narrative description where negation is a significant factor in the textual construction of character. This is illustrated in the analysis of two passages; the first, from Ben Elton's (1989) *Stark* and the second, from Harper Lee's (2001/1960) *To Kill a Mockingbird*. I argue that the analysis of negation can shed light on the textual construction of characters and first person narrator in these passages.

2 Linguistic negation

Understanding the effects of negation in discourse requires an understanding of what negation is and how readers infer meaning from its use. Key to this is the idea that interpreting negation is a matter of working out the implications of a possible, but unrealised, presence and reversing these to recover a potential implicature; the contextually determined significance of a possible presence forms the basis of the potential meaning implied by its actual absence. In effect, understanding negation is as much about presence as it is about absence. To return to our 'hero' (noted above); a 'tall, dark and handsome' hero might be assumed to be ordinary, run-of-the-mill (within the conventions of literature). An utterance that notes that our hero lacks these attributes is likely to be understood relative to these assumptions, perhaps producing the implicature that the hero is odd, peculiar or unique.

Further, while an utterance containing negation produces a contextually determined implicature, the possible presence evoked is not discarded from the ongoing discourse in favour of this implied meaning. Rather, the possible presence is retained and impacts on the ongoing discourse (Giora 2006; Giora et al. 2004, 2005, 2007). Take for example,

Basil Fawlty's famous (or infamous) injunction to his staff in dealing with a German couple visiting the Fawlty Towers hotel in the BBC sitcom of the same name:

(1) Don't mention the war.

(Cleese and Booth 2001/1977: 153)

This could be interpreted in context to mean that the staff should talk about anything but 'the war'; they should be tactful or careful to avoid offending the guests. Basil's failure to abide by his own injunction as the action unfolds is only relevant and humorous against the background of having evoked the possibility of mentioning 'the war' in the first place.

The following sections expand on this approach to understanding negation in discourse. I start by defining what is meant by *negation* in this study and go on to explore its presuppositional qualities and argue for a broadly Gricean method of interpreting its meaning in context.

2.1 Defining negation

Negation has been a recurring theme in scholarly research as attested to in Horn's (1989) seminal work in the field, *A Natural History of Negation*. It has been examined from a wide variety of perspectives including logic (e.g. Gabbay and Wansing 1999), cross linguistic variation (e.g. Miestamo 2005), grammar (e.g. Huddleston and Pullum 2002), semantics (e.g. Lyons 1977), philosophy (e.g. Westbury 2003 and Saury 2008), pragmatics (e.g. Horn 1985, 1989; Moeschler 1992; Geurts 1998), corpus linguistics (e.g. Tottie 1991) cognitive linguistics (e.g. Verhagen 2005), cognitive stylistics (e.g. Werth 1999; Hidalgo-Downing 2000; Sweetser 2006) and stylistics (e.g. Nørgaard 2007). In fact, much research has been concerned with determining just what negation is. Definitions have ranged from the view that negation is a mechanism indicating otherness or distinction (philosophy e.g. Westbury 2003), through to scholars in pragmatics defining it by its role in interaction between speaker/writer and reader/hearer as denial and prohibition (e.g. Horn 1985, 1989; Tottie 1991; Guerts 1998).

The definition used in this study adopts Jeffries' (2010) characterisation of negation as a 'conceptual practice', the recognition and linguistic realisation of absence. With this view, this broad definition of negation is a precursor to the above approaches; it tackles the issue of what brings together syntax, semantics, logic and pragmatics, and that is that prior to reversing the polarity of a sentence or denying a prior assertion, linguistic forms give expression to the underlying recognition of a salient absence. Absence, however, is contingent on the possibility of presence; there can only be an absence of something where there is the possibility of that something being there. The expression of an absence is, in large part, the process of drawing attention to unrealised possibilities.

This conceptual practice of negating can be realised through a variety of textual vehicles (Jeffries 2010). These range from the prototypical forms (e.g. *not, no, never, none, nothing*) to more peripheral realisations such as past tense conditional constructions (*if you had done x, we could have done y*) (Dancygier and Sweetser 2005); modal constructions, (e.g. *you should have done x, I wish you had done x*); grammaticalised metaphors (e.g. *we're out of x, he is far from x*) (Yamanashi 2000); and expletive forms which have migrated from their role as emphatic support for a negator (e.g. *you don't know bugger all about x/you know bugger all about x*). This variation in expression is motivated by issues of scope (which sentence and utterance elements fall under the influence of the negator) but also by questions of force and focus. It is not simply that some state, event or entity is absent, but that this meaning is expressed with variable pragmatic emphasis. This motivation for the variation of negation is complex and will not be pursued further here as the examples examined below do not exploit this potential for variable form.

2.2 Negation, expectation and pragmatic presupposition

Language users' experience of the world is one in which the presence of events, objects and attributes is perceptually prominent against a background of absence. Negation, or the linguistic realisation of absence, is a reversal of this normal view of the world, where the absence is made prominent whilst presence is the background. Givón (2001) captures this idea in relation to the notions of 'change and stasis'. He notes that 'stasis', or non-events, is the more frequent norm than change, the event, and that 'an event is the cognitively salient *figure*. It stands out against the *ground* of stasis' (2001: 372). Negation occurs where stasis and change are switched and the event becomes the ground against which the non-event becomes 'temporarily, locally-salient, more informative' (2001: 372). Consider the following example:

(2) (a) a man came into my office yesterday and said...
(b) *a man didn't come into my office yesterday and said...
(c) ?Nobody came into my office yesterday and said...
Example from Givón (2001: 373).

Within the norms of everyday experience, (a) is pragmatically acceptable in that it picks out the event, a man visiting, against a background norm that most people do not visit at all times. Against this same background, Givón notes that although (c) is possible, (b) appears pragmatically (and grammatically) odd. The reason for this is that in a situation where most people do not visit, to pick out one who does not is uninformative. However, if the background norm were one in which there is a constant flow of visitors – for example, a doctor's surgery – a non-event, the absence of a visitor, would be the salient figure against a ground of constant visits.

Givón's use of 'figure' and 'ground' here could be viewed as limited in that figure and ground elements are conventionally viewed as occupying the same perceptual space. In their explanation of figure and ground with reference to image schemas, Ungerer and Schmid (1996: 157–160) suggest that if we take a situation such as a book on a table, the book can be viewed as the figure against the ground of the table. This is reflected in the way we might describe the situation:

(3) There's a book on the table.

We are unlikely to present the same situation as:

(4) There's a table under the book.

However, if we extend this example, it is possible to extend the figure and ground relationship beyond a single perceptual space. Imagine a situation in which there are several tables and one of the tables has a book on it, the book would remain the figure against the ground of the table. We might now consider the tables without books as a ground against the figure of one table with a book. However, if there were several books and tables, but one of the tables did not have a book, although the figure and ground relationship between the tables and books would remain the same, the relationship between the tables with a book would now be the ground for the one table without. The absence of a book would be perceptually prominent.

We can now introduce the notion of time; if we take an alternate situation, that of meeting a friend who happens to be naked, we might comment:

(5) You have no clothes on!

The friend's nakedness is perceptually prominent against a generalised expectation (based on experience) that people wear clothes. The many points in time where clothes have been worn can be equated to the books on the tables. So, the ground is something usually happening (wearing clothes), the figure is the situation in which it does not happen. We can, of course, switch the figure and ground configuration; in a nudist camp where the previous points in time have included being naked, a comment such as (5) would be pragmatically dubious and we would need to assume that the speaker expected the hearer to be clothed. Similarly, we would be unlikely to refer to a newborn baby as not wearing anything as there is no prior experience of babies being born fully clothed against which the assertion of nakedness would be salient. With negation then, we can view the background experience of presence as the ground against the figure of absence and, as such, absence is perceptually prominent where presence is expected.

How then, does this experiential understanding of expectation as integral to negation relate to the use of negation in texts and the presupposition it appears to trigger? Givón (2001) posits a discoursal pragmatic presuppositional account of negation, suggesting that it triggers presuppositions regarding the expectations of discourse participants based on contextual, co-textual and generic knowledge. He argues that: 'a negative assertion is made on the tacit assumption that the hearer has either heard about, believes in, is likely to take for granted, or is at least familiar with the corresponding affirmative proposition' (Givón 2001: 336).

He notes that discoursal pragmatic presupposition must be distinguished from other types of presupposition regarding the situation in focus:

> It is clear that the notion of presupposition relevant to the discussion here is pragmatic rather than logical. Otherwise, one would be claiming that NEG-assertions assert the falsity of one proposition (NEG-P) while presupposing the truth of its logical opposite (P), a rank logical contradiction.
>
> (Givón 2001: 371)

For example, it is not possible to both assert that X is not Y and presuppose that X is Y. Rather, what is presupposed is that X was in some sense expected to be Y. Presupposition here, then, is concerned not with the situation in focus, but with discourse participants' expectations about that situation. We can, then, view negation as triggering two interrelated presuppositions:

(a) The hearer/reader expects whatever is negated to be the case.
(b) The speaker/writer believes that the hearer expects whatever is negated to be the case.

So, when a speaker produces a negated utterance, they do so on the basis that they believe or assume that the hearer expects whatever is negated to be the case. Whether or not actual readers/hearers hold these expectations is questionable. As with all theories concerned with the pragmatics of language comprehension, we can't *know* what hearers believe or expect, we can only draw plausible conclusions based on context and co-text. Although we do not know what actual hearers/reader know or believe, we do know that the speaker treats this information *as if* it is known (as per the Lewis rule of accommodation, Horn 1997: 306). We can suggest then, that an utterance projects an 'ideal' reader/hearer that may, or may not, correlate with the actual flesh and blood reader/hearer. Pagano (1994) proposes this as a solution to the problem of accounting for the difference between what an utterance appears to present as presupposed and what actual readers share. In relation to written texts, she suggests:

> The writer creates a picture of the reader, who thus becomes an 'ideal reader', and attributes to this reader certain experience, knowledge, opinions and beliefs on the basis of which a writer builds his/her message... As the writer somehow assumes what the reader's questions and expectations are, s/he tries to provide information about these.
>
> (Pagano 1994: 253)

However, the relationship of negation to expectation is not as simple as arguing that negation triggers the presupposition that the speaker assumes the hearer to expect something. This would result in the notion that only the hearer does the expecting, but it is not difficult to imagine a situation in which the speaker also expects. Imagine a scenario in which a diner in a restaurant calls the waiter over and says:

(6) There's no salt in my soup.

It is likely in such a context that the speaker is intending to complain about the lack of salt in her soup. If we take a limited scope to who expects, then we would have to say that in this situation the speaker is drawing on generic knowledge that soup has salt, or projecting it as an expectation of salt in soup on the part of the hearer. But surely, in this situation, it is not only the ideal hearer who expects salt, but also the speaker; why else would they draw attention to something in this context? The speech act of complaining then, provides a clear example of a situation where it is the speaker who expects.

The difficulty in attaching the presupposition to the speaker/writer arises as a result of the apparent contradiction between evidently knowing that something is not the case (as attested to by the proposition itself) whilst simultaneously expecting the opposite. Work by Nolke (2006) (see also Ducrot 1984) may provide some insights into how this can occur. As noted above, there is a distinction between the actual reader/hearer, the person who picks up a text or hears the words, and an ideal reader projected by the text. Nolke (2006), in his discussion of the dialogic nature of language, posits that there is equally a distinction between the speaker/writer who produces the words and the speaker/writer projected by the text (2006). Nolke argues for a polyphonic reading of utterances, that is, that several voices or viewpoints are encoded, not only in parole, but also in langue. The language system, he argues, contains instructions that utterances should be understood as containing multiple viewpoints and this is particularly evident in negation. In this model, Nolke (2006) distinguishes between the speaker and the 'locutor', where on the one hand the locutor is a product of the sentence, and on the other of the utterance. So, the occurrence of a negator encodes two points of view (POV). Nolke uses the following example to illustrate:

(7) This wall is not white.

Such an utterance encodes two viewpoints:

POV 1 – This wall is white.
POV 2 – POV 1 is wrong.

It is the locutor who holds POV 2, whilst, Nolke argues, the reader will attempt to work out who holds POV 1. Although Nolke specifically discusses the expectation of the positive in terms of the hearer's attempts to assign those expectations to a significant discourse participant, the distinction for a separation between the locutor and the speaker allows for the possibility that whereas the locutor is presenting one position, the actual speaker may have expectations regarding another. For example, if (7) had been addressed to the painter of the wall who had been asked by the speaker to paint it white but has instead painted it green, it would be consistent with the context that whilst the speaker expects what is encoded in POV 1, the knowledge that this is not the case is consistent with POV 2 (the locutor's point of view).

The final point here is to consider the location of the expectations triggered. Although negation functions as a pragmatic presupposition trigger, treating the negated information as if it is expected, these expectations can also be apparent in the co-text and context as well as projected through the process of negating:

i Explicit expectations: expectations that are explicit in the co-text

ii Implicit expectations:

  (a) based on assumptions about how the world works;
  (b) based on specific knowledge shared by discourse participants;
  (c) based on incorrect inferences from the text;
  (d) based on cultural shared knowledge;

iii Projected expectation: expectations simultaneously instantiated and defeated through the use of negation.

Understanding negation in context, then, is a case of understanding the expectations it evokes through its presuppositional nature, taking into account who holds those expectations and considering whether they are reflections of existing expectations or projections of expectations created through the act of negating.

2.3 Negation and implicatures

This presuppositional aspect to negation is only one element of understanding its complex nature and the question remains as to how readers interpret this evocation of unrealised positives in context. Moeschler (1992), in outlining problems with and rejecting a speech act theory account of negation, considers the implicatures that are potentially generated by choosing to negate a particular situation. Taking a relevance-theoretic approach, Moeschler suggests that the interpretation of negation is based on its optimum relevance in context relative to the cognitive effort required for that interpretation:

> The hypothesis I will make, and which supposes an inferential view of negation, is that the negative must be considered as the most

> relevant in the circumstances, i.e., the utterance whose effect is sufficient to balance the supplementary cognitive effort imposed by the treatment of negation.
>
> (Moeschler 1992: 66)

This is in line with Leech's (1983: 101) assertion that whilst a sentence containing negation is ostensibly uninformative, because of the assumption of linguistic co-operation, it will, in fact, be used when the utterance is more informative in context than a positive counterpart. Moeschler's (1992) account considers how the selection of state, entity or event that is negated is meaningful in context. He argues that interpreting negation is a combination of context and invited inference (1992: 67–68). He uses the following example to illustrate this:

(8) Speaker A: How is the weather today?
Speaker B: It is not nice.

Moeschler (1992) suggests the meaning of speaker B's response is dependent on context. Where there is an understanding between speakers that they will go to the beach if the weather is nice, this constitutes the context for the interpretation of B's utterance. Speaker A would be likely to recover the contextual implication of B's utterance as *they will not be going to the beach/they will stay at home*. Such an inference is based on the notion of invited inference whereby the context establishes the conditions under which the type of weather is relevant: if the weather is nice, they will go to the beach, *if p then q*. Appealing to the pragmatics of natural language (rather than the rules of classical logic), Moeschler argues that if it is the case that *if p then q*, then, by invited inference, *if not p then not q* (1992: 68–89). Consequently, the interpretation of not going to the beach/staying at home results from *if not p then not q*. Moeschler's (1992) analysis demonstrates two things of significance here; first that using negation produces meaning beyond implying its opposite (for example, *not nice/bad*) based on context and second, that recovering this implication is dependent on considering the significance of the positive.

Whilst Moeschler's approach provides a strong foundation for understanding how negation is interpreted in context, a Gricean (1975) approach allows for a consideration of the mechanisms involved in signposting a distinction between what is said and what is meant. Just which of Grice's maxims are flouted when negation is used is dependent on the context. The following example illustrates how negation is interpreted when the maxims of quantity and relation are flouted.

(9) Speaker A: Some vicious cat has been terrorising all the other cats in the neighbourhood.
Speaker B: My cat's not male.

Whilst what is said by Speaker B in (9) appears to deviate from the conversational topic (the vicious cat), as per Grice's (1975) Cooperative Principle, the hearer will assume that the utterance is appropriately informative, truthful, relevant and clear in context and work to recover the implied meaning. Speaker B's response flouts the maxims of quantity and relation in that it conveys more information than is strictly called for by the conversational context and is not ostensibly relevant to the previous utterance. Given the assumption that Speaker B's utterance is meaningful, the maleness, or not, and ownership of cats can be seen as relevant and informative in response to Speaker A's assertion that some cat is terrorising the neighbourhood. In referring to 'my cat', in opposition to some non-specific ('some') cat (a flout of quantity), Speaker B implies that the issue of who owns the vicious cat is informative. By raising the issue of the whether the cat is male or not, Speaker B highlights general background assumptions that are relevant in this context, namely that cats that are vicious tend to be male. Speaker B's assertion, therefore, implies that the sex of the cat is relevant to which cat is responsible; if 'my cat' is male, it could be responsible. Given that the maleness attribute is negated, the resulting implicature is that some other male cat is responsible. So, in flouting the maxims of relation and quantity by asserting the non-maleness of 'my cat', speaker B implies more than what is said.

Interestingly, a very similar contextual meaning could have been produced through a positive assertion of the speaker's cat being female. However, the use of negation allows speaker B to project onto speaker A the expectation that her cat is male and therefore responsible. If speaker B's cat is male, then Speaker A is correct. This is reversed in the context of negation and so, in addition to implying that some other cat is responsible, Speaker B's utterance generates the conversational implicature that Speaker B is wrong. In doing so, it is possible to see that Speaker B may have interpreted Speaker A's assertion as an accusation rather than a neutral statement of fact.

On a final note, whilst the use of a negative construction draws on potential background assumptions, this process of doing so has the potential to reinforce those assumptions; interpreting (9) is likely to involve the assumption that it tends to be male cats that are vicious and by drawing on this it feeds back and reinforces the 'truthfulness' of this assumption. Whilst this may not be of great import to whether male or female cats are vicious, it can have ramifications for the reproduction of social norms and ideologies.

Here then, we can see the interpretation of utterances containing negation as closely bound up with understanding the significance of possible presence. When we interpret negation, we are not interpreting absence, but interpreting what it means for something to be present. So, we can apply Grice's maxims, particularly the maxim of relation, to the pragmatically presupposed positive. For example:

> (10) 'Boris Johnson has no serious experience or track record of managing substantial budgets or any previous commitment to this city.'
>
> *The Evening Standard* 18 April 2008

This example is a quote from an interview with Ed Balls (Labour minister) during the 2008 London mayoral election. The context is such that Balls is commenting in support of the Labour candidate for mayor (Ken Livingstone). It pragmatically presupposes an expectation that Johnson, as a candidate for mayor, has experience of managing budgets and a commitment to London that predated the election campaign. The question is what is the relevance of Johnson having experience of big budgets and previous commitment and how does this relate to the pragmatic presupposition of this expectation?

I return here to Moeschler's (1992) notion that the positive forms the basis for interpreting the negative. Example (10) flouts the maxim of relation as there is no co-textual reference to the expectation. It also flouts quantity as it is ostensibly uninformative, it does not say what Johnson does have and it is overly informative because it does not address the topic of the discourse. It is necessary, then to calculate how the assertion is relevant to the ongoing discourse, that is, the significance of the possibility of Johnson having 'experience and previous commitment', the *if p, then q* element of Moeschler's (1992) explanation. Given the context, which includes the knowledge that:

i the role of Mayor of London includes managing the budget of one of the largest cities in the world;
ii a successful mayor would need to be committed to the city, and;
iii election campaigns focus on the potential strengths and weakness of the candidates.

the possibility that Johnson has 'experience and commitment' may imply that he would make a good Mayor of London. So, the significance of potentially having 'experience and commitment' is what it implies about the quality of the mayoral candidate who has these attributes. Now, because negation creates an absence of 'experience and commitment', the reader is required to modify what is implied by having these attributes relative to their absence:

- if Johnson has experience and commitment, then he may make a good mayor;
- if Johnson lacks (does not have) experience and commitment, then he may not make a good mayor.

Here then, we might recover the opposite of the positive implicature, *Johnson may make a bad mayor*. As the utterance pragmatically presupposes that the ideal reader expects that Johnson has experience and commitment, it also implies that this ideal reader assumes he will be a good mayor. So, the utterance further implies that the ideal reader (and actual reader if they share the assumption) is wrong. This follows Givón's assertion that negation represents a state of affairs 'where the hearer knows wrong' and 'the speaker knows better' (2001: 372).

3 Negation and characterisation

Like linguistic negation, the history of research into the concept of characterisation is long and varied. Questions have been raised as to the existential properties of characters; as Eder et al. (2010) suggest, characters appear to have a semi-autonomous existence, integral to the stories in which they appear, but recognisable as clearly demarcated entities. They are textually constructed in the fabric of the text, but also arise from the relationship of the text with readers' extratextual knowledge about real people and real interactions as well as other fictional characters (Culpeper 2001; Toolan 2001; Culpeper and McIntyre 2010). As Toolan notes, a reader's conceptualisation of Sherlock Holmes will be 'guided by' their knowledge of detectives and crimes from other sources. Character then, is a combination of existing knowledge and textual prompts. As Toolan argues:

> Character entails an illusion in which the reader is a creative accomplice. Out of words we make a person. A variety of descriptions of some posited individual, together with descriptions – implicit or explicit – of that individual's actions and reactions, suffice to lead most readers to conceive of a person of whom these references and insights are just glimpses.
>
> (Toolan 2001: 80)

The way in which readers conceptualise fictional characters is complex, involving both explicit and implicit realisations of character traits. It is frequently discussed in terms of what can be inferred about characters from their verbal behaviour and interactions with other characters (Leech and Short 1981 [2007]) and from what readers bring to a text in terms of their knowledge of real people (Culpeper 2001; Toolan 2001; Culpeper and McIntyre 2010). Characters can also be constructed directly through what narrators and other characters say about them. This chapter is concerned with this direct form of characterisation through narrative description and looks at the way in which the evocation of absent actions and attributes activates pre-existing expectations or projects expectations about characters.

The examination of the relationship between the evocation of absences and how this contributes to characterisation is still in its infancy. Notable recent contributions in this area have been made by Sweetser (2006) and Nørgaard (2007). Sweetser takes a mental spaces approach (see, for example, Fauconnier 1985) to negation and examines the effects of litotes on character construction in Trollop's *The Warden*. Here she notes that the combination of *not* and *un-* negation, each creating an alternative mental space, draws the reader through several conceptualisations of a character at the same time. This, she argues, has the effect of constructing a character who appears to be uncertain and vacillating. Sweetser's consideration of Trollop's character is concerned with mimetic effects; the reader, like the character, vacillates from one viewpoint to another.

Nørgaard, however, in her consideration of negation in Joyce's 'Two Gallants', focuses on the effect of evoking unrealised possibilities. Nørgaard's approach, based on the notion of linguistic polyphony, is primarily concerned with how negation contributes to the construction of point of view. However, within this, she notes that negation can also contribute to the construction of character. In her analysis she suggests that drawing attention to an absent action, that of speaking, on the part of a character, Corley, leads the reader to consider the significance of him not doing so. She concludes that by drawing attention to a possible, but unrealised scenario where Corley does speak, the reader may understand that withholding speech is indicative of a character who is dominant and controlling.

4 Analyses

The analyses that follow aim to expand on Nørgaard's account of negation and characterisation. Here I examine what kinds of expectations are evoked, who is constructed as expecting and what this contributes to the construction and comprehension of character.

4.1 Passage 1 – Ben Elton's (1989) *Stark*

> (11) No, Sly didn't bother Colin over much. So the guy was a billionaire, what could he really do to you? (1) Nothing. In the searing heat and natural abundance of a Carlton summer, Colin had much more pressing enemies than Sly. Let's face it, (2) Sly was unlikely to appear as if from nowhere, on Colin's breadboard and make him feel like throwing-up. He wasn't going to creep into the fridge and hide in the folded spout of the milk carton so that when Colin popped back the spout wings, there he would be! All horrid and scuttly! Then, off like a bullet, but not before he'd shocked Colin into dropping the milk and ruined Colin's day.
>
> Sly Moorcock was more powerful than God in Carlton, but (3) Colin had never had to throw the butter away because he'd found Sly having a fuck in it – it takes a special kind of bastard to make you do that. Colin's enemies were cockroaches, he had no time to worry about billionaires.
>
> (Elton 1989: 14)

This example is an extract from Ben Elton's (1989) novel *Stark*, a satirical exploration of the effects of greed, wealth and global pollution. The extract is taken from early in the novel where the reader is introduced to the two main characters, Sly Morcock and Colin. The passage is ostensibly about the character Colin and what has the power to control his life. It both projects and reflects the notion that it is usually people in power that have control (Sly Morcock), but what actually has control over Colin is the population of cockroaches that share his living space. In this passage, negation is used in the fine-grained description of a series of absent actions and attributes. Despite these absences, the reader is nonetheless required to conceptualise the evoked, if implausible, positive scenarios where Sly Morcock behaves more like a cockroach than a man. This projection of implausible expectations equates both Sly Morcock and the ultra-wealthy with cockroaches, contributes to redefining concepts of power, but also potentially gives rise to humour through the incongruity of what is projected as expected by readers.

The following (12) is taken from the previous paragraph and establishes the topic of 'power' as the issue at hand:

> (12) Yes, Sly owned Carlo, but he didn't rule the roost – not in Colin's little part of town anyway.
>
> (Elton 1989: 14)

Here, the use of the conjunctive 'but' and the negated verb phrase 'didn't rule' defeats the expectation, based on cultural assumptions about ownership, that 'owning' Carlton puts Sly in a position of power over its residents. This is modified with the negated propositional phrase, 'not in Colin's little part of town anyway', which partially negates the negation of the previous clause, producing the implicature that Sly controls some of Carlton. Reliance on the expectation of the positive triggers the mental representations of a billionaire (Sly) as, 'powerful', 'not powerful' and 'not powerful in a specific location'. As such, the readers' background expectations of the link between power, money and ownership are reinforced. This, in turn, reinforces the ideology that power comes with money. However, this is challenged in relation to what actually has power over Colin. The representation of Sly Moorcock as only having limited power is realised in part in the main passage (11). The following analysis focuses on the numbered underlined sections.

In this extract, a series of absurd and implausible expectations are projected by the text (2 and 3) in which the use of negation pragmatically presupposes that the ideal reader expects Sly Morcock to 'hide in the spout of the milk carton' and 'fuck' in the butter. This is inconsistent with actual readers' background knowledge and creates a conflict between what is projected as expected by the ideal reader and what is known by the actual reader (it would have to be a very large milk carton or a very small Sly Moorcock to avoid such a conflict). So, although it is true that Sly Moorcock is unlikely to appear on Colin's breadboard or hide in the folds of the milk carton, the process of introducing them as expectations through the simultaneous introduction and defeat of those expectations, creates a conflict between what the reader is being encouraged to expect and what they know of the world.

Although Sly does none of these actions, the reader is likely to understand from this passage that the actions take place, but that it is the cockroaches that do them. The expectation of action is encouraged initially by the question 'but what could he really do to you?', the connotations of which suggest something unpleasant. It is the specificity of the clauses that follow that implies more than what is said; where 'nothing' (1) produces an under-specified mental representation of the positive, (2) provides complex details and evaluation (e.g. use of exclamations marks and evaluative lexis – 'horrid and scuttly') of an unrealised event. This kind of specificity tends to be reserved for things that do happen rather than those that do not and therefore flouts the maxim of quantity. Assuming the writer is being cooperative, the reader is likely to draw the inference that the events take place, but that it is not Sly who hides in 'hide in the milk spout', but cockroaches, as Colin's real enemies, who do.

As noted above, this evocation of such fine-grained unrealised expectations has the effect of triggering a mental representation of Sly exhibiting the same behaviours as a cockroach. This is incremented to the mental representation of the character as a whole. This has implications for the construction of the unpleasant characteristics associated with the ultra-wealthy characters introduced later in the novel. Although the pragmatically presupposed expectations of Sly's behaviour are implausible, the reader is nonetheless required to conceptualise Sly behaving in that way.

4.2 Passage 2 – Harper Lee's *To Kill a Mockingbird*

> (13) He was much older than the parents of our school companions, and there was nothing Jem or I could say about him when our classmates said 'My father-'.
>
> Jem was football crazy. Atticus was never too tired to play keep-away but when Jem wanted to tackle him, Atticus would say 'I'm too old for that, son.'
>
> Our father didn't do anything. He worked in an office, not in a drugstore. Atticus did not drive a dump-truck for the county, he was not the sheriff, he did not farm, work in a garage, or do anything that could possibly arouse the admiration of anyone.
>
> Besides that, he wore glasses. He was nearly blind in his left eye and said left eyes were the tribal curse of the Finches. Whenever he

> wanted to see something well, he turned his head and looked from his right eye.
>
> He did not do the things our classmates' fathers did: he never went hunting, he did not play poker or fish or drink or smoke. He sat in the living-room and read.
>
> (Lee 2001/1960: 99)

Harper Lee's (2001/1960) *To Kill a Mockingbird* tells the story of the first person narrator, Scout, growing up in 1930s Maycomb in Alabama, USA. In this extract, Scout, more of a tomboy than a stereotypical little girl, is describing her widowed father, Atticus. As narrator, she is explaining why she is unable to boast about her father in the same way as her classmates boast about theirs. Whilst her schoolmates' fathers appear to engage in strong, masculine occupations and pastimes, her father, Atticus, as a lawyer, is much more sedentary. Since Atticus does nothing that would display overt signs of strength and masculinity, as the schoolmates' fathers do, Scout finds herself unable to say anything. This childlike outlook on what constitutes attributes worthy of boasting is constructed through the evocation of particular expectations about fathers through a series of potential but unrealised situations.

Characterisation in this second passage is much more complex than in the first; although it is ostensibly the narrator's description of her father, it contributes to the readers' conceptualisation of the narrator herself as much as, if not more than, her father. In this relatively short extract there are 14 negated propositions, triggered by prototypical verb phrase negators, 'not' and 'never', compared to only six positive propositions relating to Atticus. This clearly shows that, in this instance, negation is one of the main tools for the representation of Atticus. However, despite the long list of negatives, the parts of the extract being focused on (underlined) contain only one overarching negated concept – our father didn't do anything[1] that we could boast about. This 'anything' is elaborated by specifying those things that Atticus does not do for a job or a pastime; drive a dump-truck, work in a drugstore, farm, work in a garage, arouse the admiration of anyone, go hunting, play poker, fish, drink, smoke and he was not the Sheriff. There is a causal relationship between the occupations and pastimes and being able to boast; if Atticus had done any of the activities, Scout would have been able to boast (*if p, q*). Atticus did none of them (only worked in an office and read) and she was therefore unable to boast (*if not p, not q*). Given readers' plausible background assumptions, if Scout were able to boast about her father, she could be viewed as being proud of him. However, in evoking these unrealised occupations and pastimes, the passage as a whole generates the implicature that Scout is embarrassed by her father. That the implicature is generated by the passage as a whole here is interesting; had Atticus only been shown as not doing one job or pastime, it would, perhaps, not have generated the same implicature, it is the quantity of things that he lacks in comparison to the other men of Maycomb that implies that Scout is embarrassed. Scout's attitude towards Atticus is, of course, inferred not only from this isolated passage, but also from the wider text. However, the inferences drawn from Scout's description of her father here contribute to the ongoing development of the characters as the narrative unfolds. Indeed, Scout's growing appreciation of her father's qualities is noteworthy against this background of embarrassment.

Clearly, negation contributes to the representation of Atticus in this passage. What is also evident is that Scout herself is constructed through the writer's choice of negation. As I argued above, it is not only the ideal reader/hearer who can expect the pragmatically presupposed positives, but also other discourse participants. Here, it is the narrator who holds the expectations of, if not her father, then fathers in general; the selection of unrealised but possible activities creates an image of the story world in which fathers do these kinds of jobs and pastimes. The text, then, projects Scout as expecting fathers to fulfil one of these roles, and it is these roles, rather than Atticus as a lawyer, that Scout finds admirable. These expectations contribute to the reader's mental representation of Scout as someone who expects fathers to behave in a particular way, projecting the belief system of the character and developing her point of view in the narrative. As would be expected, Scout, at least at the beginning of the novel, shows a greater affinity with her school friends and their backgrounds in the more masculine conceptualisations of fathers, than with the more genteel existence of her own father. It also contributes to the tomboy image of Scout; in finding the masculine activities of her friends' fathers admirable, the reader may well understand her as displaying more boy-like activities that are stereotypically expected of girls.

Although the reader is presented with Scout's subjective, childlike view of her father, the writer's choice of presenting Atticus through a series of negated utterances has effects beyond representing Scout's view of him. In evoking the activities of the men of Maycomb and contrasting them with Atticus, the text prompts readers' conceptualisation of Atticus as different from the men of the town in characteristics and perhaps even outlook. This foreshadows the future conflict between Atticus and a group of men, some of whom he recognises as the fathers of his children's school friends, who come to lynch the black man he is defending in a rape trial.

5 Conclusions

Whilst utterances containing negation may, on a surface reading, appear to be less informative than their positive counterparts, this is clearly not the case when we consider the wealth of pragmatic processing involved in their comprehension. Negation requires readers to conceptualise the very thing that is negated and work to infer what this contributes to meaning and effect. The above analyses illustrate that projecting expectations can prompt readers to re-evaluate existing expectations. In the Sly Morcock example, the defeat of implausible expectations regarding his behaviour requires readers to re-conceptualise notions of power. Further, evoking the possibility of the character behaving like a cockroach requires the reader to conceptualise him in this way. As Giora (2006), Giora et al. (2004, 2005 and 2007) and Levine and Hagaman (2008) argue, the positive scenario is not discarded, but retained. This contributes to the range of textual prompts and extra-textual knowledge that constitutes the construction of character. Indeed, one would be hard-pressed to account for the humorous tone of the passage without accepting that readers conceptualise Sly hiding in the milk spout and engaging in unspeakable acts in the butter. It is then the possibility of presence rather than the actuality of absence that contributes to the fabric of the textual realisation of the character.

The question of who holds expectations when it comes to the presuppositional nature of negation was explored in relation to the passage from *To Kill a Mockingbird*. Here, the first person narrator's description of her father contributes not only to the realisation of Atticus, but also to that of the narrator herself. The expectations evoked through the use of negation not only present her subjective and childlike view of Atticus, but also set the scene for future conflict with the men of Maycomb against whom he is compared. In this first person narrative, the expectations reflect Scout's belief system as well as projecting an ideal reader's expectations of fathers and thus painting a picture of the types of activities the men of Maycomb engage in. There is, therefore, a wealth of indirect information available in simply pointing out what Atticus does not do for a job or pastime.

These analyses provide only a glimpse of the explanatory potential of analysing negation in relation to character. However, they do illustrate the way in which the realisation of an absence through negation can draw on and project readers' extra-textual knowledge. In the conclusions to both Sweetser's (2006) and Nørgaard's (2007) articles on negation in literary texts, they note that more research is required to fully explore the rich meaning making and stylistic potential of negation. My hope is that the above approach and analyses contribute one more step on that path and will encourage others in their explorations of this intriguing linguistic phenomenon.

Note

1. The use of 'anything' in the extract is clearly hyperbolic – it is impossible to not do anything. Grice's Cooperative Principle provides the basis for understanding 'anything' as relating to the topic at hand – things that Scout is able to boast about.

8

Intertextuality and the Pragmatics of Literary Reading

Maria-Eirini Panagiotidou

1 Introduction

This chapter focuses on the pragmatics of intertextuality, where pragmatics is seen as the broader cognitive and contextual reality that prompts readers into forming intertextual connections between texts. For our purposes, literary intertextuality is seen as the result of a co-operative process between the literary work and readers, who need to draw both on their background knowledge and on textual elements to create intertextual links. Intertextuality is a conceptually complex and much-discussed notion that, as Irwin (2004) notes, has acquired almost as many meanings as users due to the number of phenomena it has been used to describe. Among others, it has been used to refer to overt allusions forming a functional part of a narrative, marked or unmarked quotations from other texts as well as references to names of literary characters.

The chapter introduces a cognitively informed approach which differs considerably from the views of literary critics who considered intertextuality a property of the text itself (e.g. Barthes 1977, 1981; Genette 1992, 1997; Riffaterre 1978, 1980). Rather, by placing primacy on the reader, it follows the rationale underpinning theories developed in the fields of text linguistics and critical discourse analysis (CDA). In particular, it has affinities with the use of intertextuality in text linguistics to describe how knowledge of other texts influences the text's production and reception (de Beaugrande and Dressler 1981) as well as CDA's claim that intertextuality is a linguistic strategy employed by individuals in order to create a more effective discourse by drawing on generic features (Fairclough 1992a, 1992b). However, neither Fairclough's nor de Beaugrande and Dressler's approaches considered intertextuality within a literary context. The model presented here aims to address this largely overlooked phenomenon by drawing and expanding on these ideas while focusing on 19th- and 20th-century poetry.

Theorists have noted that pragmatics and literature relate from the angle of the reader, who gives life to the text through the pragmatic act of reading (for example, see Mey 2001). A significant part of the research has focused on the interplay between authorial and readerly voices that gives rise to the literary experience and enables the characters and worlds found in the text to be realised. This chapter will centre on the reader and investigate how he or she may produce innovative readings of literary texts while relying on his or her intertextual knowledge. This is facilitated by the ability of readers to adopt a particular type of cognitive stance, the literary stance, that allows them to promptly access relevant background knowledge concerning literary texts. The aim of the chapter is to illustrate how personal intertextual associations may arise due to previous textual encounters and account for the role of co-text in this process. In order to account for the reader-centred approach to intertextuality, I employ recent developments in the field of cognitive linguistics that cater for the encyclopaedic aspect of word meaning and the role of sentential context in supporting the emergence of encyclopaedic knowledge. More specifically, I draw on Evans's (2006, 2007, 2009, 2010) LCCM (Lexical Concepts and Cognitive Models) theory. Evans argues that lexical items afford access to cognitive models, i.e. stored background knowledge, depending on the context. I also introduce the concept of *semantic intertextual frames*, an online processing domain, where textual cues and the readers' background knowledge are combined and give rise to the most impressionistic and private types of intertextual links.

2 Intertextuality as a cognitive process

2.1 A cognitive linguistic approach to meaning construction

As mentioned above, this paper will look at personal associations that go beyond overt allusions to and quotations from other literary texts. For the purposes of this paper I will focus on how single lexical items give rise to intertextual connections and the effects of these types of connections on the reading experience. A recent development in the field of cognitive linguistics, Evans's LCCM theory (e.g. 2006, 2007, 2009, 2010), provides the basis of the discussion.

LCCM theory approaches meaning construction based on the notions of 'lexical concepts' and 'cognitive models'. Following Talmy (2000), we can distinguish between *closed class* and *open class* lexical concepts, which activate respectively the grammatical and the lexical subsystem. In the following example, the characters in bold are closed-class items that give rise to part of the information encoded by a lexical concept.

(a) **The** child chas**ed** **the** cat**s**

On the other hand, *child, chase* and *cat* are open-class items, describing the nature of the participants, the relationships between them and the action described. According to Evans, lexical concepts contain linguistic information and are used for modelling the semantic structure of words. Cognitive models refer to extensive bodies of non-linguistic knowledge that are coherently organised and are used as a means of modelling conceptual structures. This distinction allows the theory to account for the interaction between linguistics and conceptual knowledge and how this interaction may lead to linguistically mediated communication. Thus, meaning generation is seen as the combination of linguistic meaning with non-linguistic knowledge. The distinction between lexical concepts and cognitive models also captures the intrinsic connections between different layers of meaning through the introduction of *primary* and *secondary* cognitive model profiles. Primary cognitive models are accessed directly via a lexical concept while secondary models are accessed directly via primary cognitive models and thus, indirectly via lexical concepts.

Evans (2006) offers the following example as an illustration of the basic principles of his theory. The lexical concept [FRANCE] potentially provides access to a large number of knowledge structures divided into primary and secondary cognitive models. Individuals may have stored knowledge about [FRANCE] in terms of the following primary cognitive models: GEOGRAPHICAL LANDMASS, NATION STATE and HOLIDAY DESTINATION. In turn, these primary models may contain a large number of subordinate knowledge structures, namely the secondary cognitive models. For example, the primary cognitive model NATION STATE may afford access to the secondary models, which include NATIONAL SPORTS, POLITICAL SYSTEM and CUISINE. Evans notes that people may be familiar with the fact that the French engage in sports like rugby, football and athletics and that they take part in competitions such the FIFA World Cup, the Olympics and the Rugby World Cup. In addition, people may have even more refined knowledge concerning the social or economic conditions relevant to these particular sports as well as rules and practices that apply to them. All these pieces of information are available to us through a large number of sources and the knowledge associated with cognitive models is of a non-linguistic nature acquired through the interaction of individuals with the world around them. Depending on the sentential context, [FRANCE] will provide access to different cognitive models:

(b) France voted against the EU constitution in the 2005 referendum.
(c) France beat New Zealand in the 2007 Rugby World Cup.

Evans (2010: 616)

As Evans (2010) notes, in the first example France relates to the French electorate and particularly to those who took part in a vote about the EU constitution in 2005. In the second example France refers to members of the French national rugby team or squad that represented the country in the 2007 World Cup. Therefore, in the first case, the secondary cognitive model POLITICAL SYSTEM will be activated, while in the second case, access will be afforded to knowledge contained in the secondary model 'NATIONAL SPORTS. These examples highlight the fact that words appear 'to be protean in nature: [their] meaning[s] are flexible, in part dependent upon the context of [their] use' (Evans 2010: 616).

The above example demonstrates another significant principle of LCCM theory, namely the *semantic potential* of words. Words are seen as providing access to large depositories of knowledge whose activation depends on the sentential context and sometimes varies from one person to another. A major advantage of Evans's theory is that it comprehensively looks at the role and nature of encyclopaedic knowledge in meaning construction. Other theories in cognitive linguistics, such as Fillmore's frames (e.g. 1982, 1985), and Langacker's domains (e.g. 1987), offer less detailed discussions, or treat word meaning as comprising relatively stable knowledge structures (e.g. Lakoff 1987; Pustejovsky 1995). Conversely, Evans's theory successfully accounts for the multiple levels of meaning generation and the multi-faceted nature of word meaning as shown in the above example.

2.2 Intertextuality as a cognitive process

The main argument supporting my approach is that intertextuality is better understood not as a property of the text itself, but as a cognitive modality of perception. In other words, 'intertextual' is an adjective that should be applied to the way readers respond to a (literary) text rather than the text itself. The benefit of this approach is that the reader's role in the creation of intertextual links acquires primary focus and becomes the centre of our discussion about intertextuality. The reader's background knowledge and co-textual factors are the two factors influencing the creation of links among texts. A basic starting point relates to the way they position themselves and adjust their cognitive tools by adapting a particular *cognitive stance*. A cognitive stance can be defined as 'a readiness to accept things, to deal with [...] processes, events, people' (Wagner 1983: 102). When reading literature, readers are capable of adopting a particular type of cognitive stance, namely a *literary stance*, which enables them to engage with this 'genre' and its sub-genres. This cognitive positioning facilitates the activation of knowledge associated with the norms of the genre as well as their previous reading experiences. It is worth noting that the formation of intertextual links per se does not require adopting a literary stance. For example, an intertextual connection with a literary work could arise unpredictably while engaged with a non-fictional text. However, this discussion focuses on literary intertextuality and cases where readers of literary texts generate intertextual connections with other literary works, as a result of their cognitive positioning. These connections would resonate and enhance the understanding and interpretation of the text as a literary object.

Readers need to combine their own background knowledge with the sentential context to make sense out of the text (see also Emmott 1997). When it comes to intertextual links, readers need to bring together two types of information, namely text-specific information and their intertextual knowledge triggered by a lexical item. These are brought together in an online processing domain termed an intertextual frame. Intertextual frames contain lexical items present in literary texts and the intertextual knowledge the latter may trigger. The quality and effect on the reading experience of these frames may vary depending on the number of textual items that trigger the link and the detail the reader is able to bring to mind. In this chapter I will look at looser word associations that provide access to particular types of frames, namely *semantic intertextual frames*, by drawing on examples from a range of 20th century poetic texts. Being succinct and self-contained, poems allow us to examine aspects of intertextuality fully and efficiently.

Semantic intertextual frames refer to the intertextual connections that arise from a reader's personal associations and reflect idiosyncratic readings of literature. In other words, semantic intertextual frames refer to intertextual connections that are not dictated by the text, such as explicit quotations from other literary works or thematic allusions. Intertextuality arises from the identification of a single lexical item that triggers the readers' intertextual knowledge stored in the cognitive model LITERARY ENTITY. This model contains knowledge readers have associated with a particular lexical item and originates from previous encounters of the same item in other literary works as argued by Panagiotidou (2012). Cognitive models that give rise to intertextual connections are accessed directly or indirectly via lexical concepts. In the first case, there is a direct access route between the cognitive model and the lexical concept, while in the latter, the cognitive model LITERARY ENTITY is accessed directly via another (primary) cognitive model and thus indirectly via the lexical concept. In the following section I will consider the different ways semantic intertextual frames may arise via direct access routes.

2.3 Direct access routes

As mentioned above, direct access routes are created when a lexical concept affords access directly to the primary cognitive model LITERARY ENTITY triggering the formation of an intertextual frame. This takes place when the same lexical item is identified in the source and the activated text alike. Any open-class lexical item is capable of triggering this type of connection, contributing to the highly idiosyncratic nature of semantic intertextual frames. Nevertheless, there is a particular set which may afford access to less idiosyncratic readings, namely lexical items that designate mythological figures and literary characters. This is due to the strong associations between these figures and the texts from which they derive. As Müller (1991) points out, many authors and poets have inserted pre-existing literary entities into new fictional contexts or into re-writes and sequels to earlier texts. For instance, Stoppard (1968) structured his play *Rosencrantz and Guildenstern Are Dead* around two minor characters in Shakespeare's *Hamlet*, while Hamlet himself assumes a minor role. Authors may also alter the names of characters in an attempt to establish intertextual relations among texts (see Müller 1991: 102).

Nevertheless, in order for these connections to arise during the reading process, readers need to be familiar with the text from which the characters originate. The more details readers can bring to mind concerning a character, that is his or her attributes, the world he or she inhabits, his or her relations with other characters of that world, the stronger and richer the intertextual connection will be. There are also cases where this type of knowledge originates from a plurality of sources and it is closely related to the readers' cultural knowledge. Such an example is mythological knowledge and the possible intertextual connections that arise due to the identification of mythological figures in a text. An illustration of this type of connection can be seen in the lines of William Carlos Williams's poem 'Asphodel, that greeny flower': 'All women are not Helen,/I know that,/but have Helen in their hearts./My sweet,/you have it also, therefore/I love you' (1955, ll: 142–147).

In this example, an intertextual link may be constructed if the lexical concept [HELEN] provides access to the cognitive model MYTHOLOGICAL ENTITY. The lexical concept necessarily consists of the primary cognitive model FEMALE PROPER NAME, enabling readers to interpret the vehicle Helen as a reference to a female figure. If readers are familiar with the myth of Helen of Troy, then these lines may also point to an intertextual reading, activating their background knowledge about the myth. As Figure 8.1 shows, the model MYTHOLOGICAL ENTITY will in turn provide access to a number of secondary cognitive models, such as BEAUTY, INFIDELITY and VANITY. Interestingly, the lines of the poem are vague with regard to the invoked qualities of Helen, inviting readers to project their own view of Helen in the lines. Therefore, the traits of Helen that women may carry in their hearts possibly include treachery, infidelity and feminine allure, among others. Readers thus may arrive at different interpretations of these lines depending on the secondary models they activate. If the cognitive model INFIDELITY is more prominent in his/her view of Helen of Troy, given this context a reader may project this trait to the poetic persona's addressee. On the other hand, if a reader is more familiar with Helen as the personification of vain beauty, then the vehicle Helen provides access to the cognitive model

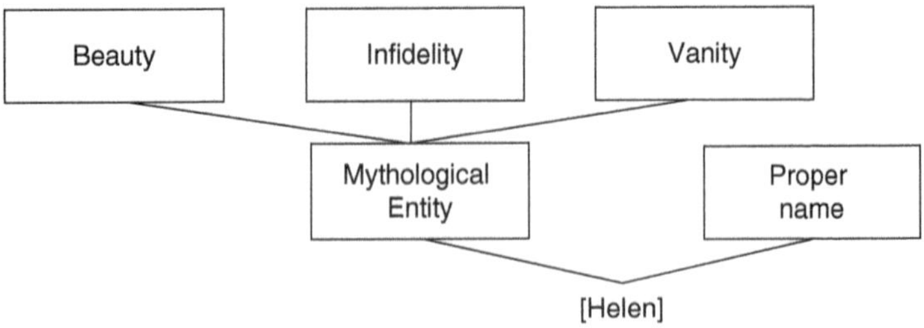

Figure 8.1 Partial cognitive model of [HELEN]

VANITY. Finally, if readers with none of this knowledge come across these lines, they would activate the cognitive model FEMALE PROPER NAME and assume that further knowledge is expected to determine the referent.

Apart from cultural knowledge, mythological entities may act as triggers of semantic intertextual frames by providing access to other literary texts that have employed the same entities. In this case, instead of accessing the model MYTHOLOGICAL ENTITY, readers access the model LITERARY ENTITY, which contains their knowledge concerning previous encounters of the same lexical items in other texts. The vehicle Helen may provide access to texts that have employed Helen of Troy as a subject matter or have referred to her. Examples include Poe's 'To Helen' (1845), H. D.'s 'Helen' (1928) or Yeats's 'Leda and the Swan' (1924). To choose one example, if a reader is reminded of Poe's 'To Helen', then a semantic intertextual frame will be created containing elements from both poems. Williams's lines and phrasing referring to Helen and the persona's addressee will be brought together with Poe's poem. It should be noted that the role of context in the creation of the frame is crucial, as apart from the vehicle that provides access to the cognitive model, the intertextual link should be supported by the presence of other contextual elements that bind the two texts together. In this example, the link is supported by the poetic persona's expression of love towards his addressee, to whom he refers as 'My sweet', coinciding with the tone of Poe's poem and the persona's feelings towards Helen. The emergence of the frame may also serve as the basis for investing the addressee of Williams's persona with qualities that have been left vague. Poe's Helen is portrayed as the archetype of classical beauty, so activating this knowledge will allow readers to feed it back to Williams's poem and assign importance to the reading of the lines as a reference to the addressee's beauty. The amount of detail that is incorporated in the frame depends on each reader's ability to bring to mind elements from Poe's (or any other) text and the frame's quality is intrinsically tied to this ability. The more elements a reader can trace, the richer the intertextual frame will be and the stronger the effect it will have on the reading experience (see Panagiotidou 2010).

2.3.1 *Same lexical item*

Apart from literary and mythological figures, the construction of intertextual links may also be based on the identification of other open-class items, such as nouns or verbs, and the subsequent emergence of semantic intertextual frames. To illustrate this, I turn to W. B. Yeats's 'Broken Dreams':

> Broken Dreams
>
> There is grey in your hair.
> Young men no longer suddenly catch their breath
> When you are passing;
> But maybe some old gaffer mutters a blessing
> Because it was your prayer
> Recovered him upon the bed of death.
> For your sole sake – that all heart's ache have known,
> And given to others all heart's ache,
>
> W. B. Yeats (2000, II: 1–8)

A semantic intertextual frame may be created via the vehicle grey in the first line 'There is grey in your hair'. A reader may be reminded of another poem by Yeats, namely 'When You Are Old' (1893), due to the presence of the same lexical item in both literary texts. In particular, the lines 'When you are old and grey and full of sleep' (l. 1) may come to mind. In the latter poem, the poetic persona asks the female addressee to consider her life in old age and the possibility of growing old without appreciating and reciprocating his love. The construction of the frame is possible if the lexical concept [GREY] provides access to the cognitive model LITERARY ENTITY, which in turn encompasses the particular reader's knowledge about the use of grey in the latter poem. The semantic intertextual frame that results from the knowledge activation is idiosyncratic since there are no explicit textual cues pointing overtly to 'When You Are Old'. The link is created and sustained by the particular reader's intertextual knowledge and his/her familiarity with the theme of both poems and their dialogic relationship. While 'When You Are Old' muses upon the future of the female addressee, 'Broken Dreams' takes place in that future; the addressee already is an old woman faced with the realities of old age. Moreover, a more extensive elaboration on the theme of 'When You Are Old' seems to be embedded in 'Broken Dreams' through lexis and imagery. I have included here only the first eight lines of the poem, but both 'Broken Dreams' and 'When You Are Old' elaborate on the theme of loss. For instance, in the above lines we read that when one is older, one's physical appeal diminishes: 'young men no longer catch their breath' when the addressee passes and only an old man occasionally acknowledges her. At the same time, the love she has inspired and the heartache she has caused or suffered belong to the past. As the poetic persona notes in 'When You Are Old', love has fled and 'hid his face amid a crowd of stars'. Therefore, the construction of a semantic intertextual frame that bears a significant effect on the reading experience should contain elements from both poems with the reader recalling lines from 'When You Are Old'.

2.3.2 Cognitive synonyms and plesionyms

So far I have discussed the emergence of intertextual links prompted by the recollection of the same lexical item in both the source and the activated text. Nevertheless direct access routes can also be afforded when readers bring to mind closely related lexical items, which have been termed *cognitive synonyms* (Cruse 1986) and *plesionyms* (Cruse 1986). Cognitive synonymy has been defined as follows:

> X is a cognitive synonym of Y if (i) X and Y are syntactically identical, and (ii) any grammatical declarative sentence S containing X has equivalent truth-conditions to another sentence S', which is identical to S except that X is replaced by Y.
>
> (Cruse 1986: 88)

An example of a pair of cognitive synonyms provided by Cruse is *hide* and *conceal*. The truth-conditions of the sentences containing these lexical items are the same in both 'John concealed the money' and 'John hid the money' as both sentences entail each other. The difference between cognitive synonyms lies in their *expressive meaning*, which Cruse associates with style, namely 'the language characteristics which mark different relations between the participants in a linguistic exchange' (Cruse 1986: 284). Here, for example, is a selection of cognitive synonyms for *die*: *kick the bucket, buy it, pop off, peg out, expire, perish, pass away, decease,* etc. (Cruse 1986: 285).

As cognitive synonyms differ with regard to their expressive aspect while sharing the same propositional meaning, these lexical items will provide access to identical lexical concepts and cognitive models. Evans refers to the notion of association areas as the 'location in the conceptual system with which a specific lexical concept is associated' (2009: 205), so it can be suggested that cognitive synonyms share by and large the same association areas. An example of this type of intertextual connection can be provided by considering the poem 'A Narrow Fellow in the Grass' by Emily Dickinson.

A narrow fellow in the grass
Occasionally rides;
You may have met him, – did you not,
His notice sudden is.
The grass divides as with a comb,
A spotted shaft is seen;
And then it closes at your feet
And opens further on.

Emily Dickinson (1866, ll: 1–8)

This poem describes an encounter with a snake and the feeling of frisson it causes. The lexical item 'snake' is not employed in the poem but readers can infer that the noun phrase 'a narrow fellow in the grass' is used to describe the reptile. A semantic intertextual frame can be activated if a cognitive synonym of 'snake' is brought to mind, such as the word 'serpent'. For example, Dickinson's poem may be linked with Shelley's poetic fragment 'Wake the Serpent Not' (1819, in Shelley 1991). The link will be based on the fact that 'snake' and 'serpent' are cognitive synonyms and their difference lies in their expressive meaning. Due to cognitive synonymy, the two lexical items share most of their association areas and thus cognitive models. Therefore, it is possible for a reader who comes across the phrase 'a narrow fellow in the grass' and the vehicle *snake* to connect it to the lexical item 'serpent', activating the cognitive model LITERARY ENTITY. An illustration is shown in Figure 8.2. The double arrow represents the cognitive synonymy of the items and the fact that they can be used almost interchangeably in the given context as a result of their shared cognitive models. The link between the two poems may be further sustained due to a number

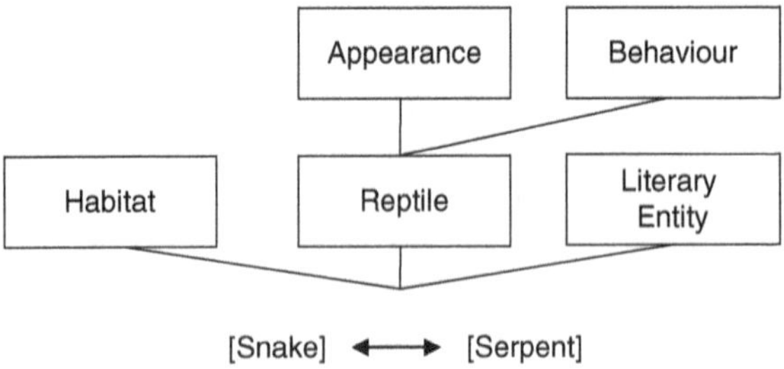

Figure 8.2 The activation of cognitive models of the cognitive synonyms *snake* and *serpent*

of lexical items present in Dickinson's poem. For example, the poetic personas in both poems present the bond the snakes have with their natural environment and their swiftness and they also express a feeling of uneasiness triggered by the encounter.

Finally, apart from cognitive synonymy, direct access routes can be afforded in cases of *plesionymy* (Cruse 1986: 285). This is distinguished from cognitive synonymy 'by the fact that they yield different truth-conditions: two sentences differing only in respect of plesionyms in parallel syntactic positions are not mutually entailing' (Cruse 1986: 285). In other words, plesionyms 'designate very similar concepts and at the same time exhibit slight meaning differences so that they cannot be considered identical in meaning' (Storjohann 2009: 2140). For this reason, Cruse (2012) has also used the term *near synonyms* (144) as an alternative. An example offered by Cruse is: 'He was not *murdered*, he was *legally executed*' (1986: 285, my italics). An interesting feature of plesionyms is that they shade gradually into non-synonymy, or in other words that '[t]here is always one member of a plesionymous pair which it is possible to assert, without paradox, while simultaneously denying the other member' (Cruse 1986: 285). When reading literary texts, readers may recall other texts by connecting lexical items that designate similar concepts and provide access to similar cognitive models. Such a semantic intertextual frame arises when the lexical item 'mist' is linked to its plesionym 'fog' and an intertextual link between two texts containing these lexical items is created. An illustration follows: in the second stanza of Larkin's poem 'Waiting for Breakfast, While She Brushed Her Hair', the poetic persona describes the view from a hotel window: 'for the stones slept, and the mist/Wandered absolvingly past all it touched,/Yet hung like a stayed breath; the lights burnt on,' (2012, ll: 9–11). The lexical item 'mist' along with the line 'Wandered absolvingly past all it touched' may conjure up an intertextual connection by invoking the plesionym 'fog' and the famous lines of the second paragraph of Dickens's *Bleak House* (1853):

> Fog everywhere. Fog up the river, where it flows among green aits and meadows; fog down the river, where it rolls deified among the tiers of shipping and the waterside pollutions of a great (and dirty) city. Fog on the Essex marshes, fog on the Kentish heights. Fog creeping into the cabooses of collier-brigs; fog lying out on the yards and hovering in the rigging of great ships.
>
> (Charles Dickens 2003 [1853]: 1)

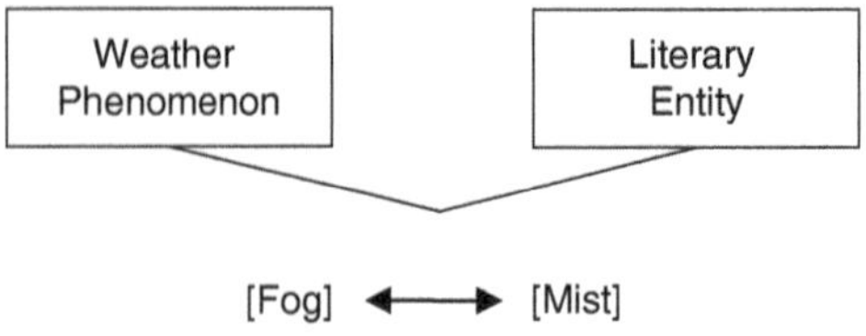

Figure 8.3 Partial cognitive profile for plesionyms *fog* and *mist*

In Larkin's poem, the activation of the cognitive model LITERARY ENTITY relies on the identification of the plesionyms 'fog' and 'mist'. The lexical concepts [FOG] and [MIST] share the majority, but not all, of their association areas, as they designate similar but not identical phenomena. In Figure 8.3 the double dashed arrow represents the fact that they are plesionyms.

The overlap of association areas facilitates the activation of the cognitive model LITERARY ENTITY, while at the same time the intertextual link is sustained due to the presence of a number of related textual elements in the two texts, which enter the semantic intertextual frame and contribute to their interrelation. In *Bleak House* the fog's omnipresence is marked by both the adverb *everywhere* and the repetition of the item 'fog', while in the poem the mist covers 'all it touch[es]'. They also seem to share the same quality of being simultaneously in motion and still; the mist appears to be both in motion and static, as it wanders absolvingly yet hangs 'like a stayed breath' (l. 11). In Dickens's extract, the lack of a finite verb component attached to the fog and the use of infinite verb forms (e.g. 'lying', 'hovering') reinforce the tension between motion and stillness. Another factor that may bring the two texts together is the parallel imagery created through blending of the urban and rural: in Dickens's passage the fog unifies the meadows and the polluted tiers of London, whereas the poetic persona's past makes a startling appearance like a deer as he gazes outside his hotel window ('beyond the glass/The colourless vial of day painlessly spilled/My world back after a year, my lost lost world/Like a cropping deer strayed near my path again' (ll. 9–15)). These co-textual factors may influence the creation of semantic intertextual links and the association of elements in the frames. A lexical item may offer access to encyclopaedic knowledge and initiate the intertextual link, but other textual elements and the ability of the reader to recall and combine them play a crucial role in the creation of a resonant link. In this example, readers may be able to bring to mind exact phrases from Dickens's text or they may be reminded of the general quality of the description of the fog and London.

2.4 Indirect routes

In the previous section, I focused my attention on the construction of semantic intertextual frames that were created through the identification of proper names or the same lexical items. In addition, I suggested that a direct link may be triggered in the case of cognitive synonymy and plesionymy, where closely related lexical items give rise to similar or identical cognitive models. However, intertextual connections may also be formed as a result of looser lexical associations. This is particularly true in the case of *hyponymy*, where readers associate a lexical item with a more general concept. Hyponymy has been defined by Croft and Cruse (2004) as follows: '[I]f X is a hyponym of Y, then the semantic content of Y is a proper subpart of the semantic content of X' (142).

With regard to LCCM theory, this means that a number of primary cognitive models afforded by the lexical concept of X also delineate aspects of the lexical concept of Y. In other words, primary cognitive models may provide access to knowledge about a superordinate concept. In the example of *snake* that was discussed above, the primary cognitive model REPTILE would contain a reader's knowledge concerning the major characteristics of snakes including that they are long, limbless reptiles. Readers may be reminded of other literary texts on the basis of this more generic type of knowledge, which in turn triggers the cognitive model LITERARY ENTITY. For an illustration, let us consider the poem 'The Crows' (1923) by Louise Bogan. A reading of this poem highlights the unceasing feeling of desire experienced by a woman 'who has grown old'. However, this feeling is not tamed by age; the woman seeks love, disregarding the knowledge that she must subdue her desire. The result of her choice is to hear 'the crows' cry', metaphorically standing for old age and death. In the lines 'The heart's laughter will be to her/The crying of the crows,/Who slide in the air with the same voice' (ll. 7–9), the lexical item *crows* may also act as a trigger of an intertextual link. This is possible through the association of *crow* with a superordinate, such as *bird*.

More specifically, the association creates a semantic intertextual frame, with the cognitive model LITERARY ENTITY being accessed via an indirect access route as follows: the lexical concept [CROW] affords access to the primary cognitive model BIRD, which in turn provides access to the secondary model LITERARY ENTITY, thus establishing the intertextual link. The frame will be constructed owing to the identification of the superordinate-hyponym pair 'crow' and 'bird' and it will be activated by the particular reader's knowledge about the nature of crows and his or her intertextual knowledge. The intertextual knowledge will enable him or her to identify a specific occurrence of the lexical item *bird* in other literary texts, such as W. B. Yeats's 'The Second Coming' (1921, in Yeats 2000). A connection may be established between the two poems with regard to the latter poem's reference to birds: '...while all about it/Wind shadows of the indignant desert *birds*' (ll. 16–17, my emphasis). Interestingly, the link in this case goes beyond the hyponym-superordinate connection with the tone and the imagery of both poems. In Bogan's poem the crows are croaking and flying over open fields, while in Yeats' poem the birds are described flying in circles indignantly over the desert. The tone is also unsettling as references to death are made directly and metaphorically in 'The Crows'. The use of symbols of death, namely 'scythe' and 'mow', and the association of 'hardened stem' with the stiffening of a dead body may be paralleled with the disturbing appearance of the beast and the darkness it casts ('She is a stem long hardened/A weed that no scythe mows', ll. 5–6). Thus, it can be suggested that the ominous quality that the birds acquire along with the similarities in the imagery fosters the creation of the semantic intertextual frame. After bringing these two texts together, a reader may go beyond the initial idiosyncratic connection and inform his or her interpretation of Bogan's poem using imagery and even feelings triggered by Yeats's poem.

Apart from hyponyms, intertextual links among texts may be built via the association of a lexical item with other open class items that trigger related cognitive models. Since they provide access to related types of knowledge, the lexical item in the source text may prime the reader for other lexical items that are usually encountered in the same contexts as the item in the source text. This idea of priming goes back to psycholinguistic literature (e.g. Neely 1977; Swinney 1979; Anderson 1983) and to semantic priming, used to describe 'how a "priming" word may provoke a particular "target" word' (Hoey 2005: 8). Hoey highlights the role of context in priming, noting that our knowledge of a word includes 'the fact that it co-occurs with other words in certain types of context' (2005: 8). This notion of priming is compatible with LCCM theory, where context plays a deciding role in the types of cognitive models afforded by a lexical concept. Evans (2009) describes the phenomenon of attributing resonance to one or more cognitive models to which a lexical concept provides access as activation. Contextual factors contribute to the activation of the appropriate cognitive model and also to the priming process by setting the reader's expectations and activating words which belong to the same semantic set. For instance, particular words in the poem 'Here, Bullet' by Brian Turner (2005) may bring to mind Wilfred Owen's 'Arms and the Boy' (1918, in Owen 1965). In the latter poem, Owen ascribes human traits to weapons of war in order to call attention to the innocence of the boy and the absurdity of war, while at the same time reminding readers that weapons are merely the tools of violence and death and not their true agents: 'Let the boy try along this bayonet-blade/How cold steel is, and keen with hunger of blood/... Lend him to stroke these blind, blunt bullet-heads/Which long to muzzle in the hearts of lads./Or give him cartridges of fine zinc teeth,/Sharp with the sharpness of grief and death' (ll. 1–2, 5–8). In Turner's poem, the poetic persona dares the bullet to penetrate the body and 'finish what you've started': 'if a body is what you want/then here is bone and gristle and flesh' (ll. 1–2).

The occurrence of the word *bullet* may provoke a connection with Owen's references to military equipment, namely the bayonet-blade, muzzle (an interesting word-play on two meanings of the word) and cartridge. The connection is a result of the fact that these words provide access to encyclopaedic knowledge concerning weaponry and warfare and thus to related cognitive models. This can be further reinforced later on in 'Here Bullet' when other references to similar lexical items are made: 'here is where I moan/the barrel's cold esophagus, triggering/my tongue's explosives for the rifling I have/inside of me, each twist of the round/spun deeper' (ll. 11–15). Co-text plays a major role in bringing these words together; there are similarities in the narrative technique and both poems focus on the horror of war. Apart from the presence of semantically related words, the way these words have been employed may serve as another parameter reinforcing the priming process. In 'Here, Bullet' the poetic persona addresses directly the bullet, for example 'if a body is what *you* want' (my italics), while in 'Arms and the Boy' the narrator 'encourages' his addressee to introduce the child to the use of weapons. Moreover, the personification of *bullet* may prime the reader for the similarly personified weapons in Owen's poem. More specifically, the bayonet blade is described as keen with hunger of blood, blue with malice and famished for flesh, the bullet-heads are blunt and blind, ready 'to muzzle in the hearts of lads', while the cartridges have sharp teeth.

The construction of this type of intertextual link is based on accessing the secondary cognitive model WAR via the primary model WEAPONRY and the lexical concept [BULLET]. The secondary cognitive model contains a reader's knowledge concerning the nature of bullets, their use in warfare and other types of weapons and military equipment. Accessing this type of knowledge facilitates the priming of related words, such as *gun*, *cartridge* and *missile*. If, while activating the cognitive model WAR, the reader is reminded of other literary texts that contain possible target words, he or she will activate the cognitive model LITERARY ENTITY and connect the texts. This is the case for Owen's poem, as described above. It should be noted that the role of co-text in the creation of these indirect access routes is crucial, as it should support the priming of target words that will enable the creation of the intertextual link. The activation of the cognitive model WAR along with the similarities in the descriptions allow the reader to bring 'Here, Bullet' and 'Arms and the Boy' together and establish a dialogue between them. Therefore, this approach to the creation of intertextual links points to a more creative and simultaneously systematic way of examining intertextuality; it can be used to account for more idiosyncratic connections between literary texts using linguistic tools and taking into consideration contextual factors and the readers' background knowledge.

3 Intertextual misreadings

Up to this point, I have examined cases where the intertextual link was successfully constructed and supported by the co-text. Readers may also establish intertextual links based on the activation of particular cognitive models but soon afterwards realise that particular links are not sustained by the text. Thus, they have to re-interpret the lexical item that led them to the construction of the link and modify their reading of the text retrospectively. This process has been termed *frame repair* in a different context by Emmott (1997: 160–162). In narrative comprehension, frame repair refers to the instances where readers miscue and wrongly interpret textual elements. Once they realise that they are using the wrong frame, they are forced to change their assumptions and 'repair' their representation. The same may occur with semantic intertextual frames. Readers may initially establish an intertextual link based on cognitive model activation but the textual cues might direct them towards reassessing the link and repairing the semantic intertextual frame or erasing it. As an example, I provide here an account of my own reading where a semantic intertextual frame was activated but at a later stage had to be repaired, as I felt that the co-text did not support my intertextual link. The poem I started reading was Hughes's 'Daffodils' (1998). The first lines of the poem set its melancholic tone: 'Remember how we picked the daffodils?/Nobody else remembers, but I remember./Your daughter came with her armfuls, eager and happy,/ . . . She has forgotten./She cannot even remember you' (ll. 1–5).

Upon reading the title of the poem, the lexical item *daffodils* afforded access to the lexical concept of [DAFFODILS] and this in turn provided access to the primary cognitive model LITERARY ENTITY bringing to mind William Wordsworth's famous poem 'I wandered lonely as a cloud' (1815). My knowledge concerning the content of Wordsworth's poem surfaced and in this way an intertextual link between the two texts was created. Consequently, I made the initial assumption that the two poems are related to each other and based on that I anticipated more points of contact between the two. However, as I continued reading Hughes's poem, I realised that the intertextual frame I had established could not be sustained. From the very beginning, it becomes apparent that the theme of Hughes's poem is radically opposed to Wordsworth's. The poetic persona is the only one who remembers the daffodil harvest and the fact that they were sold afterwards. The images of death, poverty and harsh living conditions of the first stanza contrast starkly with the beauty and serenity of nature described in the other poem. While reading this stanza, I was monitoring the text in order to track further lexical items that would support the established intertextual link. In other words, I was employing the principle of *intertextual chaining* (Panagiotidou 2012) so that I could validate the accuracy of the link and enrich the texture of the connection. However, the poem does not contain any lexical item that would allow the activation of additional knowledge concerning the activated text, such as specific word occurrences or further similarities based on the content. Thus, I had to reassess the previous assumption concerning an intertextual connection between the two and neglect the constructed frame. Nevertheless, it should be stressed that despite the fact that the link is neglected, the original connection and subsequent juxtaposition of the two poems may affect the reading experience by foregrounding the hardships that the poetic persona and the addressee have to endure. Thus, the description of these events as 'misreadings' should not be taken too strongly; it implies that the intertextual connection must be reassessed and perhaps discarded, but not that it was wholly invalid or even unintended by the author.

4 Conclusions

The aim of this chapter is to bring together literary pragmatics and the cognitive approaches to reading literature. Intertextuality is approached as a cognitive process active throughout the reading process, allowing readers to form links between literary texts. For the purposes of our discussion, single lexical items and the cognitive models to which they provide access are seen as the primary triggers of intertextuality. For this reason, I maintained that this type of link should be considered as the most idiosyncratic and private one and as the one that has the more localised effect. Connections are formed in terms of direct or indirect access routes to the readers' intertextual knowledge: cognitive synonyms, plesionyms, hyponyms and also words that tend to co-occur can be brought together in a semantic intertextual frame and produce intertextual effects.

The advantage of approaching intertextuality as a cognitive process is that it allows us to focus our attention on the role of the reader in uncovering or discovering connections between texts, while accounting for the role of co-text in facilitating this process. As such, it follows the basic premise of pragmatics that language users and their conditions affect the way an utterance is understood. As reading is often a solitary experience, individuals need to turn to their background knowledge, previous readings and ability to adopt a literary stance in order to understand and experience literature. So, instead of passive receivers, readers become active agents in the creation of the literary experience and, ultimately, of the literary work. By investigating the creation of intertextual links, we are offered an interesting outlook into this process as well as into the ways that context and encyclopaedic knowledge influence the reading process.

Nevertheless, this is not to say that authorial intention or co-textual factors do not influence the ways readers approach texts. Williams's choice to include a reference to Helen of Troy can be read as an effort on his part to engage the reader and invite him or her to employ knowledge about Greek mythology to interpret the meaning of the lines. The reader's ability or inability to evoke such knowledge determines his or her ability to form the intertextual link. Moreover, throughout the chapter I pointed to the importance of co-text in shaping the texture of the intertextual link. To strengthen their interpretation, readers have to look for other co-textual elements that would support and strengthen the connection between the two texts. When these were not present, the link would be discouraged, as was the case with Hughes's 'Daffodils'. Despite this, one may suggest that semantic intertextual frames have a rather local effect on the reading experience due to the fact that they mostly arise from single lexical items and they cannot account for links based on larger-scale similarities, such as the theme of literary works. Finally, I would like to stress that even though emphasis was placed on literary texts, this model can be used to account for the creation of intertextual links in non-fictional texts as well.

In conclusion, this chapter's purpose was not only to direct the discussion towards the readers' role in the generation of intertextual readings but also to bridge literary pragmatics with cognitive linguistic approaches to literature and provide a framework that can be expanded so that we are able to consider more extensive cases of intertextuality.

9
'I've never enjoyed hating a book so much in my life': The Co-Construction of Identity in the Reading Group

David Peplow

1 Introduction

Literary texts are put to many different uses outside academia. Books are used to decorate rooms, stimulate conversation and even prop open doors. Research is growing into the social uses to which literature is put in wider society, with much of this work focusing on the ways in which non-academic readers talk about texts. A popular site of study in this research is the book group, as these social contexts provide readers a space to meet and discuss a text that all members should have read. Swann and Allington (2009: 249) suggest that book groups offer researchers the opportunity to study reading in an environment that is 'natural' for readers. The present study forms part of this growing body of research into natural reading and, in particular, research into book groups (Devlin-Glass 2001; Hartley 2001; Allington and Swann 2009; Benwell 2009; Swann and Allington 2009; Allington 2011). Researchers in this field share a desire to study reading as it occurs in the world (as opposed to studying reading in rather more artificial experimental contexts) and share a belief that non-academic literary reading is a legitimate object of enquiry in its own right.

Gathering book club data allows researchers to consider a range of issues that are of interest to literature scholars and linguists alike: how fiction is experienced and appreciated by members of the public; the language that readers use to discuss texts; and how issues of reader taste and identity affect literary interpretation and evaluation. In this chapter, I consider all three of these aspects of book group talk, paying closest attention to the third issue of how identity operates in this context. I look at the way that interpretive and evaluative work is performed by one particular book group, referred to as the *Forest Group*. I focus on one meeting held by this group, in which the readers discussed *The Shack* (Young 2007), a bestselling evangelical Christian novel. Through detailed analysis of transcripts from this group's meeting, I consider the ways in which the readers co-construct a position of collective resistance against *The Shack*. I argue that evaluative and interpretive work in this context is a product of two elements: the group's invoked sense of collective identity and salient aspects of the individual readers' personal identities. Members of the group invoke aspects of their group history and use counter-dispositionals (Edwards 2007) to strengthen rhetorically their resistant stance toward the novel (with readers saying, for example, 'this must be the first time we've all agreed on a book'). Also focusing on individual identity, I look at the stance taken by one reader in the group towards the novel. As the only self-defining Christian in the group, this reader (Frank) seeks to present his own faith as credible by disassociating himself from the brand of evangelicalism espoused in *The Shack*.

In the next section, I provide an overview of research into reading groups; then introduce the *Forest Group*, discussing the members and the history of the group. In the analysis section following this, I focus on one short extract of conversation from the group's meeting on *The Shack*, providing a turn-by-turn analysis of the interaction and the group's resistance against the perceived ideology of the novel. Following this analysis, I discuss the construction of group identity and personal identity in this meeting and the specific interactional ways in which these identities are achieved.

2 Reading groups and reading group research

In this section, I give an overview of research into reading groups, before moving on to discuss my own contribution to the field. The modern day book group originated in the USA and has been growing in popularity in the UK and the USA over the last 20 years. Although a study by Knulst and van der Broek (2003) has suggested that the proportion of people reading for pleasure across Europe has declined, Hartley (2001) noted that reading groups have become increasingly popular, estimating that there were over 50,000 people in UK reading groups in 2001. Many UK broadsheet newspapers now run book clubs, while celebrity couple Richard Madeley and Judy Finnegan have hosted a highly-popular TV book club since 2004, *Richard and Judy Book Club*. These media encourage the public to read collectively, sharing their experience of texts with a wider community of readers.

The growing importance of book groups to reading practices in the UK and the USA has led to an increased academic interest in the phenomenon. Scholars have researched the reading group from a number of different academic areas: sociology (Rehberg Sedo 2003; Fuller and Rehberg Sedo 2006), English Literature (Hartley 2001; Long 2003) and areas of linguistics (Benwell 2009; Swann and Allington 2009; Whiteley 2011). Within linguistics, ethnographic socio-linguistic work has been carried out on reading groups, with much of this research focusing on the collaborative nature of talk in these groups. In a large-scale study, Swann and Allington (2009) offered qualitative analysis of reading group meetings, concluding that these are spaces in which interpretations of texts 'are collaboratively developed rather than being the property of individual speakers' (Swann and Allington 2009: 262). Benwell has similarly argued that readers within book groups offer 'shared discourses on particular texts', with the 'cultural regimes of value informing the interpretations that are collaboratively arrived at' (Benwell 2009: 301). Other linguists have used reading group data to inform stylistic analysis, focusing on how the features of a text can lead readers to particular interpretations. For instance, Whiteley's (2011) study into group readings of Ishiguro's *The Remains of the Day* considered how the readers constructed 'counterparts' of themselves in order to 'fill the addressee role that is demanded by the text' (Whiteley 2011: 34). She also looked at how readers reconstructed particular scenes from the novel and how they inferred the mental states of the characters when these were not explicitly referred to in the narrative (2011: 35–36). Whiteley concluded that the readers did this through projecting 'psychologically into the perspectives' of the characters when processing the narrative (2011: 37).

The research presented in this chapter follows the former, ethnographic and discourse-analytic tradition described above. This chapter considers how aspects of personal and group identity can be brought to bear on the discussion of the text in the book club setting. Although the stylistic features of *The Shack* may have contributed to, or determined, the group's evaluation and interpretations, this chapter is primarily interested in the identity work that this kind of social reading performs.

3 The *Forest Group*

The *Forest Group* is a book club run by a library based in a city in the East Midlands, UK. The group meets once a month throughout the year. The texts read tend to be bestselling contemporary literary and popular fiction, as those are the titles that are held in plentiful supply by the local library authority. Over the six months of my fieldwork (described in more detail below), the group read *Wolf Hall* by Hilary Mantel (over two months), *Room* by Emma Donoghue, *Somewhere Towards the End* by Diana Athill, *Beatrice and Virgil* by Yann Martel, and *The Shack* by William P. Young. The population of this urban area is vibrant and ethnically diverse and a strong sense of community is shared by many of the locals. However, it is one of the poorer areas of the city and there is a perception shared by many who do not live in the area that this is a dangerous neighbourhood rife with drug and gun crime.

Forest Group has been meeting regularly for four years in this library. Membership in these library book groups can be quite loose, with mostly peripheral members who attend occasionally. By contrast, the *Forest Group* has a core membership that attends every month. More than half of the group members were good friends prior to joining the group and in the group there are two married couples: Frank and Joan, and Daniel and Jess. Both couples have been married for over 30 years. Table 9.1 below gives some very basic details about the individual *Forest Group* members:

Table 9.1 Details of individual *Forest Group* members

Reader name	Age	Length of membership
Frank	60–65	4 years
Joan	60–65	4 years
Daniel	70–	4 years
Jess	70–75	4 years
Lucy	40–45	4 years
Samuel	60–65	4 years

As the above table shows, all of the current members of the *Forest Group* have belonged to the group since it began four years ago. There is an even split in terms of gender and, with the exception of librarian Lucy, the age-range of the readers is between 60 and 75. As librarian and group facilitator, Lucy's position in the group is somewhat specialised and her role notably different from that of the other members. She is responsible for ensuring that the meeting room is booked and that other groups vacate in time for the *Forest Group*'s meetings to start on time. Lucy also plays an important role in the book-selection process, compiling a shortlist of titles from which the group can choose.

Before discussing the details of the particular meeting under analysis in this chapter, I shall situate the *Forest Group* within my wider research into reading groups. The book group data discussed in this chapter is taken from a much larger study into reading groups (Peplow 2011, 2012, forthcoming). This research looked at six book groups that were based in a variety of settings: libraries, private homes and workplaces. These groups were recorded and observed over a period of six months and interviews were conducted with the groups at the end of the fieldwork. The discourse produced by the book groups was considered through detailed analysis of meetings and the groups were evaluated as communities of practice. Originating in Lave and Wenger's (1991) and Wenger's (1998) accounts of teaching and learning environments, the community of practice (CofP) model has been taken up by a number of socio-linguists in recent years as a way of describing particular social groups, most notably in Eckert and McConnell-Ginet's (1992) and Eckert's (2000) accounts of gendered language variation. Defined as 'a group of people brought together by some mutual endeavor', members of a CofP engage in a 'common enterprise... to which they bring a shared repertoire of resources, including linguistic resources' (McConnell-Ginet 2003: 71). As I have shown elsewhere (Peplow 2011, 2012, forthcoming), reading groups exist for a particular purpose (the discussion of texts) and engage in particular ritualised practices, with certain ways of interpreting and evaluating prized in some groups and not in others. All of the groups, however, had a propensity for 'mimetic' reading, with readers evaluating and interpreting literary texts in light of their own personal experiences and their personal identity (for more detail, see Swann et al. in press, ch. 4). This 'reading for real life' was often realised discursively in the form of category entitlements (Potter 1996: 133), where readers directly invoked a text-relevant personal experience in order to rhetorically strengthen their view of the text (Peplow 2011: 302–303). This 'mimetic' reading is in evidence in the discourse of the meeting analysed in this chapter, particularly in Frank's invocation of his Christian identity (see Analysis and Discussion sections below).

Social groups become CofPs over a period of time, with particular practices established as the norm within a group. Membership in CofPs can be dynamic, with long-standing members who engage in most or all of the group practices attaining 'full' participant status and newer members in a group occupying a 'peripheral' status. In the context of my wider study, the *Forest Group* was an unusual book group because the membership was rather static, with the same readers attending regularly since the group's inception (see Table 1.1). As the below analysis shall show, however, this fixed membership of *Forest Group* has resulted in a strong sense of a shared group history and a reification of particular group practices.

4 The meeting

The meeting that forms the present study took place in February 2011. The book that *Forest Group* read for the meeting was *The Shack*, an evangelical Christian novel written by Canadian author William P. Young and published in 2007. Although there is not space here to describe the plot of the novel at length, the publisher's blurb on the back-cover of the book provides an account of the issues addressed in the novel and gives a sense of the style:

> Mackenzie Allen Philips's youngest daughter, Missy, has been abducted during a family vacation and evidence that she may have been brutally murdered is found in an abandoned shack deep in the Oregon wilderness. Four years later in the midst of his great sadness, Mack receives a suspicious note, apparently from God, inviting him back to that shack for a weekend. Against his better judgement he arrives at the shack on a wintry afternoon and walks back into his darkest nightmare. What he finds there will change Mack's world forever.
>
> In a world where religion seems to grow increasingly irrelevant THE SHACK wrestles with the timeless question, 'Where is God in a world so filled with unspeakable pain?' The answers Mack gets will astound you and perhaps transform you as much as it did him. You'll want everyone you know to read this book!
>
> (Young 2007)

During the meeting, librarian Lucy justified picking *The Shack* because she had heard that it was a book club 'favourite' and that the book had 'gone down well' with other reading groups that her colleagues had facilitated. Indeed, the novel was hugely popular in the USA, topping the *New York Times*'s bestseller chart for 52 weeks and has experienced similar (albeit more moderate) success in the UK market. Readers in the *Forest Group*, however, were not enamoured with *The Shack* at all. The novel provoked strongly negative reactions from all readers, with Lucy remarking that reading the novel had made her 'feel sick' (see Extract 3 below) and Frank claiming that never in his life had he 'enjoyed hating a book so much'.

Although all six readers in the *Forest Group* reported disliking the novel, it was clear to me (and the other readers) that Frank's reaction was more extreme than that of the other readers. In addition to his comment that he had 'never enjoyed hating a book so much' in his life, Frank had written down 'the 17 reasons why it's the worst book in the world'. Like Lucy, Frank also reported that the novel had made him feel 'physically ill' (see Extract 3 below). Other members of the group picked up on Frank's extreme reaction, variously remarking at the end of the 45-minute meeting that *The Shack* had really 'touched a nerve' (Joan) and had 'wound you up' (Daniel). It is worth noting that Frank's extreme reaction to the novel was somewhat out of character. Although a frequent contributor to discussion, Frank tended to be more measured in his evaluations than was the case in this meeting. Frank would often seek to discuss the good qualities of a text even if his general opinion was negative, and vice-versa.

It was clear that the *a priori* fact of Frank's Christian belief played a central role in the discourses produced in this meeting, both in terms of his own evaluation of the novel and in how the other readers reacted to the text. Although Frank had discussed this aspect of his identity in previous meetings, his Christianity was primed by the evangelical themes in *The Shack* and, at times in the meeting, he defended his own faith against the doctrine espoused in the novel.

Across the meeting, Frank discussed how the act of reading the novel had affected him. For instance, he recounted his experience of discussing the novel with other members of the congregation at his church, at one point describing his relief that one of his fellow parishioners had also disliked the novel (for a transcription key, see Appendix):

Extract 1

[00:03:16.16] *Forest – The Shack*

FRANK:	luckily the – there is a chap wh – who goes occasionally (.) I said > what did you think of it < he said oh it's crap y'know (.) I was kinda relieved in a way
LUCY:	ohhhhh right yeah

A few minutes later, Frank reported his discussion with the vicar, who conversely enjoyed the book:

Extract 2

[00:11:02.18] *Forest – The Shack*
FRANK: I said to him (.) I've got a feeling that I'm not going to like it he said (.) oh really y'know
LUCY: =oh really
FRANK: (*exasperated tone)* hhohh (1.0)
LUCY: [xxxx]
FRANK: [but] he's a nice chap and I can't let him down by not going any more

Frank also discussed the physical and social impact that the novel had made upon him. The novel acted as a 'covenant' (a religious and legal term meaning an agreement to engage in or refrain from performing a particular action) and discouraged him from attending church for one week:

Extract 3

[00:02:12.06] *Forest – The Shack*
LUCY: it made me feel sick [it give]
FRANK: [it was s-] like a covenant it made
me feel physically ill (.)
and when it came to Sunday
I just couldn't bring myself to go to church
[for]
LUCY: [rea]lly
FRANK: for the first Sunday (.) I thought you know (.) because I feared that people there might like it you know

These three short extracts give a sense of Frank's extreme reaction towards *The Shack*. Far from just offending his sense of taste, Frank reported the visceral effect that reading *The Shack* had on his physical and social behaviour.

In the next section, I analyse a short but highly illustrative segment of transcript taken from the *Forest Group*'s discussion of *The Shack*. In this passage of talk the group articulates a collective resistance to the perceived ideology of the novel. The readers achieve this in two ways: invoking elements of group history *and* creating an out-group target audience for the novel. Frank's role in this is crucial and I also consider how he uses aspects of his own (in his eyes, more reasonable) Christian belief to debase the Christianity in the novel.

5 Analysis – 'This must be the first time that we've all agreed on a book'

The passage of conversation analysed in this section appeared just one minute into the *Forest Group*'s meeting. Prior to this extract the readers had offered only brief negative evaluations of the novel. At 70-seconds long this passage is obviously only a fraction of the group's overall conversation on *The Shack* (running to an hour); however, it crystallises important aspects of the readers' reactions to the novel and is illustrative, to some extent, of the group's collective resistance to the text. Following the reproduction of the transcript, I give a turn-by-turn analysis of the readers' conversation.

Extract 4

[00:1:13.02] *Forest – The Shack*

LUCY:	i – it were kinda like (0.5) aimed at (2.5) I thought it was aimed
	at Christians (1.0)
JESS:	I don't think it was aimed at anybody
? :	=[mmm]
LUCY:	=[don't] you
JESS:	=no::
LUCY:	(0.5) REAlly↑
JESS:	=no::
LUCY:	cos they are the kinda people that (0.5)° they are the kind of
	people° (.) erm (.) a lot of (.) I g – I get the impression that a
	lotta church groups (.) reading groups like that
FRANK:	=god it would absolutely terrify me
LUCY:	=but maybe it's Am – maybe it's Am – American[s]
DANIEL:	[Am]ericans
LUCY:	=American [groups]
DANIEL:	[I can't] can't imagine [British groups going in for it]
LUCY:	[xxxxxxxxxxxxxxxxxxxxxxx]
FRANK:	=I find it really scary that American (0.5) Christians you know
	could (.) kind of [go in for this]
JESS:	[yeah cos]
FRANK:	makes you think that
JESS:	=but I think [one thing that we]
FRANK:	[they must be utter] simpletons y'know (0.5)
JESS:	could all agree on (.) this must be the first time (.) that (.)
	[we've all agreed on a book]
JOAN:	[all agreed]
DANIEL:	[all agreed]
SAMUEL:	[on a book]
LUCY:	[hehehehe]

30 JESS: because usually > we're sort of I hated it (.) some say I lov[ed it
31 and <]
32 LUCY: [yeah
33 yeah]
34 JOAN: = yeah

To summarise this passage of talk, the readers begin by imagining the target audience of *The Shack*. As mentioned, in the short time before this extract the readers have given brief and critical evaluations of the novel. Concurrently, members of the group are aware that *The Shack* is a bestseller, and so spend this early part of the meeting trying to understand (and account for) other readers' love for the novel in light of their own resistance to it. Once they have established that the audience is 'American Christians' the group move on to discuss how unusual it is for all members to agree on their evaluation of a text.

Lucy is the first to speculate about whom *The Shack* is 'aimed at'. Her first claim (lines 1–2) is that the novel is 'aimed at Christians'. The design of Lucy's turn displays her tentativeness in making this presupposition. Although her turn begins as a categorical statement, her assertion displays hesitation features in the form of disfluency ('i-it') and two pauses, one of which is a relatively lengthy 2.5 seconds. In addition, the first half of her turn contains hedging ('kinda like'), also suggesting her uncertainty and her difficulty at making this claim. Following the 2.5 seconds mid-turn pause, Lucy moves away from attempting to make a categorical statement. Instead, she foregrounds her own perspective and stresses that the speculation is *her* view rather than a general statement of fact: 'I thought it was aimed at Christians' (ll. 1–2). On the face of it, Lucy's claim that an overtly evangelical Christian novel (see publisher's blurb above) might be aimed at Christians is not controversial, so the degree of Lucy's mitigation could be seen as unusual. As I go on to suggest in the Discussion section below, however, her tentativeness is likely a result of Frank's presence in the group. At this stage, Lucy's imagined target audience of 'Christians' includes Frank, making it difficult conversational work for Lucy to accomplish.

Following Lucy's turn, Jess offers disagreement at line 3: 'I don't think it was aimed at anybody'. I interpret Jess's comment as suggesting that *The Shack* is so bad that the author did not have any particular audience in mind when writing the novel. From lines 5 to 8 Lucy and Jess continue to disagree as to whether the novel had a specific audience, with Lucy questioning the basis of Jess's opinion at line 7: 'REAlly?'

In her next substantial turn across lines 9–11 Lucy responds to Jess's disagreement by justifying her claim that the novel has a specifically

Christian audience. This turn follows a similar pattern to Lucy's turn at lines 1–2. At line 9, she begins to make a seemingly categorical assertion about Christians: 'they are the kinda people'. As before, this assertion is aborted, presumably because Lucy realises that it constitutes a potentially problematic and sweeping categorisation, especially in light of Frank's presence in the group. Again, the features of her turn indicate the difficulty of her assertion. Lucy abandons her assertion by using repair and mimicking her own speech, seemingly ridiculing what she has just said in a noticeably quieter voice: '°they are the kind of people°'. As before, Lucy hedges her unqualified original statement to a more personal assertion, individual to her: 'I g – I get the impression that...' (l. 10). Lucy also softens her assertion by moving away from commenting on the attributes of Christians ('they are the kinda people') and towards making a claim about whom the book is very specifically aimed: 'church groups (.) reading groups like that' (l. 11).

Latching on to Lucy's turn, Frank takes the floor for the first time in this passage at line 12. He seeks to distance himself from the 'Christians' and the 'church groups' that have been posited as the target audience of *The Shack*. His comment 'god it would absolutely terrify me' overtly displays his sense of revulsion towards these other Christians and this demonstrates his desire to dissociate himself from this out-group created by the *Forest Group*. This is achieved through Frank's use of what Pomerantz (1984) refers to as an extreme case formulation (ECF), an expression that indicates a speaker's position on a matter rather than being a pure description or a statement of fact. Frank's report that he is 'absolutely' terrified at the prospect of a Christian who would enjoy *The Shack* is clearly an exaggeration and serves the rhetorical purpose of distancing his own faith from that of the perceived target audience of the novel. As I go on to argue later, this distancing is something that it is acutely important for Frank to achieve, as he has the most to lose by being associated with the ideology of *The Shack*.

Between lines 13 and 17, the *Forest Group* engage in more detailed out-group creation, further specifying a target audience for *The Shack* that is increasingly distanced from the identity of Frank and the group. At line 13, Lucy qualifies her previous comment on 'church groups': 'but maybe it's Am – Americans'. From lines 14–17 there is co-constructed talk between Daniel and Lucy. Daniel agrees with Lucy at line 14, offering affiliative overlap (Kitzinger 2008) with the terminal point of her turn. He echoes Lucy's specification of groups of 'Americans' that comprise the captive audience for *The Shack*. As Lucy completes her turn at line 15 ('American groups'), Daniel overlaps again stating that he 'can't imagine

British groups going in for it' (l. 16), creating an 'Us vs. Them' binary between sensible British groups on the one hand and duped American groups on the other. For the *Forest Group*, this relatively specific out-group of 'American groups' works successfully as a demonised audience for *The Shack*, with Frank continuing with this out-group creation over the next few lines.

Across lines 18–19, Frank picks up on Lucy and Daniel's focus on the target 'American' audience of *The Shack*. Frank claims to 'find it really scary that American (0.5) Christians you know could (.) kind of go in for this'. In expressing this incredulity Frank creates further distance between himself and the other 'American Christians'. Frank elaborates on this out-group across lines 21 and 23, between Jess's bids for the floor. Across these lines Frank makes inferences about the literary taste and subsequent mental capacity of these 'American Christians'. He makes the link between the two explicit at line 23 when he claims that those who do enjoy the novel 'must be utter simpletons'. As before, Frank displays the most outrage at the perceived ideology of *The Shack*, going further than the other readers in chastising the imagined fans of the novel.

In the final part of the passage, the evaluative and interpretive work performed by *Forest Group* is focused on the group's sense of collective identity and its shared history. The invocation of this shared history seems to strengthen the group's resolve against *The Shack*. During her bids for the floor across lines 22–24, Jess remarks that a negative assessment of the novel is 'one thing we could all agree on'. Having secured the floor at line 24 she goes on to say that 'this must be the first time that we've all agreed on a book' (ll. 24–25). As I go on to discuss in the next section of this chapter with reference to interview data from *Forest Group*, it is part of this group's identity and folklore that the members do not agree on books; indeed, they actively seek disagreement at times. Jess's invocation of this shared history across lines 22–24 further fortifies the group's negative assessment of the novel, as the readers *naturally* have no predisposition to agree with one another. The implication of this is that *The Shack* must be objectively bad in order to prompt such agreement among the readers.

Jess's turn across lines 24–25 reflects an important aspect of the *Forest Group*'s sense of shared identity. Even more interesting, however, are the ways in which the other readers go about agreeing with Jess across lines 26–29. Joan, Daniel and Samuel all successfully project the end of Jess's turn with overlapping agreement. Remarkably, Joan, Daniel and Samuel articulate 'all agreed' in very quick succession, while Samuel utters 'on a book' simultaneously with Jess. Coates (1996: 118) refers to this kind of collaborative talk as 'joint construction', where speakers 'work together so that their voices combine to produce a single utterance or utterances'. The co-construction of shared meaning between the different readers here shows shared opinions and thought in the *form* of the conversation as well as in the *content* of what is said.

This display of group identity and the invocation of a shared history are continued in the final turns of this extract. As in her previous turn, Jess uses the plural pronoun 'we' to refer to the group at line 30, which constitutes a clear example of collective identity (Pennycook 1994; O'Keefe 2002): 'because usually >we're sort of I hated it (.) some say I loved it<'. Also in her turn, Jess summarises the common disagreement that typifies the group's normal meetings. She shifts into the imagined direct speech of the readers to represent these 'usual' disagreements: some say 'I hated it (.) some say I loved it' (l. 30). Research by Holt (1996) into such examples of direct reported speech has found that it serves to provide evidence for a particular state of affairs or an opinion. Wooffitt (2001, 2007) has similarly found that the use of direct reported speech by mediums (those supposedly in contact with the dead) acts to establish the 'authority and authenticity' of the medium. In this instance, Jess's direct reported speech does not attempt to quote literally anything that has actually been said at previous meetings. The 'I hated it' and 'I loved it' quotations are approximations of previous utterances, rather than representations of actual conversations. However, this 'unspoken speech' (Myers 1999) still establishes a link between the here-and-now of the present interaction (discussing *The Shack*) and the history of the group, providing evidence and authenticity for the group's evaluation of the text and thus is similar to the direct reported speech analysed by Holt (1996) and Wooffitt (2001, 2007).

In the next section, I extend elements of this analysis into the Discussion. I concentrate on two aspects that I have referred to throughout the analysis, both of which relate to identity work in the talk: how the group establishes a collective identity and how Frank's personal identity comes to the fore in this discussion of *The Shack*.

6 Discussion

Establishing group identity

Throughout the passage of conversation in Extract 4 the members of *Forest Group* co-construct a sense of shared identity. This sense emerges from the readers' unanimous response to *The Shack* and the group's response to the novel is seemingly strengthened by this invocation of a shared history and identity. In this way, the readers' collective reaction to the novel and their strong sense of group identity exist symbiotically, mutually reinforcing one another. In order to discuss further the establishment of group identity in the *Forest Group* I focus on three elements introduced in the Analysis section: specific discursive features that index group identity, the invocation of shared history and the construction of an out-group readership for *The Shack*.

As discussed in the Analysis section above, there are particular discursive features in the passage of conversation that indicate a sense of group identity. Most obviously, Jess's repeated use of the first-person pronoun 'we' to refer to *Forest Group* (ll. 22, 25, 30) indicates not only her own 'group membership' (van Knippenberg and Ellemers 2003: 31) but also the existence of a group above and beyond each individual reader. More interesting than this, however, are the collaborative features of turn exchange that are particularly evident towards the end of the extract, with the readers building on others' turns. The joint construction at the end of the extract is illustrative of this (ll. 25–28), displaying 'understanding, affiliation and agreement' between the speakers (Lerner 2002: 250). The presence of these features in addition to the frequent turn-latching and lexical repetition constitutes a highly collaborative floor (Edelsky 1981; Coates 1996), with the speakers seemingly 'on the same wavelength' (Edelsky 1981: 391) as they discuss the novel.

At the end of Extract 4, these collaborative turn features are used to establish a group identity based upon the shared history between the readers. Jess's comment that 'this must be the first time that we've all agreed on a book' (ll. 24–25) explicitly cites the *Forest Group*'s normal propensity for disagreement; a history that others in the group quickly ratify across subsequent lines (ll. 26–28). Jess's turn at the end of the extract (ll. 30–31) builds on her previous comment, as she enacts the voices of the members in a typical meeting in which disagreement occurs between readers: 'usually we're sort of I hated it... some say I loved it'. Edwards (2007: 36) describes this kind of rhetorical formulation as a counter-dispositional – a claim that is 'reluctantly arrived at, or even precisely counter... to one's own presumptions and biases'. With the help of the other readers, Jess flags up that the group does not have a history of agreeing, thus making the agreement in this situation exceptional and counter to normal business.

The *Forest Group* members' predisposition towards disagreement in their usual meetings was something I discussed with the group at interview. The question I (DP) ask at the start of Extract 5 is one that I posed to all the reading groups that comprised my fieldwork:

Extract 5

[00:03:32.18] *Forest – Interview*

DP:	ok (.) do you tend to find that you all react in a similar way
JOAN:	no [no]
FRANK:	[no]
?:	[no no no::]
DP:	[to the books]
JOAN:	there's only one book that we all said we didn't like and I can't [remember]
FRANK:	[it was the] shack
JOAN:	=oh [the shack]
?:	[xxxxxxxxxxxxxxxxxxxxxxx]
JESS:	[one we all agreed on]
SAMUEL:	=universally disliked
FRANK:	haha[hahahaha]
JOAN:	[otherwise] we all have different opinions
FRANK:	=yeah

In the interview the readers were quick to deny that they agree in their literary taste, with Joan citing the discussion of *The Shack* as the only occasion when the group 'all' agreed. Jess and Samuel support this point, with the latter remarking that the novel was 'universally disliked'. Just as in the meeting data (Extract 4), this conformity of opinion between the readers over *The Shack* was worth the group remarking upon because it was so unusual for the members. As Joan remarks, usually the readers 'all have different opinions'.

In the meeting data, the group's reference to their usual practices not only invokes an important aspect of their group identity but also serves to strengthen their position against *The Shack* through the use of a counter-dispositional. If this is the 'first time' (Extract 4, l. 24) the readers have agreed on a book, the implication is that the novel must have been exceptionally bad. In summary, these comments from the group's meeting and the interview reinforce the group's sense of shared history and identity, while also strengthening their position against the novel and the readers' perception of its ideology.

Finally, the *Forest Group* establish a group identity by way of creating and demonizing an out-group of readers who, they believe, would enjoy *The Shack*. The group was aware of the novel's bestseller status and, given the group members' highly negative opinion of the text, positing the likely identity or identities of these fans was an important discussion point for the group. As Branscombe et al. (1999: 48) argue, this kind of out-group creation can serve specific functions for the in-group: 'for those who value the identity in question, derogation of the threatening out-group can serve collective self-esteem restoration purposes'. Across Extract 4, members of the group construct an increasingly specific readership for the novel, moving from 'Christians' to 'church groups' to 'American Christians'. As the out-group becomes more specific, it becomes more geographically distant and ideologically removed from the readers in the *Forest Group*. This distancing is crucial work for Frank to achieve, as discussed in the next sub-section. Fans of the novel are portrayed as terrifying (l. 12), 'scary' (l. 18) and as 'utter simpletons' (l. 23). Conflating literary taste and mental capacity, the group censure this out-group of other readers as inferior and gullible. This offers an implicit contrast to the readers in the *Forest Group*, who are able to see the novel for what it *really* is: 'the worst book in the world'.

In summary, the readers in *Forest Group* engage in various practices in order to establish a particular group identity. In Extract 4, the construction of this collective identity is comprised of two elements: the group's usual predisposition towards disagreement and the creation of an imagined out-group of readers who constitute the fanbase of *The Shack*. Rather than being the 'utter simpletons' duped by the evangelical ideology and the hype surrounding the novel, readers in the *Forest Group* portray themselves as a sensible and rational 'British group' (l. 16) who can acknowledge the objective *fact* that the novel is terrible. This group identity is demonstrated on a turn-by-turn level, with collaborative turn features occurring across the extract.

Frank's personal identity

The readers in the *Forest Group* first and foremost regard *The Shack* as a Christian novel and it is an important factor that one member of the group is a Christian. Frank's religious faith is an aspect of his identity that he frequently raises and the themes of the novel under discussion in this particular meeting afforded him the chance to talk about his faith in opposition to another brand of Christianity. As the only self-defining Christian in a group of agnostics and professed atheists, Frank perhaps has greater 'stake' or interest (Potter 1996) in adopting a more negative view of the novel than the other readers. In other words, Frank's need to disassociate his faith from that of the novel is more pressing than that of the other readers.

As Extract 4 demonstrates, the other readers seem acutely aware of the salience of Frank's personal identity in this meeting. Across the first few turns of the extract Lucy tentatively discussed the target audience of 'Christians' (l. 2), then moving on to make suppositions about Christians as a particular 'kinda people' (ll. 9–10). The formal features of these turns showed the difficulty that Lucy experienced in making these assertions, with her comments becoming increasingly more personal (as opposed to categorical) and her turns replete with disfluency features. The difficulty that Lucy experienced is likely a result of Frank's presence in the group and her mitigated and tentative remarks show her performing facework to Frank, softening the potential offence caused to him as a Christian. As becomes apparent, however, Frank is not offended by this categorisation of *The Shack*'s target audience as 'Christians' and he seems even keener than the others to chastise the kind of Christian who does like the novel.

In Extract 4, Frank goes further than the other readers in criticising the target audience of the novel by explicitly linking literary taste with intellect (l. 23). Frank presents himself as a different kind of Christian from those who enjoyed the novel and (judging from the behaviour of the other readers) he is afforded greater rights to make these comments. While other members of the group are tentative in making inferences about the audience of the novel (Lucy at ll. 1–2 and ll. 9–11), Frank's forthright comments might suggest he experiences no such difficulty. It is Frank's Christian identity that provides him with the 'epistemic primacy' (Raymond and Heritage 2006: 694) to criticise other types of Christians in a much stronger way than the other readers in the *Forest Group*. In Extract 4, Frank couches his response to the novel in more extreme terms, using extreme case formulations (Pomerantz 1984) and making explicitly disparaging comments about the 'American Christian' out-group. Throughout the meeting Frank consistently offered more extremely negative evaluations of the novel than the other readers in the group. In Extract 3 for instance, Frank 'upgrades' (Pomerantz 1984: 65–66) Lucy's comment that the novel had made her feel 'sick'. Frank agrees that the novel made him feel 'physically ill' but goes further than this, remarking that the novel acted as a religious 'covenant' and prohibited him from attending church for a week.

For Frank, reading and discussing *The Shack* had a surprisingly therapeutic effect, affirming his Christian faith rather than damaging it. At the end of the meeting he made the following comment about his religious belief:

Extract 6

[00:42:10.17] *Forest – The Shack*

FRANK:	in spite of everything erm (1.0) what faith I have I wouldn't sell for a 1000 million pounds (.) couldn't do without it (.) I really couldn't (1.0) erm life would be totally meaningless in in unless I (0.5) had some kind of faith in in (.) life being (1.0) underpinned by some (.) greater reality than my own individual self [y'know]
DANIEL:	[mmm]
FRANK:	= my own consciousness erm (1.0) but it – it's but to be expressed in these terms (.) or even in orthodox Christian terms couldn't I couldn't do it

Here, Frank directly contrasts his own faith with the perceived form of faith promoted by *The Shack*. His personal faith is something he 'wouldn't sell for a 1000 million pounds' and he reports that he could not conform to the ideology of *The Shack* or express his faith 'in orthodox Christian terms'. So although Frank was at various points across the meeting dismayed and disgusted, he was also keen to stress the (unintentional) cathartic effect of the novel on him. For Frank, the novel was so terrible that it served to affirm his conviction in his own, different brand of faith.

7 Conclusion

The book group data presented and analysed in this chapter suggest that evaluative and interpretive work in this context can be seen as a product of two elements: a group's invoked sense of collective identity and salient aspects of individual readers' personal identities. The members of *Forest Group* unanimously agreed on a highly negative assessment of *The Shack* and, as such, collectively and collaboratively offered resistance to the perceived Christian ideology of the novel. This group response to the text was positioned in relation to their history and how the readers usually respond to the books they discuss. The unanimous agreement among the readers was seen as highly unusual in this respect. This was worth the group remarking upon, not just for the reason that agreement between the members is rare, but also because this backdrop of a shared history confirmed to the readers that they were correct in their assessment of the novel. The readers reported their predisposition to disagree and the resulting claim was that *The Shack* must be objectively bad in order to lead to such conformity. In addition, it is clear from the data presented here that features of readers' personal identity can be brought to bear on the discussion of literary texts. An important part of Frank's identity is his religious faith and this was made salient by the themes of the novel under discussion. The analysis suggests that Frank felt that his own Christianity was being denigrated by the evangelical form of Christianity presented in the novel. His reaction to the book, therefore, appeared more extreme than other reactions from the group, not only because (as a Christian) he was more affronted by the novel but also because (as the *only* Christian in the group) he ran the risk of being associated with the novel's ideology.

If reading in the book club context involves the constant negotiation and updating of interpersonal relations and group identity, then it also involves readers engaging in dialogue with absent voices. Readers are not merely interacting with other members of the group, but are also in dialogue with characters, authors and the voices (imagined or real) of other absent readers and critics. In *Forest Group*'s discussion of *The Shack*, the readers' reaction prompted them to consider reasons for the popularity of the novel. This involved out-group creation and vilification, which in turn served to reinforce and justify the group's negative assessment of the text. Paying close attention to the ways in which readers in book clubs talk about texts allows us to consider how non-academic readers perceive the act of literary engagement and the resources that these readers bring to bear on the discussion of books. It is often important for these groups to establish and sustain some kind of group identity, but aspects of the readers' personal identities are never far from the discussion. Aspects of group and personal reader identity were highly salient during *Forest Group*'s discussion of *The Shack*, with the text priming these invocations of identity. As researchers, we must be attentive to the possibility that non-academic readers will bring particular resources to bear on the discussion of texts (for example, personal identity and experience) that many 'trained' academic readers would actively seek to avoid.

Book talk in the reading group setting is, therefore, rarely just talk about books. When people get together to discuss books there are a variety of other contextual factors at play affecting the discourse. For example, the interpersonal relationships among and between readers, politeness norms and aspects of personal and group identity are likely to produce particular kinds of responses. Far from being a private activity, reading becomes a highly social activity in the book group context.

Appendix

Transcription Key

(.)	very brief pause
(0.5)	timed pause
=	no pause between speakers' turns
[yeah]	
[yeah]	overlap
REAlly	emphasis (where capitalised)
> yes <	speaker speeds-up
xxxxxx	inaudible speech
↑	rising intonation
^{0}they^0	quieter section of talk
No::	elongated vowel sound
(exasperated tone)	manner of delivery
?	unknown speaker

10

The Narrative Tease: Narratorial Omniscience, Implicature and the Making of Sensation in *Lady Audley's Secret*

Ruth Schuldiner

1 Introduction

Mary Elizabeth Braddon's 1861 sensation novel *Lady Audley's Secret* is narrated in a somewhat counterintuitive fashion. On an explicit level, the novel anticipates the detective mode which would become popular with the publication of Wilkie Collins's *The Moonstone* (1868): as in much detective fiction, the blatant crimes which motivate Braddon's narrative are left unstated until near the end of the novel. While they are not made explicit, however, these crimes are strongly implicated, so that the coherence of the narrative depends upon the reader's recognition of the text's implicatures.

The centrality and sustained quality of these implicatures provides material for an inquiry into the potential reaches of implicated fictional narrative. In *Lady Audley's Secret*, the use of implicature takes on a particular salience, and the indirect method of communicating the constitutional occurrences of the plot is as conspicuous as the narrative facts themselves. The narrative voice ostensively remains silent on key points of the narrative, oscillating playfully between limited and full omniscience. The conspicuous semi-articulation of these key points adds a dysphemistic tenor to their communication and taints otherwise benign local implicatures with a sinister (if humorously overdone) quality. This tone impacts what Clark (2009: 191) terms the reader's 'global inferences', or 'the interpretation of the book as a whole and the development of literary interpretations'. In other words, the dysphemistic tenor of the text's implicatures allows the reader to infer the sinister trajectory of the narrative.

This chapter examines passages within *Lady Audley's Secret* and critical scholarship on the novel to evidence two interrelated claims. The first relates to how the implicatures examined here rely on a context of narratorial omniscience and, correspondingly, a context of fictionality: the narrative's notable silences may only be interpreted as giving rise to implicatures if the reader assumes the narrative voice to be omniscient, and this reader assumption is only possible if the reader also assumes the narrative he or she is reading to be fictional. In specifying this reader 'assumption of fictionality' I mean to indicate something other than Mary Louise Pratt's well-known 'assumption of literariness'. In her seminal book *Toward a Speech Act Theory of Literary Discourse*, Pratt (1977: 86) indicates that 'Literature itself is a speech context' that must be assumed in order for the reader to experience literature as literature: the assumption of literariness is the appropriateness condition that must be met in order to experience the literariness of a text. This assumption is meant to indicate the reader's appreciation of the text's prolonged and deliberate preparation and is intended to account for the reader's relative unwillingness to interpret textual aberrations as errors (1977: 170). Pratt's assumption of literariness does not account for readers' willingness to believe the evident omniscience of fictional narrators: no amount of preparation could enable a nonfictional narrator to unproblematically read nonfictional characters' minds. It is only when readers assume a text to be fictional that they can interpret the omniscience exhibited by a narrator as a narrative effect rather than as a textual error. Fiction authors may then exploit the perceived omniscience of their narrative voices to create implicatures such as those discussed in this chapter.

My second argument contributes to an ongoing discussion on the nature of the 'sensation novel' and, specifically, its relationship to literary realism. I argue that the humorous elements of *Lady Audley's Secret* are intentional and indicative of the novel's satire on more realistic fictions, an argument that deviates from previous characterisations of sensation fiction generally and of *Lady Audley's Secret* in particular. An analysis of some of the novel's central implicatures uncovers a relationship between the laughter these passages often evokes and the novel's popular categorisation as a 'sensation novel': some of the reader impressions reported by previous literary theorists were in reaction to Braddon's conspicuous use of implicature. Evidencing a stance on this perennial debate within scholarship on Victorian literature with a discussion of implicature indicates the general pertinence of pragmatics to mainstream literary criticism. Only a discussion of the implicatures within *Lady Audley's Secret* is capable of articulating the mechanics behind prominent narrative effects within the novel; greater acknowledgment of implicature within mainstream literary criticism would inform not only studies of individual novels but also studies on the literary genres formed by them collectively.

The body of this chapter is made up of three sections: an introduction to the first argument, an introduction to the second, and supporting close readings of passages from *Lady Audley's Secret.* I place emphasis on the author's, rather than the reader's, role in the literary communication (that is, on the creation, rather than the interpretation, of the text's implicatures). This emphasis reflects my narratological background, as does my preoccupation with narratorial omniscience and the potential distinctions between fiction and nonfiction. My discussion of the text's implicatures, however, also draws on relevance theory as delineated by Sperber and Wilson (1986/1995). Relevance considerations determine the extent to which an utterance gives rise to implicatures, their strength and the salience both of particular implicatures and of the process of deriving them. I attempt to relate these perceived implicatures to the context of narratorial omniscience in which the utterances are found. An analysis of the implicatures that result from a demonstrably omniscient narrator's abrupt reticence must consider the reader's expectations of narratorial omniscience; the text's implicatures are created by the author's manipulation of these reader expectations.

2 Narratorial omniscience and implicature

Implicature is employed heavily in communicating the plot of *Lady Audley's Secret*; without an unusual amount of inference on the reader's part, the basic narrative is incomprehensible. The reader's inferences rely on the background assumption that the narrator is omniscient, an assumption made possible by the text's perceived status as fictional and the narratorial omniscience practiced throughout the text. It is only by interpreting the gaps in explicit communication as purposeful that the reader can regard them as indicative of implicatures and can infer the inexplicit progression of the plot.

The plot of *Lady Audley's Secret* involves a deserted wife ('Helen Talboys', née 'Maldon') who has changed her name (to 'Lucy Graham') and bigamously married the established and wealthy Sir Michael Audley (becoming 'Lucy Audley'). When her estranged first husband, George

Talboys, returns from Australia, his chance encounter with his close friend Robert Audley (Sir Michael's nephew) places George within the social sphere of his bigamous wife, whom he has been told is dead. Lady Audley is intent on avoiding exposure and subsequently pushes George down a well with the intention of killing him. Upon the disappearance of his friend, Robert actively occupies the role of amateur detective, following various leads until 'circumstantial evidence' leads him to confront Lady Audley about her guilt. In a rare narrative twist, Lady Audley confesses to madness at the end of the novel, blaming her criminal actions on insanity. In an attempt to handle her humanely (and to save his family from scandal), Robert commits Lady Audley to a Belgian asylum. In a last narrative twist, George suddenly reappears, have fled to New York after his wife's murderous attempt.

Until her confession, all of Lady Audley's criminal activities are communicated only through implicature; her status as George Talboys's wife, as well as her attempt to murder him, is left inexplicit. Without the reader's inferences, many of the explicitly depicted scenes of the novel would appear to lack causality and would keep him or her from following the general development of the narrative. In other words, the text's reliance on implicature is such that a reader's basic comprehension of the plot is only possible alongside his or her recognition of its implicatures. In a somewhat circular fashion it is possible to claim that the centrality of these implicatures distinguishes them from both weaker implicatures and implications: cumulatively, these implicatures are responsible for the communication of the plot itself, apart from any tonal or qualitative effects the reading of the narrative might also engender. These implicatures evoke what Clark terms 'salient inferences'; he explains that '...the nature of some communicative acts makes aspects of the inferential processes more salient and sometimes it is hard, arguably impossible, not to notice them' (2009: 173). The implicatures discussed in this chapter can similarly be distinguished from non-communicated implications: because the text's narrative appears coherent only if the reader assumes that the undocumented events have occurred (because the implicatures communicate information which is, in other words, integral to the coherent development of the plot), they must be interpreted as intended by Braddon herself.

My first argument relates to the narrative technique through which many of these implicatures are made ostensive: the obtrusive, superficially unexplained alternations in the narrator's status as omniscient. These alternations implicate, first, the unarticulated relationship between Lady Audley and George Talboys; second, her attempt to murder him. These implicatures function by way of the puzzle inherent in the unorthodox silences of the omniscient narrative voice: the puzzle of why an omniscient narrator – definitively capable of providing the reader with all narrative information – would leave integral developments inexplicit becomes the puzzle of the information that these ostensive narrative gaps are intended to communicate. It is these implicitly posed questions that motivate readers to decipher the meaning of the text's ostensive gaps; in other words, they play a large role in effecting the text's implicatures.

I intend to discuss all implicatures as posed by the omniscient narrator, although it is necessary to keep in mind that the narrator is purposefully fashioned by the author. I highlight the use of the narrator, as opposed to the author, for two reasons. The first involves the 'teasing' quality of the narrative voice that is at times created by its heavy use of implicatures: the use of implicatures helps to create, at times, a distinguishable narratorial persona. The second involves a long-standing controversy and confusion between the roles of the author and the narrator in narrative theory. Almost every prominent narrative theorist (including those who could be considered to practice pragmatic stylistics, such as Mary Louise Pratt and Marie-Laure Ryan) has weighed in on the controversy and (despite decades of discussion) no sure consensus has been reached. As a compromise most narrative theorists refer to a 'narrative voice' when the narratorial persona is not individuated; I adopt that term throughout most of this chapter, but with the consciousness that it implies the presence of a narrator.

Because intentional vagueness or ellipses are especially suspect in a context of omniscient narration, and because omniscient narration is only possible in a fictional context, the effect of many implicatures found within omnisciently narrated texts relies on that context. While critics are far from being in agreement on what constitutes fiction, few will dispute that omniscient narration is only present in fictional discourse. Readers rarely read – nor are they expected to read – nonfictional discourse as if it were narrated omnisciently; the possibility of knowing everything as a certainty is a known fiction. The fictionality of omniscient narration translates into an overarching fictionality of discourse, making omniscient narration perhaps the sole sufficient marker of fictionality.

Clearly this assertion depends on how one defines 'omniscience'. The 2009 edition of the *Oxford English Dictionary* defines literary omniscience as 'an attribute of the author or a third-person narrator: a full and complete knowledge concerning all the events of a narrative, and the private motives, thoughts, etc., of all the characters'. It is this definition of omniscience that is used here. 'Omniscient narration' can, for instance, imply that a narrator is impartial or has a very large, if not infinite, knowledge of his subject matter. I am not concerned with the narrator's impartiality, or 'distance' from the narrative communicated; I focus primarily on the epistemic connotations of 'omniscience', although I will at times comment on the narrative voice's distance from the characters it discusses. I am also not concerned with instances in which a narrator's knowledge is large but limited: while there are nonfiction narrators who provide readers with expert knowledge (such as a specialised scientist detailing his or her research to laypeople), these narrators are not truly 'omniscient', in that they cannot know everything. Conversely, a fictional narrator may possess unlimited knowledge of the narrative and third-person omniscient narrators regularly do know the impossible (such as their characters' thoughts) and are perceived by readers as possessing all narrative information (unlike nonfiction narrators, who are identified with the only-human implied author).

Within narrative theory, there is an active tradition that associates narratorial omniscience with fictionality. Cohn (1999) provides a definition of fiction that is closely aligned with a potential for narratorial omniscience:

> In fiction cast in the third person, this presentation involves a distinctive epistemology that allows a narrator to know what cannot be known in the real world and in narratives that target representations of the real world: the inner life of his figures.... this fictional stamp, as one theorist proposes, makes such a text 'epistemologically illegitimate' to the point where its speaker must appear as 'insane' to someone who mistook it for a historical text.
>
> (Cohn 1999: 16)

Cohn is careful to point out that her claim follows earlier propositions by Hamburger (in Cohn 1999: 23). Cohn's own work has been carried forward in other narratological texts: both Fludernik (2009: 6) and Palmer (2004: 5) have echoed her close alignment of fictionality with a potential for narratorial omniscience in their respective writings. Cohn's use of the term 'fictional stamp' is telling, in that she (and the other narrative theorists named) tend to view omniscience as a convention potentially exhibited by fictional texts, rather than as a convention potentially assumed by readers of fictional texts. In the analyses that follow, I discuss narratorial omniscience as a contextual assumption made by readers (fully aware that this assumption may be instigated and/or strengthened by evidence of narratorial omniscience within the text). This formulation of how assumed narratorial omniscience impacts the interpretation of fictional texts allows for an exploration of how authors are able to manipulate this reader assumption, exploiting the reader's expectations in order to effect implicatures.

3 Sensation fiction and implicature

The implicatures found in *Lady Audley's Secret* impact both the communication and the tone of the narrative. Cumulatively, communicating many narrative facts through conspicuously indirect means can act as the verbal equivalent of the physical wink and nod that might accompany oral storytelling; it can indicate a jocular knowingness which the storyteller shares with his or her audience. The sheer number of salient, central implicatures found in *Lady Audley's Secret* creates this same tone, communicating Lady Audley's ludicrous actions with a tone that registers an implicit reaction to that ludicrousness. The same use of implicature satirises the ideal of 'objective' narration in much realist fiction, carrying it to an absurd – ludicrous – extreme.

Sensation fiction is known as an unconventionally racy school of fiction that flourished throughout Britain in the 1860s. *Lady Audley's Secret* helped found the mode it participated in and is still considered today as definitive of the movement. These novels are known for having placed significant emphasis on detection and this quality is perceived as one of the characteristics that differentiate them from more 'realistic fiction'. Knight (2010: 43) notes that 'detection was a recurrent element in these first major sensational novels, and in some it can dominate' (2010: 43). In *Victorian Sensation Fiction*, Radford (2009: 6) writes that 'the typical sensation narrative has been assessed as a "novel with a secret" in which the solving of puzzles becomes a principal ingredient in its extraordinary commercial impact'.[1] However, there is traditionally more scholarly attention paid to this fiction's content (which was, historically, perceived as far more 'sensational' than that of realist fiction) and to the conditions of its historical emergence. *The Woman in White* (1860) by Wilkie Collins is often described as the movement's watershed novel (Law 2006: 97; Pykett 2006: 50; Levine 2008a: 100; Knight 2010: 40). It was followed closely by *Lady Audley's Secret* (1861) and Mrs. Henry Wood's *East Lynne* (1861) (Radford 2009: 19; Knight 2010: 41–42). Together, these three novels were perceived as defining and leading the sensation movement.

Although sensation fiction was hugely popular it was regularly criticised for its perceived deviations from realism. This criticism often claimed that the content of sensation novels (such as representations of multiple murders, bigamous marriages and hidden identities) was both immoral to depict and depicted unrealistically (Levine 2008a: 102; Radford 2009: 2). Sensation fiction became derogatorily associated with the lower reaches of the press; in countering this criticism, sensation authors claimed that the similarities between their stories and those in the press evidenced sensation fiction's faithful representation of reality (Brantlinger 1982: 10; Radford 2009: 1; Knight 2010: 31). The mode declined in popularity near the end of the decade, but it is thought to have been an important precursor to the more 'decadent' literary movements that would characterise the end of the 19th century.

Although the sensation mode is often associated with an emphasis on detection and narrative secrets, scholars often fail to differentiate between characters' secrets that are nonetheless communicated to the reader (those which create dramatic irony, for example) and narrative secrets in which information is kept from the reader for a significant portion of the text (true omissions). Narratives which include the former kind may employ the type of salient implicature that has been discussed above; the presence of implicatures naturally emphasises information's secret status by communicating it inexplicitly. When 'novels with a secret' make salient use of implicature, the narrative is often designed to encourage the reader's inferences to parallel those of a protagonist or detective; in the absence of a detective figure, it is the reader's inferences which may be said to form the detection with which the narrative mode is closely aligned. This teasingly, ostensively withheld information draws attention to the author's ultimate control of what is communicated and how it is communicated. In *Lady Audley's Secret,* the emphasis placed on the text's narration calls attention to its exaggerated use of realist conventions, emphasising that the ideal objectivity of realist narration has been, in the sensation mode, transmogrified into incongruous abdications of omniscience.

This discussion is partly inspired by the connection that scholars have made between what is often taken to be sensation fiction's non-serious tone and its poor moral standing. While the classic definition of sensation fiction concentrated on its 'sensational' content (Brantlinger 1982: 1; Radford 2009: 1–2), scholars have long remarked that it was how authors treat this content, rather than the presence of it, that was controversial. Brantlinger believes that the style of these novels fed their reputation; he writes that 'subjects were broached in sensation novels that many good Victorians thought inappropriate, and the fact that these subjects seemed not to be addressed seriously but merely "sensationally" made them all the more disreputable' (1982: 7). The sensational, rather than serious, discussion of 'inappropriate' topics effected an implicit commentary on the trite quality of face-saving implicatures.[2] The characterisation of these implicatures as trite undermined the realist objective of works in which they were earnestly employed and implicitly satirised the attempts at presentational politeness which often accompanied discussions of serious topics by realist authors.

Many of the implicatures in *Lady Audley's Secret* function as dysphemism, causing otherwise seemingly innocent events and activities to be interpreted with suspicion. Correspondingly the implicatures used to communicate central issues are often communicated through the presence of several, less central implicatures that build upon one another. These higher-order implicatures render the narrative technique more conspicuous, calling attention to the reader's complementary inferential processes and highlighting the relative absence of explicit communication. It is the unusual salience and number of these implicatures that lead readers to consider sensation fiction as excessive in its 'stylistic mannerisms' and to note especially the entertaining 'feeling of narrative wilfulness' that results (Brantlinger 1982: 14).

While Brantlinger's discussion of sensation fiction is especially articulate about the 'feeling of narrative wilfulness' that arises in readers, he only cursorily speculates as to its source. Much of Brantlinger's analysis of 'narrative wilfulness' focuses on sensation authors' use of third-person omniscience and specifically the temporary renunciation of it in some sensation texts. His discussion informs the one presented here, but I argue that it underestimates the pivotal role that implicatures play in these sensation narratives. Brantlinger does not distinguish between narratives that omit central information and those that use implicature to communicate it inexplicitly. He describes the general tenor of Braddon's implicatures, although without acknowledging that they are implicatures:

> Without any consciously experimental intention, she pushes third-person omniscient narration to its logical limits. The narrator, even while foreshadowing with fatalistic implications, ceases to convey all information and begins to disguise much of it as hints, clues, hiatuses.... The central mystery, the disappearance of George Talboys, involves the same pattern. We sense that the narrator is being willful

> and even capricious when George and Robert view Lady Audley's portrait, but George – and the narrator – give no sign of recognition. (1982: 14)

I agree and intend to develop Brantlinger's characterisations of the narrative voice's indirect style of communication. However, I disagree with some of Brantlinger's other characterisations of the narrative voice and believe that they misrepresent the narrative techniques responsible for the general narrative effects which Brantlinger describes. Brantlinger believes that the narrative voice 'disguise[s]' information when, in contrast, it shares that information with the reader. Information may be only partly given in a fictional text, but it may not be 'disguise[d]': it is either (perhaps only partly) on display for the reader to perceive, or is nonexistent. If a narrative voice truly 'cease[d] to convey all information' there would be no narrative. Far from being secretive, the narrative voice echoes the cant of obtuse yet hyperbolically 'objective' report, providing a humorously ironic, implicit commentary on the popular endeavour to portray fictional acts as 'realistically' as possible.

In *How to Read the Victorian Novel*, Levine notes that sensation fiction 'calls into question the epistemological authority that the omniscient narrator of most Victorian novels implies' (2008a: 122). According to Levine, both realism and omniscient narration are dominant features of Victorian fiction, although the exact natures of both concepts are controversial and variable from author to author (2008a: ix, 33). Levine believes that realism 'aspires, above all, to truth-telling' (2008b: viii). This objective necessarily complicates processes of representation: realism, Levine writes, 'makes the difficulties of the work of representation inescapably obvious to the writer; it makes inevitable an intense self-consciousness, sometimes explicit, sometimes not' (2008b: 189). That self-consciousness motivates but also complicates 'objective' modes of writing, such as those which employ omniscient narration. Levine's discussion of Victorian realist fiction emphasises authors' attempts at objectivity and equates objectivity with 'truth-telling' (adding a moral urgency to the pursuit). However, because authors, unlike their narrative voices, are never omniscient, it is a pursuit that sets standards for itself which it cannot meet; at least not within the framework of an earnestly narrated fiction. 'Ironically', Levine writes,

> realism, the Victorian novel's primary method, whose determination to get at the truth entailed at least an overt rejection of merely literary forms, is thoroughly literary. It is so in two ways, primarily: first,

> it sets itself up as rejecting earlier literary representations and thus frequently satirically re-enacts aspects of more traditional literature. Satire is intrinsic to realism, and satire depends in part on knowledge of that earlier literature.
>
> (2008a: 12)

Levine asserts that realist fiction must continuously break previous literary conventions in order to evoke an objective reality. That 'objective reality' can be, simply, the exposure of previous literary conventions as subjective cants. Whether or not 'objective' information is presented, this effect is simulated by the reader's realisation that the debunked conventions are merely conventions. Essentially, irony effects the revelation with which the realist mode is ideally associated. As Levine notes elsewhere of *Vanity Fair*, 'it creates its reality by satirizing conventional literary form' (2008b: 195).

While both Brantlinger and Levine characterise sensation fiction as an evolution of, rather than a separate school from, realist fiction, neither considers the possibility that sensation fiction's problematic relationship with more realistic fiction might be explained by ironic elements in sensation fiction's narration.[3] Similarly, while they both note the subversive use of omniscient narration in sensation novels, they do not specify why the 'fluid' omniscience found in sensation fiction seems subversive. A relevance-theoretic discussion of the omniscient narration found in *Lady Audley's Secret* sheds light on these issues. While 'fluid' omniscient narration (or, the occasional renunciation of narratorial omniscience) is not found in all sensation fiction, its acknowledgment could enrich the ongoing debate concerning sensation fiction's relation to more realist fiction. The implicatures found within *Lady Audley's Secret* are what identify the novel's narrative omniscience as echoic: it is only with the inconsistent, incongruent use of a literary convention that it may be recognised as ironic and consequently as both participating in and building on the realist conventions of the past.

4 Close readings

In general, the emphasis on content-related issues in *Lady Audley's Secret* has resulted in relatively little attention to the novel's narratorial style (with Brantlinger's analysis being an important exception). While Braddon's ability to represent Lady Audley 'subtly and incrementally as a crazed killer' (Knight 2010: 41) is almost universally noted, little has been said about how Braddon achieves the narrative effect of 'subtl[e] and incrementa[l]' communication. This section discusses some of the most implicature-heavy passages of the novel, although the context described is built up steadily through seemingly 'irrelevant' details mentioned on almost every page.

After the title of the narrative (which tells us that Lady Audley has or will develop a 'Secret') the existence of Lady Audley's 'hidden' identity is first suggested to the reader in her own soliloquy: after Lady Audley ruminates about 'every clue to identity buried and forgotten – except these, except these', the reader is told that she keeps 'a ring wrapped in an oblong piece of paper' hidden under her dress (Braddon 1998: 17). Lady Audley's rumination is in reaction to Sir Michael's marriage proposal, which is narrated on the same page. In this context, the ring (defeasibly) signals a prior marriage and, correspondingly, her bigamous intentions towards Sir Michael (she has accepted his proposal). How the reader is meant to detect that Lady Audley is George Talboys's deserted wife is less easy to articulate, partly because the communication of the information spans most of the novel, until Lady Audley confesses to having pushed him down a well. The information is partly communicated through persistent alternations between scenes which primarily follow Lady Audley and scenes which primarily follow George Talboys: these alternations are in place before any explicit connection has been made between their social spheres, so that the ostensive lack of narrative coherence between the passages implicates an inexplicit connection between the two characters.

With this context established, Braddon employs foreshadowing to cement the reader's expectations of the mystery that is already forming. After Robert receives a letter from Sir Michael's daughter by his first marriage, Alicia, the reader is informed that

> If any one could at that moment have told the young barrister that so simple a thing as his cousin's brief letter would one day come to be a link in that terrible chain of evidence afterwards to be slowly forged in the one only criminal case in which he was ever to be concerned, perhaps Mr. Robert Audley would have lifted his eyebrows a little higher than usual.
>
> (Braddon 1998: 54–55)

Although the criminal nature of the ensuing plot is made explicit, it is telling that it is framed within a conjecture based on the mention of the future crime, the discussion of which is itself hypothetical: the narration of the future 'criminal case' is several removes from factual report.

It is not only that the information is found within a counterfactual conditional, but also that it is the nonfactual information (the presence of a 'criminal case') on which the counterfactual (telling the 'young barrister' about it) of the conditional operates. Moreover, it is noteworthy that the crime already communicated through implicature (bigamy) is unmentioned, with only the mention of a 'criminal case' to indicate the serious and mysterious quality of the unfolding plot. Like the 'secret' that is present in the novel's title, the foreshadowing explicitly communicates the mysterious quality of the plot; this emphasis on mystery alerts the reader that the narrative's incoherence is indicative of as yet 'secret' information. In effect, it acts to turn otherwise irrelevant, incongruous narrative details into ostensive communicators of the inexplicit storyline.

A mockery of the ideal of objectivity is discernible in the unexplained details which, together, implicate Lady Audley's guilt. The inability of Brantlinger's schema to explicate the effect of these narrated details is evident in his treatment of a scene in which Lady Audley orders her maid to send what would be, if revealed, an incriminating telegram: ' "And now listen, Phoebe. What I want you to do is very simple." It was so simple that it was told in five minutes, and then Lady Audley retired into her bed-room' (ch. 7, p. 39). The central mystery [Brantlinger comments], the disappearance of George Talboys, involves the same pattern (1982: 14).

Brantlinger uses this scene as an example of how the narrative 'ceases to convey all information and begins to disguise much of it as hints, clues, hiatuses' (1982: 14). He rightly compares the tactic Braddon uses to communicate Lady Audley's request with the tactic Braddon uses to communicate what happened to George Talboys (although Brantlinger does not mention that it is the accumulation of scenes such as these that implicate what has happened to George; in effect, the described scene is a microcosm of the way implicature operates in the narrative as a whole). However, Brantlinger's specification of the 'hints, clues, hiatuses' Braddon uses to 'disguise' narrative information is misleading. As discussed above, the narrative information presented here is not, and cannot be, disguised, but is rather only partly given: Braddon's narration carries distanced 'objective' report to a satirical degree, reporting only what can be 'overheard' and providing none of the usual narrative commentary that accompanies such report. This narratorial restraint functions as a purer form of narrative objectivity than is found in most realist texts, but also satirises the narrative distance that is often entangled with that objectivity. While narrative omniscience and the aim of objectivity do not necessarily entail narratorial distance, they do often consist of an element of narratorial restraint, in that 'intrusions' (in the form of commentary) are frowned upon. In many passages in *Lady Audley's Secret*, Braddon takes this philosophy to an extreme by refusing to comment on the significance of narrated acts. Although the context of this scene allows the reader to reconstruct the missing narrative information, the very information that the narrative voice omits is the most relevant to the narrative: Lady Audley has ordered Phoebe to send a telegram, requesting that Lady Audley visit London on the same day that George Talboys is expected at Audley Court. The passage implicates not only these concrete details of the plot but also the lengths to which Lady Audley will go to avoid meeting George. Instead of explicitly disclosing this significant information, the distanced narrative voice narrates only a relatively immaterial conversation that could realistically be 'overheard'. In *Lady Audley's Secret*, narrative 'distance' equates with obtuseness, and that obtuseness both satirises the broad aims of realist fiction and makes ostensive the 'mystery' which the passage is instrumental in (inexplicitly) dispersing.

Brantlinger's analysis does not consider that the reader draws on textual context in interpreting the passage quoted in this last excerpt and in effect does not describe how the reader infers that 'Lady Audley orders her maid to send what would be, if revealed, an incriminating telegram'. An examination of the passage's context clarifies how that implicature is constructed. A few sentences prior to giving the instruction, Lady Audley introduces her request by saying 'I want you to go to London by the first train to-morrow morning to execute a little commission for me...I shall give you a five-pound note if you do what I want, and keep your own counsel about it' (Braddon 1998: 61). From these sentences we learn that the task requires Phoebe's presence in London and that it is incriminating or at least delicate enough to warrant a substantial bribe. The larger context and succeeding paragraphs of the passage communicate the task's relevance to the narrative: the reader has previously been made aware that George Talboys's initial visit is expected at Audley Court the next day (Braddon 1998: 58) and soon afterwards learns that a telegraph has reached Lady Audley from London, asking for her immediate presence at the side of an ill former employer (Braddon 1998: 61–62). Because Lady Audley's absence will conveniently allow her to avoid George, the reader infers that it has been prearranged by Phoebe's dispatch of a telegraph.

Other key passages in the text work similarly to evoke a picture of Lady Audley's secret guilt. George's first recognition of Lady Audley is spurred not by meeting her, but by viewing her portrait while she is in London. Braddon writes that

> strange as the picture was, it could not have made any great impression on George Talboys, for he sat before it for about a quarter of an hour without uttering a word – only staring blankly at the painted canvas, with the candlestick grasped in his strong right hand, and his left arm hanging loosely by his side. He sat so long in this attitude, that Robert turned round at last.
>
> 'Why, George, I thought you had gone to sleep!'
>
> 'I had almost.'
>
> 'You've caught a cold from standing in that damp tapestried room. Mark my words, George Talboys, you've caught a cold; you're as hoarse as a raven. But come along.'
>
> Robert Audley took the candle from his friend's hand, and crept back through the secret passage, followed by George, very quiet, but scarcely more quiet than usual.
>
> (Braddon 1998: 72–73)

The phrase 'it could not have made any great impression on George Talboys' is clearly facetious, as the context of the passage confirms. The narratorial irony results from the incongruence between the display of the narrative voice's powers of clarifying commentary in the first paragraph and the converse lack of narratorial clarification in the dialogue underneath and afterwards. As in other key passages of the text, the narrator remains playfully silent as to the factive status and significance of the assertions depicted in the latter half of the passage: whether or not George had almost fallen asleep and whether or not he caught a cold is never explicitly resolved. But the information they suggest – that George spent an unexpectedly long time in front of the portrait and that his voice is now hoarse – provides evidence for the reader (who has narrative context to draw upon) that George has recognised his wife. In this passage's dialogue, Robert plays the role of the unreliable commentator, voicing an obvious misconstruction of narrative information. Brantlinger's analysis does not capture the dramatic irony which arises from Robert's obtuseness (which the narrative voice echoes). Robert, of course, is not privy to as much context as the reader possesses; he has not followed the scenes which sharply alternate between George Talboys and Lady Audley; more importantly, his interpretation is not subject to the conventions of fiction which allow the reader to perceive the ostensiveness with which certain narrative details are or are not presented. The silence with which George's response is communicated, then, not only depicts Robert's obtuse perception of the situation, but functions as a narrative joke of which Robert is the butt: he has been unable to solve a narrative puzzle which is clear to the reader. This silence is ostensive primarily because the reader has become accustomed to the narrator's overt omniscience.

Braddon's use of implicature extends to her depiction of the act that defines the narrative: Lady Audley's attempt to murder her husband. Unlike the previous passages discussed, it does not immediately implicate the information which, in retrospect, it is gradually perceived to have represented; instead, it merely indicates that the primary 'secret' denoted in the novel's title has occurred. When interpreted in the context of narrative information later given, however, the passage implicates Lady Audley's murder of George Talboys. Braddon writes:

> ...my lady had strolled, book in hand, into the shadowy lime-walk; so [Audley Court] had never worn a more peaceful aspect than on that bright afternoon when George Talboys walked across the lawn to ring a sonorous peal at the sturdy, iron-bound oak door.
>
> The servant who answered his summons told him that Sir Michael was out, and my lady walking in the lime-tree avenue.
>
> He looked a little disappointed at this intelligence, and muttering something about wishing to see my lady, or going to look for my lady...strode away from the door without leaving either card or message for the family.
>
> It was full an hour and a half after this when Lady Audley returned to the house, not coming from the lime-walk, but from exactly the opposite direction...
>
> (Braddon 1998: 80)

After the omitted 'hour and a half' of the narrative George Talboys disappears from the text and as this disappearance is sustained the implicature asserting George's death gains strength. By reducing the scene in which Lady Audley pushes George down a well to the undisclosed action of 'an hour and a half', Braddon forces all information the reader has about the pivotal scene to be inferred from the scene's context. While the scene does not immediately implicate George's murder, it is physically demarcated (and rendered relevant) by the explicit mention of the passage of time, thereby manifesting its relevance to the interpretation of the overall narrative. The passage is further foregrounded by the detail with which the (unnarrated) encounter is introduced. The scene is set for the long-awaited first interaction between George Talboys and his estranged wife; after this scene is omitted, the reader is told that Lady Audley returns to the house from the opposite direction in which she had been walking – implying that something has interfered with the expected course of her walk and that something (of considerable duration) has happened. What has happened, however, is only communicated by the passage's context and by the accumulation of further speciously irrelevant details in the narrative that follows. At a local level, Braddon's narration is limited in both the strength of its communication (it 'implies', rather than 'implicates') and what it communicates (it communicates only that something has happened). But these local implications help build the global implicature on which the most prominent narrative effect of *Lady Audley's Secret* relies: the indirect communication of the plot's central action (the attempted murder of George Talboys).

Unlike 'true omissions' within narratives, this gap in explicit narration does not truly omit or 'disguise' the information it purportedly does not communicate. Instead, the gap demarcated by the explicit mention of a lapsed 'hour and a half' calls attention to the information which surrounds it, characterising it as related to the 'secret' and 'criminal case' already introduced into the narrative. Because there are 80 preceding pages on which the reader may draw, the passage reliably communicates that Lady Audley and George have just met; however, it coyly backs away from describing more than how long the meeting took. When reading passages further along in the narrative, the reader is able to recall the omission of this scene; in the context of information that the narrator later adds, it implicates that Lady Audley has killed George Talboys.

The implicatures on which the story builds continue from this point, echoing the deductions Robert makes but teasingly stopping short of the conclusions he reaches. Robert begins to suspect Lady Audley when, shortly after George's disappearance, he notices a bruise on her wrist. When asked how the bruise occurred, Lady Audley responds

> I am rather absent in mind, and amused myself a few days ago by tying a piece of ribbon round my arm so tightly, that it left a bruise when I removed it.
>
> 'Hum!' thought Robert. 'My lady tells little childish white lies; the bruise is of a more recent date than a few days ago; the skin has only just begun to change colour.'

> Sir Michael took the slender wrist in his strong hand.
>
> 'Hold the candles, Robert,' he said, 'and let us look at this poor little arm.'
>
> It was not one bruise, but four slender, purple marks, such as might have been made by the four fingers of a powerful hand that had grasped the delicate wrist a shade too roughly. A narrow ribbon, bound tightly, might have left some such marks, it is true, and my lady protested once more that, to the best of her recollection, that must have been how they were made.
>
> Across one of the faint purple marks there was a darker tinge, as if a ring worn on one of these strong and cruel fingers had been ground into the tender flesh.
>
> 'I am sure my lady must tell white lies,' thought Robert, 'for I can't believe the story of the ribbon.'
>
> (Braddon 1998: 91)

In introducing a discussion of Robert's deductive skills, Carnell notes of this passage that the 'reader and Robert Audley think she has George's blood on those hands. Robert shows detective abilities, as he notices clues that no one else does, and Braddon succeeds especially in details like this because the reader follows his thoughts, sharing his investigation' (2000: 253). While Carnell's discussion aptly explains Robert's position as 'detective' in the narrative, she does not address the broader narrative problem of how it is that the information presented in the above passage convinces the reader and Robert that Lady Audley 'has George's blood on those hands'. On an explicit level, Robert only notices that Lady Audley must be lying, a conclusion explicitly linked to the colour of her bruise. According to reader interpretations that are based only on the passage's explicit content, the two paragraphs lying between Robert's assertion and reassertion of this conclusion must be irrelevant; there is no explicit link made between their content and the conclusion that is attributed to Robert. Carnell's assertion that the above details are indicative of Robert's thoughts is untenable, considering that Robert has not yet begun to consider that George might have been physically harmed (two pages later he leaves for London, expecting to find George there). It would also be socially incongruous for an unrelated man to grasp Robert's aunt's hand as the details suggest: in Robert's social context and his current state of awareness, it would be a surprising mental leap for him to form such conclusions.

The paragraphs are jarringly specific and detailed for an analysis of a bruise; the passage provides a suspiciously detailed speculation as to what 'might have' produced an ambiguous mark. In this passage, the narrative voice abruptly pulls back from the objectivity it has supposedly practiced and encourages lurid conjectures that far surpass what their context evidences. Moreover, it is only, on an explicit level, a hypothesis that is detailed; the narration leaps from one extreme of minimal commentary to another which details an unlikely hypothesis. This incongruity implicates the truth of what is being posed as conjecture: the specificity of the cause's description clashes with the vagueness expected of discussions concerning hypothetical occurrences, causing the reader to re-evaluate his or her view of the description as hypothetical. In relevance-theoretic terms, the space devoted to a concept that is explicitly designated as nonfactual is disproportionate. As Sperber and Wilson note,

> Information processing involves effort; it will only be undertaken in the expectation of some reward. There is thus no point in drawing someone's attention to a phenomenon unless it will seem relevant enough to him to be worth his attention . . . ostension comes with a tacit guarantee of relevance. (49)

It is the length and excessive detail of this passage that necessitate an effort on the reader's part which is not commensurate with the hypothetical status of the information communicated. The detailed conjectures in these paragraphs act ostensively, leading the reader to expect 'some reward' more relevant to the overall storyline than a hypothetical aside. The 'tacit guarantee of relevance' which ostensive communication carries spurs the reader to reconsider the information's status as nonfactual.

While an interpretation that includes Pratt's assumption of literariness would conclude that the passage's implicated factuality is a result of the reader's perception of the description as deliberately disproportionate, an interpretation that includes an assumption of narratorial omniscience would be more specific, claiming that the passage is felt to be deliberately disproportionate because the omniscient communicator of the narrative would not devote so much space and detail to a description it knows to be irrelevant to the narrative. This fictional-level attribution of narratorial (as opposed to authorial) intention allows the reader to conclude that the information itself is factual and that it is the proposed nonfactiveness of it that is facetious. The reader's assumption of narratorial omniscience, then, is capable of explaining not only why the nonfactual language of the passage seems motivated (which a reader's assumption of literariness explains) but also what specifically that motivation is, why it leads the reader to assume that Lady Audley 'has George's blood on those hands'.

5 Conclusion

The above discussion of *Lady Audley's Secret* attempts not to interpret it in a new light, but to explain existing interpretations of the novel. The reader interpretations assumed by my pragmatic analysis are evidenced by contemporary reactions to the novel as well as the more recent ones discussed above. An early review in *The Morning Post* claimed, for instance, that the 'identity of Helen Talboys and Lucy, Lady Audley is apparent at once to the reader'. The writer goes on to remark upon 'the slow and deliberate revelation of crime' ('Lady Audley's Secret' 1862: 6). This narrative revelation is the result of sustained, central uses of implicature that exploit the reader's assumption of the narrator's omniscience. Although the novel is judged as stylish and clever, the reviewer feels the need to point out that the 'story is unredeemed by any touch of the higher sentiments of human nature, and in this lies the grave defect of the author' (1862: 6). A deliberate humour in the narration of the plot's serious events, enacted by these same implicatures, is responsible for the lack of '[high] sentiments' attributed to Braddon; this same humour, however, enables her to both exploit and comment quietly on realist conventions.

Notes

1. In fact, Radford's phrase 'novel with a secret' is taken from Kathleen Tillotson's well-known characterisation of sensation novels as 'novels with a secret' (Brantlinger 1982: 1).
2. Face-saving implicatures are implicatures which arise in an attempt to minimize the effect of a 'Face-Threatening Act' (as discussed by Brown and Levinson 1987). These implicatures are often used in Victorian novels to indicate sexual acts and other impolite topics.
3. Despite Brantlinger's doubts concerning 'the secretive or somehow remiss narrator-author' in *Lady Audley's Secret* (which stem largely from his conflation of narrative omission and implicature), he characterises sensation fiction as a subversive subgenre of the dominant realist mode and its 'undoing [of] narrative omniscience' as indicative of this subversion (1982: 26).

11

Literature as Discourse and Dialogue: Rapport Management (Facework) in Emine Sevgi Özdamar's 'Blackeye and His Donkey'

Chantelle Warner

1 Introduction

When national newspaper *Die Zeit* requested that she express her opinion about current (here: early 1990s, post-unification) relations between Germans and minorities (*Ausländer*), highly acclaimed author, actress and playwright Emine Sevgi Özdamar responded with a vignette titled, 'Blackeye and His Donkey' ('Schwarzauge und sein Esel'). Özdamar, who was born in Turkey but has lived much of her adult life in Düsseldorf and Berlin, warned the editors in a letter, 'I am writing something. But it is completely different from what you expect' (1993: 1).[1] With the final clause Özdamar locates her text within a particular field of linguistic practice in which expectations are managed and negotiated based on previous textual experiences and in this way the author points directly to the 'horizon of expectations' or 'discourse world' or 'frame of relevance' that she anticipates her readers share. Her response, a literary anecdote about her experiences directing the play *Blackeye in Germany* (originally titled in Turkish and German as *Karagöz in Alemania* and *Schwarzauge in Deutschland* respectively), is also, importantly, an act of what Erving Goffman called 'footing' (1981), in that Özdamar aligns herself differentially to the interaction initiated by *Die Zeit*. While the first observation relates to discourse in the post-Foucauldian sense in which it is most often understood in contemporary literary and cultural studies,[2] this second observation opens up a very different line of interrogation. What do these expectations say about her readers as people who expect certain kinds of things? Why would they expect it from her? What does this say about their image of her? What claims does she make for herself by flouting these expectations? These questions pertain less to the cognitive and socio-culturally embedded processes by which writers and readers make sense out of the text and more to what their discourse, in the sense of social acts of meaning-making, might say about them and the dynamic relationships between them.

Like few other terms, the word 'discourse' has become deeply embedded in the lexicons of numerous and diverse fields of language and literature-focused disciplines. Whereas scholarship in contemporary literary criticism and cultural studies has tended to emphasise the ways in which literary works manifest discursive formations in the sense of socially endorsed values, beliefs, attitudes and identities, scholars in stylistics and literary linguistics have tended to focus on how stretches of literary language function as discourse in the sense of actual events of communication.[3] The relation between these two levels of discourse (one referring to individual encounters between writers and readers, the other referring to institutionalised ways of being and thinking in the world – has often been neglected, in part perhaps because the shared term 'discourse' somewhat obscures the very distinction between the two.[4] Within areas of interpersonal pragmatics, however, scholars have productively analysed how the social and linguistic behaviours of interactants position them vis-à-vis the situation at hand and the other participants, and in doing so work to maintain or disrupt existing social orders.[5] In this chapter, I look to this work in interpersonal pragmatics and in particular interactional theories of face and rapport management as a model for analysing published literary utterances as dialogic and relational acts in which both levels of discourse intersect. Using the aforementioned piece by Emine Sevgi Özdamar, 'Blackeye and His Donkey,' which was published in *Die Zeit* in a special feature on multiculturalism in Germany, I demonstrate how illocutionary and stylistic choices might function as strategies for rapport management in encounters with real readers and explore some of the potential benefits and analytical problems that arise in an interactional approach to the pragmatics of literary texts.

2 Societal discourse and social discourse

Since the 1970s and 1980s, work in literary studies in North America and many European countries has been informed by cultural studies and historicist paradigms (e.g. New Historicism), which regard literary works as manifestations of socio-political discourses. Discourse here is understood as referring to structures of knowledge and power relations embodied in language and other signifying practices. According to this view, the task of literary scholars is to locate the work(s) in a web of historical conditions, relationships and influences (see Gallagher and Greenblatt 2000). Impassioned by critical theories from feminism, postcolonialism and cultural materialism, to name a few, the study of literature has also often taken on political commitments; through critical analyses of old and new literary writings, scholars aim to retrace and explore historically misrecognised mechanisms of repression and subjugation. The role of literary studies, now augmented by cultural studies, became in general more anthropological and socio-political and less linguistic (see Klein 2005 for a discussion of these shifts within the humanities).

The somewhat hasty sketch provided here points to a general trend in literary studies over the past few decades towards historicist methods and a preoccupation with the societal implications of literary discourse. This has yielded many valuable insights into the intersections between literary and other symbolic practices; however, the tendency to treat literary texts as manifestations of culture has disconnected the actual social and cognitive act of reading from the participation of the literary utterance in more diffuse discursive fields. Within cultural studies, real readers and their concerns are often either neglected or relegated to a more or less rhetorical role as generic arbiters of cultural evaluations and predispositions (seen in the ubiquity of expressions such as 'the sophisticated reader').

Parallel to the cultural turn in literary studies, stylistics and literary linguistics have evolved semi-independently into equally inter – and transdisciplinary fields of research. Whereas literary studies moved in the direction of cultural studies, stylistics and literary linguistics were shaped by advances in linguistics, including areas such as discourse analysis, socio-linguistics and pragmatics. Stylistics has taken on discourse as both an analytical object and a pre-modifier (e.g. 'discourse stylistics'; see Simpson and Hall 2002), as literary-linguistic inquiry moved beyond more formalist analysis of sentence-level phenomena and towards the study of complex stretches of text in their contexts of use. Stylistic effect and meaning have been understood not as stable and fixed features of texts but as products of a 'dialogic interaction' (Weber 1996: 3) between writers and real readers, both those contemporary with the author and those who encounter the work in less immediate historical and cultural circumstances. An interest in literature as discourse in the sense of *language in use* also led to the emergence of a number of allied and subordinate fields related to discourse stylistics, including most importantly for my purposes here, literary pragmatics and pragmatic stylistics.[6] Scholars working in these areas use principles and concepts from pragmatic theory in order to explicate various textual effects and stylistic phenomena including implicature and *impoliteness*.

In recent years, literary pragmatic scholarship inspired by relevance theory and neo-Gricean approaches (see this volume) has yielded valuable insights into how readers make sense out of literary language. However, it has had less to say about the social dimension of literary reading practices – the ways in which acts of writing, reading, interpretive response and uptake (see Freadman 2002) are interpersonal events of communication. To develop a model of literary pragmatics that can bring together the study of literary discourse as an interpersonal event and as a stakeholder in socio-historical discussions and debates requires that we treat literary works as not first and foremost representational or informational but as interactional. That is to say that in order to take up, take on, challenge or critique societal discourses, literature must also participate in social acts of encounter with actual readers. The object of such study is, to quote pragmatics scholar Jacob Mey, 'the kinds of effects that authors, as text producers, set out to obtain, using the resources of language in their efforts to establish a "working cooperation" with their audiences, the consumers of the texts' (Mey 1999: 12). As was the case with the call and response that led to Özdamar's piece in *Die Zeit*, a 'working cooperation' does not necessitate that the author meets the exact expectations put upon her, but it does compel her to carefully negotiate the constituent dialogical dynamics.

The scholarly reception of Emine Sevgi Özdamar's works has tended to situate her writings within discussions (read: societal discourses) of minor literatures, migration and transnationalism (e.g. Jankowsky 1997; Seyhan 2000; Johnson 2001; Shafi 2003; Ergin 2013). These same aspects of the author's identity were invoked in the editor's initial request that she speak to the relations between Germans and immigrants in German society. Özdamar first came to the Federal Republic of Germany in 1965 along with the waves of guest workers who were recruited through a government programme to ameliorate the labour shortage experienced in West Germany in the wake of the economic upturn and the suspension of Eastern immigration. While working in a factory in Berlin for nearly two years, Özdamar was exposed to the work of famed playwright Bertolt Brecht and ultimately decided to go back to Turkey in order to commence her study of the theatre in 1967. She then returned to Germany in 1976, to pursue a career in the theatre. In 1982, her first play *Karagöz in Alemania*, also known under the German title *Schwarzauge in Deutschland* (*Blackeye in Germany*), began production with the Bochum Schauspielhaus. It is this play that is referenced in the title of Özdamar's contribution to *Die Zeit*, 'Blackeye and His Donkey'.

Although her earliest literary pursuits were theatrical, by the mid 1990s, Özdamar had received much recognition as an author of poetry and prose works, in particular for her collection *Mother Tongue* (*Mutterzunge* 1990) and the novel *Life is a Carawanserai Has Two Doors I Went in One I Came out the Other* (*Das Leben ist eine Karawanserei, hat zwei Türen, aus einer kam ich rein, aus der anderen ging ich raus*, 1992). Although her literary acclaim would have certainly contributed to the editors' choice of Özdamar as a respondent, it was likely based on her biographical profile, her personal experiences as an immigrant and her identity as a member of Germany's largest and most visible minority group that she was asked to offer her viewpoint on the state of affairs for minorities living in Germany.

Scholars and authors have criticised the 'biographical trap' into which minority authors fall as soon as they take up writing (e.g. see Şenocak 2006) and because of this authors who are identified as members of ethnic and cultural minorities are often made to function as pseudoethnographers rather than as legitimate literary authors. In these discussions, the focus often remains representational, although the author is positioned not in a cultural niche or social milieu, but on the stage of national or world literature, and the tenor tends to be prescriptive in that it more or less overtly privileges certain practices of writing and reading. The pragmatic dynamics of these literacy practices are, however, not the subject of analysis. Exploring the illocutionary force and the potential perlocutionary effects of literary utterances and how these are negotiated stylistically within systems of politeness and rapport requires a social theory of literary speech acts, which acknowledges that authors and readers only act as arbiters of societal discourses through actual events of communication.[7] In the sections that follow, I draw on Erving Goffman's (1967) interactional theory and Helen Spencer-Oatey's (2000, 2005, 2007, 2009) adaptation of some of his concepts into a relational model of what she calls 'rapport management' in order to consider the discursive, stylistic and illocutionary resources Özdamar takes up in her literary response to *Die Zeit* and in doing so, to propose a more interactional model for studying literary discourse.

3 Literature as social rapport

One of the most influential concepts within interactional theories continues to be Erving Goffman's notion of face, 'the positive social value a person effectively claims for himself by the line others assume he has taken during a particular contact' (1967: 5). Facework, for Goffman, corresponds to how social actors claim for themselves and acknowledge in others certain social values attributed to the verbal and nonverbal actions they undertake in a line of talk (1967: 5). Like comparable terms from cultural studies such as representation and identity, face is linked to the maintenance of social orders. Through facework we maintain, reinforce, or even contest hierarchies and social positions. Thus, it pertains, as Goffman claims, not to 'men and their moments, but moments and their men' (1967: 3). But whereas cultural representations and social identities are positioned within systems of discourse, for example as ways of talking about and symbolising multiculturalism, face as an inherently relational concept emerges in a particular moment of interaction.

From the then nascent field of pragmatics, scholars Brown and Levinson embraced Goffman's work on face as a foundation for theorising politeness. In their much-cited book *Politeness: Some Universals in Language Use* (1987) Brown and Levinson construed politeness as the interactional rituals through which we protect face – both our own and that of our interlocutors. In their work, they develop a detailed typology of face and politeness. Included in their framework is a distinction not found in Goffman's writing between positive face – one's desire to have the self-image that one claims recognised, appreciated and approved of by others – and negative face – the individual's need not to be imposed upon, to act freely and to claim their own space (both figuratively and literally) (Brown and Levinson 1987: 61). According to Brown and Levinson, all adults in society have positive and negative face and they must actively negotiate their own wants and needs with their interlocutors in the midst of interaction.

The detailed typology of facework provided in *Politeness: Some Universals of Language Use* (1987) has proved productive for many scholars who wish to identify linguistic forms of politeness. At the same time, many scholars in pragmatics and social interaction theory have criticised Brown and Levinson's model for being overly individualistic (see Werkhofer 1992; Spencer-Oatey 2000, 2007, 2009; Bargiela-Chiappini 2003; Arundale 2006, 2009, 2010). In particular Bargiela-Chiappini (2003), Arundale (2006, 2009) and Spencer-Oatey (2007) have stressed that face is an interactional and dyadic phenomenon. For Brown and Levinson, face needs and wants are something that we carry around with us as psycho-social beings and which come under threat in interaction. For the pragmatics scholars that I have cited here, face meanings are not held by the individual actors but are as co-constituted as emergent properties of social interaction.

It is in this way that face differs importantly with identity. Whereas face is an *in situ* phenomenon, identity is a more durable, dimension of self-image (e.g. Arundale 2006; Spencer-Oatey 2007). Returning to Goffman's work, Spencer-Oatey (2007) has further argued that face, unlike identity only relates to the positive attributes that an individual wishes to claim and have acknowledged in a particular moment of interaction. As Tae-Seop Lim writes, 'face is not what one thinks of oneself, but what one thinks others should think of one's worth' (1994: 210). Because identity is a broader concept, that describes a person's sense of belonging in the social world, it is constituted by both positive and negative traits. Both levels of self-image – face and identity – are constructed dialogically and dynamically through our interactions with others, but identity holds a certain historicity, while the specific attributes that are sensitive to face vary greatly across interactional contexts. Spencer-Oatey does see overlap between the two levels of self-image in what she calls *identity face*, an individual's claims to social identities and group roles. *Identity face* is opposed to *quality face*, which relates to positive, personal attributes such as kindness.

Spencer-Oatey's understanding of face is embedded within a model of what she calls 'rapport management.' Rapport management involves the ways in which language is used to construct, maintain and/or threaten social relationships between interactants. Along with face, Spencer-Oatey posits a second concept, *sociality rights*, which encompasses our social expectancies with regard to 'personal/social entitlements... fairness, consideration, social inclusion/exclusion and so on' (2000: 14). She further divides sociality rights into two subcategories – *equity rights*, which are premised on the fundamental belief that each person has the right to personal consideration and fairness, and *association rights*, the fundamental belief that we are entitled to receive empathy and respect from others (2000: 14). Because face is an emergent phenomenon, speech acts are not inherently threatening to face or sociality rights. Participants' intentions and perceptions of speech acts depend upon the context of interaction, interactants' social (behavioural) expectations and how they orient themselves in interaction (for example, challengingly or positively) (Spencer-Oatey 2005).

The earliest theories of politeness and facework tended to adopt a Gricean view of communication as typically cooperative. More recently, several scholars have taken up the notion of 'aggressive facework' or impoliteness, a form of interaction which Goffman mentions but hardly develops in his essay on the subject (see Bousfield 2008; Bousfield and Locher 2008; Culpeper 2011). Jonathan Culpeper, for example, develops a framework for the study of impolite behaviours along the same conceptual orientations theorised by Spencer-Oatey in her model of rapport management, namely face and sociality rights (Culpeper 2011: 256). Among those impoliteness strategies targeting face are deliberate insults and pointed criticism, unpalatable questions and uncomfortable presuppositions. Various forms of exclusionary behaviour constitute impoliteness strategies that are oriented towards the association rights of interactants. Finally, equity rights can be infringed upon through patronising behaviour, failure to appropriately reciprocate behavioural norms, literal and metaphorical encroachment on the other's personal space and the display of taboo behaviours.

While her identity as a prominent Turkish-German may have motivated the editors of *Die Zeit* to invite Özdamar to write for the issue, the ways in which she manages readers' expectations beyond the content of the message pertain to what I have described above as rapport management. Rather than contributing an opinion piece, Özdamar begins by telling the story of her first play. This is an overt decision to select a speech act that is different from that which was requested (i.e. an anecdote instead of a opinion piece) as an initial shift in footing which frames the rapport for the remaining duration of interaction. In what follows, I argue that we can consider a published piece such as Özdamar's as a turn in an extended dialogue, which includes public reviews and the author's previous works so that we can then productively analyse how linguistic and stylistic elements of the text are implicated in processes of rapport management with an indeterminate but nevertheless very real audience of readers.

4 Özdamar's writing in dialogue: Managing rapport with readers across illocutionary, discourse and stylistics domains

The request from *Die Zeit* that is referenced in the introduction to 'Blackeye and His Donkey' frames the work as a dialogic rejoinder in a conversation between Özdamar and the editors. But the participant structures of published pieces such as this are never straightforward dyads and the broad and varied public audience in relation to whom a published author positions herself and with whom she must build rapport presents an analytical problem for the study of facework in literary works; however, published works often do carry with them documented histories of reception including, for example, reviews from both professional and non-professional readers. In all likelihood it was this kind of published reception that informed Özdamar's anticipation of what the editors (and other potential readers) might or might not expect. For this reason, it is necessary to look beyond the immediate co-text of 'Blackeye and His Donkey' in order to frame Özdamar's contribution within an extended dialogue between her and her reading public.

In 1991, Özdamar became the first non-native speaker of German to win the prestigious Ingeborg Bachmann Prize for literature based on an excerpt from her novel *Life is a Caravanserai, it has two doors I came in one I went out the other* (*Das Leben ist eine Karawanserei, hat zwei Türen, aus einer kam ich rein, aus der anderen ging ich raus*, 1992), often shortened to *Caravanserai*. This led to a public debate about the status of German literature as some commentators viewed Özdamar's award as a turning point towards expanded definitions of 'Germanness' and 'German literature' (see Janowsky 1997), while others contended that it was her minority status rather than her talents that were being rewarded (see also Jankowsky 1997; Johnson 2001; Gramling 2010). Özdamar's *Caravanserai* was juxtaposed with the work that came in second, Urs Alleman's avant garde novel *Babyficker* (*Babyfucker* 1992), a work noted for its experimentalist prose and language play. Özdamar, on the other hand, was cast as the moral but naïve storyteller whose clumsy language 'vouches for its authenticity' (Bohl 1991: 7). Even in some of the most positive critical reception of the work, it was not the magical realist elements of her writing that were praised, but rather the 'beloved oriental ingredients' (Ebel 1991).

In the afterword to the collection *Mother Tongue* (1990), Özdamar writes that she was accepted into the German literary scene, 'but only as a guest writer,' a play on the phrase 'guest worker', which was used by the West German government in their recruitment campaigns. The implication is that Turkish writers, like Turkish workers, certainly enrich the German host society and German literary traditions, but their participation status in also only ever contingent, fleeting and marginal. It is worth noting that Özdamar's *Caravanserai* was involved in another literary scandal in 2007, when author and media personality Feridun Zaimoğlu was accused of plagiarising aspects of her novel in his book *Leyla*. In his defence, Zaimoğlu confessed that his novel was in fact predicated on an ethnographic source, namely interviews that he had conducted with his mother.[8] In the plagiarism scandal, again questions of social identity, authenticity, creativity, aesthetics and social relevance were raised, similar to those that framed the debate around Özdamar's 1991 Ingeborg Bachmann Prize. Although she has been the recipient of numerous literary prizes in the decade and a half that had ensued, public attention once again turned to the documentary aspects of her work as Zaimoğlu insisted that any parallels between the two works must stem from the similarities in his mother's and Emine Sevgi Özdamar's biographies.

The word 'literature' in contemporary society, and certainly in German society, bears a particular *symbolic power* (Bourdieu 1993) and the status of *literary author* its own prestige, honour, and attention. In his writings on the field of cultural production, Bourdieu argues that the value of literature, as least in Western cultural traditions since the 18th century, lies in its cultivated claim to be pure, disinterested creation, in short, art for art's sake (1993: 34). Literature can thus be contrasted with other cultural practices, such as documentary representation. Whereas quality literature is evaluated based on its creativity and originality, documentary works are at their best authentic and mimetic (see Warner 2011, 2012). While these two positions often become polarised, as they did in the two debates that surrounded Özdamar's *Caravanserai* in 1991 and 2007, the author herself seems to call this into question at the beginning of 'Blackeye and His Donkey' when she tells her readers that after reading the aforementioned letter from a Turkish guest worker, 'I wanted to write a drama about him and to invite him to Germany for the premier. I wanted to show him that his life was a novel – just like he had claimed in his book' (1993: 1).[9]

Although the editors of *Die Zeit* had asked Özdamar to express her opinion about current events, she did so by writing about her art, indicating that the two are closely linked, but also that this would not be what the editors would expect. Spencer-Oatey has noted that face is only affectively salient when there is incongruency between an attribute claimed or denied and a trait perceived as being ascribed by others (2007: 11). Given the critical reception of her earlier works and the request from *Die Zeit* that she should submit what is in effect a piece of folk ethnography based on her personal experiences as a member of the Turkish–German minority, it seems reasonable that Özdamar's social identity face as a literary author was affectively salient. Adopting a literary style in the response to *Die Zeit* can thus be viewed as a move of facework through which she attempts to claim for herself the values that are associated with the role of literary author rather than those that have been bestowed upon her as a member of a minority group.

I have argued elsewhere that experiential testimonies from individuals who are identified with socially marginalised groups, such as ethnic minorities, are often perceived by some readers as face-threatening acts, since they may sense that they are directly or indirectly implicated in the author's feelings of oppression and exclusion (see Warner 2012, ch. 6). If rapport is not managed accordingly, readers may feel that their individual or collective face as a member of dominant society is unduly threatened, they may become antagonistic to the narrator's account, refusing to acknowledge the positive face that they claim for themselves and even refusing to 'listen' by simply ceasing to read or, in the case of Özdamar's text, refusing to publish. For this reason, politeness and impoliteness are often overtly thematised in these works to the extent that facework and sociality rights relate both to the content message of these works and the desired perlocutionary effects they bring about in their readers.

Lim and Bowers have noted that facework may be influenced by perceptions of the speaker's right to performance of a given act in a given situation more than the absolute face threat of an act, (Lim and Bowers 1991: 10). This pertains to what researchers including Spencer-Oatey (2000: 19–20) have identified as the *illocutionary domain* of rapport management, the interactional repercussions of different speech acts. Following work by other scholars, Spencer-Oatey notes that this is the domain to which Brown and Levinson (1987) devote the most attention in their model of politeness, since they are most concerned with speech acts that are typically associated with facework, such as requests, compliments and apologies; however, within the more emergent model of facework and rapport management that I am working with here it becomes clear that facework encompasses a much broader body of speech acts than those acknowledged by Brown and Levinson. The choice of illocutionary act (narrative versus commentary) performs the initial shift in footing in 'Blackeye and His Donkey' but the management of rapport does not end there. In order to examine how face and sociality rights are negotiated throughout the text, I turn my attention now to two of the other domains of rapport management: the discourse domain and the stylistic domain.

In responding with a literary prose piece, Özdamar may not have given the editors of *Die Zeit* the illocutionary act that they expected, a choice which I have interpreted as a move of aggressive facework through which she asserts her position and prowess as a literary author.

She does however maintain their choice of topic. While the decision to depict the relations between minorities and Germans in response to a request that she write on exactly this topic, might seem uninterestingly obvious, given that Özdamar disregarded the text type assigned by the editors, Özdamar's management of this topic is worthy of attention.

In Spencer-Oatey's model, the selection and negotiation of topic relates to what she calls the *discourse domain*. From the purview of Spencer-Oatey's interpersonal pragmatics, discourse in the sense of what gets talked about is a communicative resource for rapport. The strategies through which Turkish–German authors cope with what Tom Cheesman calls the 'burden of representation,' the thematic demand placed on minority authors by virtue of their social identity, seem to me to be examples of rapport management in the discourse domain. Authors can choose to overtly explore issues of identity and difference (what Cheesman calls *axialism*), to parody discourses of migration and multiculturalism by exaggerating the clichés and stereotypes to the point of absurdity (*parodic ethnicisation*), or to widen the cultural-historical perspective beyond minority issues into the broader study of the individual and society (Cheesman 2006: 486). In addition, Cheesman lists 'refusal' as one of the strategies, in effect pointing to the pragmatic effect of this thematic lacuna, a present absence (Stockwell 2009: 25) experienced by readers when a minority author writes about something other than a minority theme. With these options in mind, all of which respond to a compulsion to write about minority experiences, Özdamar's choice of laconically narrated autobiographical anecdotes, in which she depicts the very specific, local experiences that she had as a playwright and producer in Germany can be recognised as an element of the deliberate design of her text and the relations between her and her readers (including the most explicit addressees, the editors of *Die Zeit*).

By conceptualising distinct domains within which face and sociality rights are negotiated, Spencer-Oatey illustrates the complexity of rapport management, while also providing a framework within which different dimensions of facework and sociality rights can be clearly identified. When applied to the analysis of literary texts, Spencer-Oatey's model highlights the social, interpersonal dimensions of the writing and reading, which are often obscured in studies that focus only on the text as a manifestation of societal-level discourses. Within the framework of pragmatics, the illocutionary act of authoring a literary text is no more a given than the acceptance of the topic, relationships between minorities and ethnic Germans.

Two of the other dimensions that Spencer-Oatey identifies – the *participation domain,* which relates to procedural aspects of interaction (e.g. turn-taking, overlaps, pauses) and the *non-verbal domain,* (e.g. gesture, intonation, multimodality) are vital in many face-to-face encounters, but they are less relevant to works of written discourse that adhere to conventionalised publication formats, such as a piece in a newspaper. The final domain, the *stylistic,* which Spencer-Oatey associates with tone, lexis, syntax, address and honorifics (2000: 20), could also be understood as including the full range of effects studied by researchers in stylistics.

In 'Blackeye and His Donkey' two aspects of style are most salient in the management of rapport: indirectness and irony. The piece consists of numerous anecdotes from the creation and production of the play, which was first performed in Germany featuring a cast of international actors (plus a sheep and a lamb), delivered in a style that is almost bereft of commentary. She begins 'Blackeye and His Donkey' by revealing the original inspiration for the play, the letter that she had found from a Turkish guest worker. She then describes how she set off on a trip to Turkey, travelling in a train car filled with Turks, Greeks and Yugoslavians, to invite the guest worker to come to view the play. Her observation that many of the Yugoslavian builders who boarded the train in Austria 'had intentionally broken their own fingers with a hammer, so that they could receive sick leave, and rode with bandaged hands to their wives in Yugoslavia' (2) is left to stand alone at the end of a paragraph. She then goes on to describe the Turkish fathers who join them with empty coffins. They were on their way to pick up the bodies of their dead sons in Yugoslavia, where they had perished in a car accident on the drive back to Turkey from Germany. She ends this section with the following:

> ... the common language was German. A sort of oratory emerged, and the mistakes that we made in the German language were us. We had nothing but our mistakes.

In these final two sentences, Özdamar departs gently from the relatively laconic narrative style of the preceding paragraphs, although it is still left open to the reader to interpret what is meant in these final moments of reflection. The lack of direct commentary invites what in relevance theory might be described as weak implicatures, which contribute to the poetic effect of the passage (see Pilkington 1991, 1992, 2000). They also invoke what in politeness theory following Brown and Levinson is called off-record politeness, a strategy for diminishing the face threat associated with a given speech act by performing it only implicitly (Brown and Levinson 1987: 12, 14). In other words this intended meaning is conveyed indirectly, leaving the reader largely responsible for determining the possible import of what is said, for example any possible parallels between the rhetorical artistry in the mistakes implied by the word 'oratory' (as opposed to talk or chatter) and the supposed naïveté of Özdamar's novelistic prose alleged in the wake of the Bachmann Prize scandal. In a sense, Özdamar compounds her rejection of the requested illocutionary act, an opinion piece, by implicating the reader in the act of evaluation.

Özdamar devotes the second half of 'Blackeye and His Donkey' to the interactions between the actors and stage crew from the play *Blackeye in Germany*. As she describes it, the mood on stage was in the first days of production 'hallow'. 'For the first time a theatrical work about Turks! Quiet voices – love glances. Slow movements.' This reverent atmosphere lasted a week, she writes. 'After a week, the normal difficulties of rehearsal started up.' By prefacing the interactions that follow as examples of the 'normal difficulties' that arise in the production of a play, Özdamar seems to undercut a presupposition inherent in the topic suggested by *Die Zeit*, namely that relations between Germans and minorities are somehow qualitatively different from other social relations. In this sense, there is a slight shift of footing within the discourse domain towards the strategy that Cheesman dubbed *glocalism* in that the specific relations of the actors in her play are located within the larger context of theatre productions; however, this same shift is potentially undercut by the series of ethnically-shaded insults that follow. For example:

> The Turkish star wanted to show the German star, who was playing the Turk, how to play a guest worker. The German star told him: 'You caraway-Turk, learn how to speak proper English for once.' The Turkish star said to him: 'You SS Man, you are SS man.'

In each of these instances the primary interaction involves the assignment of an ethnic stereotype to the addressee. In terms of rapport management, each of these quotes from the cast contains a deliberate insult to the quality face of the collective of which the individual is a member. The juxtaposition of utterances also makes clear that each turn is simultaneously an act of impoliteness and a face-saving move. For example, the code-switch to English functions both as a face-saving act, since it indexes at least a rudimentary knowledge of English, and as a more aggressive move of facework, since it associates the German actor (and possibly all Germans?) with Nazis. If these episodes are intended to be representative (a deduction that is only weakly implicated by the text), then Özdamar seems to suggest that intercultural relations are in general dominated by aggressive facework.

At the same time, Özdamar's presentation of these reported speech acts is delivered in an ironic tone. This is perhaps especially clear in the first two exchanges. The apparent absurdity of a Turk teaching a German how to play a Turk and of the German's suggestion that English proficiency would better qualify the Turkish star to do this would not be lost on most readers. A similar device can be found in a later passage where Özdamar tells the reader:

> The artistic director was a nice man. He loved the work. When an actress had to say, 'I staying back. My husband Germany. Staying fucking German women,' he said: 'Please, don't say that word, otherwise all Germans will think that Turkish literature consists of that kind of language.'
>
> From then on in the rehearsals the actress said: 'My husband Germany. Staying funking German woman.'

In effect, the director – who is presumably a German although this is left unclear – attempts to protect the collective face of Turkish people by protecting Germans' evaluation of their literature. At the same time, what he is asking her to do in the name of face could be perceived as an infringement on the sociality rights of the character, the actress and potentially a larger group of Turkish women whom she is meant to represent, since she is being denied a form of expression that is available to other speakers of German. (At this point, it is worth remembering that the title of the other work in the scandal around the Ingeborg Bachmann Prize two years earlier was *Babyfucker*.) There is also something potentially ironic in the assertion that the taboo broken by the use of the word 'fucking' is more impolite and more threatening to the quality face of an entire culture than the behaviour of the husband, which the illicit language is used to describe. Culpeper notes that the strongest differences in perceived politeness are often 'brought about through changes in the power condition, whether low to high or high to low.' (e.g. Culpeper 2011: 200). The protectionism surrounding Turkish literature, the stress on taboos and the precarious imposition of euphemism index the social processes of rapport management that are only necessary because of the power imbalance and unequal statuses of practices marked as German or Turkish in the cultural field in which Özdamar was writing and producing in the early 1990s. In light of this, Özdamar's positive opening comments can be read ironically, as echoes of the director's thoughts, rather than her own.

'Blackeye and His Donkey' ends six years after the curtain had fallen on the production of Özdamar's play. Özdamar tells the reader that she still meets or telephones the actors who were in the cast. She then presents a series of sentences that appear to be instances of free direct speech:

> She has a child, did you know that?
> I met up with him in Berlin.
> She's singing now on the Mailänder Scala – Have you heard anything from him?
> Winter's coming. Do you think she will wear that long coat of hers again?

The final sentence, which follows immediately after these quotations, appears to come from the voice of the authorial narrator: They track each other like lovers (5–6). MacMahon (1996) has suggested that in some cases indirectness (a category in which she includes ironic discourse) can be associated with social power, since the listener or reader must be willing to work hard at interpreting the message and the speaker must have the luxury of accepting the consequences of a misinterpretation. By offering the readers of *Die Zeit* literary anecdotes which convey meanings through indirectness and irony, Özdamar asserts what can be understood as literary equity rights to creative and indirect expressions that have been denied to her in the past (for example, by the reviewers of *Caravanserai* and potentially by the editors of *Die Zeit*).

Final comments

Viewing Özdamar's contribution as part of an extended dialogue between the author and her reviewers allows us to conceive of the work as an act of aggressive facework. After Özdamar's writing was demeaned as effectively un-literary by the press, her face as a legitimate literary author and artist was made salient in her discourse with the editors of *Die Zeit* (and a vicarious reading public as well). Her decision to respond with a literary text and her employment of indirect forms of commentary such as irony can be construed as an off record criticism of the request itself and the implied infringement of Özdamar's equity rights embedded in the recognition awarded to her minority status rather than her literary prowess. It should be noted that, by this same logic, the editors' decision to publish the piece and to frame it within its dialogic context can also be seen as an attempt to redress what may have been an inadvertent threat to the author's face, thus claiming their own quality face. In short, an analysis of rapport management allows us to consider how it is most poignantly her *right* to *write* literarily that is foregrounded in this literary act.

Without a doubt, scholars who are more interested in locating the piece within the author's complete body of writings or within the field of literary practices will doubtless find other aspects of the vignette that warrant careful attention; however, by introducing the concepts of facework, rapport management and sociality rights as categories of analysis for literary works, I hope to encourage scholars within stylistics and literary studies to also consider the interactional aspects of literary utterances. Published literary texts pose some challenges for existing pragmatic theories, because of the complexity of their participation structures and their ability to communicate across multiple time scales; however, by adopting these frameworks to extended, published written utterances, scholars of literary pragmatics and pragmatic stylistics can add to these models in the development of a pragmatics of literary discourse.

Notes

1. An English translation of this text is available under the title '"Blackeye and His Donkey" A Multicultural Experience' in the volume *Turkish Culture in German Society Today* (1996) along with an analysis by David Horrocks and Frank Krause (Horrocks and Kolinsky 1996).
2. Michel Foucault's theories of discourse and social power have been influential in the human and social sciences over the past few decades. For an introduction to Foucault's conceptualisation of discourse and control, see his essay 'The Order of Discourse' (1981 [1970]).
3. The two uses of 'discourse' described here correlate to the distinction linguist James Gee makes between 'capital "D" Discourses' and 'little "d" discourse'. See *Social Linguistics and Literacies: Ideology in Discourses, Critical Perspectives on Literacy and Education* (1990).
4. For an overview of the use of the term 'discourse' in various disciplines see the introduction to Teun van Dijk's volume *Discourse Studies: A Multidisciplinary Approach* (2011).

5. I borrow the term 'interpersonal pragmatics' from Locher and Graham's (2010) volume with the same title. They define interpersonal pragmatics as the study of 'the dynamic of relationships between people and how these relationships are reflected [and I would add constructed] in the language choices that they make' (2).
6. It is worth noting that no conventionally agreed upon distinction between literary pragmatics and pragmatic stylistics exists. In fact the choice between terms seems in many cases institutional rather than intellectual, i.e. based on professional affiliations rather than key conceptual or methodological differences.
7. In associating literary utterances with particular illocutionary forces and to some extent with certain perlocutionary effects, I am leaning gently on the earlier work of Richard Ohmann (1971) and Sandy Petrey (1990), who both worked to ground poetics in a social theory of speech acts in recognition that the act of putting a literary text into the world is a specific way of doing things with words (compare Austin 1962). I agree with Ohmann's assertion that 'Our readiness to discover and dwell on the implicit meanings in literary works – and to judge them important – is a consequence of our knowing them to *be* literary works, rather than that which tells us they are such' (1971: 6), as well as with Petrey's caution that the illocutionary forces derived by literary texts vary across communities and contexts.
8. For an extended discussion of the suggestions of plagiarism see Warner (2011, 2012).
9. This and all subsequent translations are my own.

Bibliography

Adamson, Sylvia. (2001) 'The rise and fall of empathetic narrative: A historical perspective on perspective', in van Peer, W. and S. Chatman (eds) *New Perspectives on Narrative Perspective* (New York, NY: SUNY Press).

Allington, Daniel. (2011) '"It actually painted a picture of the village and the sea and the bottom of the sea": Reading groups, cultural legitimacy, and description in narrative (with particular reference to John Steinbeck's *The Pearl*)', *Language and Literature*, 20.4: 317–332.

Alleman, Urs. (1992) *Babyficker* (Vienna: Deuticke).

Allington, Daniel and Joan Swann. (2009) 'Researching literary reading as social practice', *Language and Literature*, 18.3: 219–230.

Anderson, John R. (1983) *The Architecture of Cognition* (Cambridge, MA: Harvard University Press).

Anderson, John R. (1990) *The Adaptive Character of Thought* (Hillsdale, NJ: Lawrence Erlbaum Associates).

Anderson, John R. and Lael J. Schooler. (2000) 'The adaptive nature of memory', in Tulving, E. and F. I. M. Craik (eds) *The Oxford Handbook of Memory* (Oxford: Oxford University Press) 557–570.

Arndt, Michael, Dayton, Jonathan and Valerie Faris. (2007) '*Little Miss Sunshine*': *The Shooting Script* (New York, NY: Newmarket Press).

Arundale, Robert. (2006) 'Face as relational and interactional: A communication framework for research on face, facework, and politeness', *Journal of Politeness Research*, 2.2: 193–216.

Arundale, Robert. (2009) 'Face as emergent in interpersonal communication: An alternative to Goffman', in Bargiela-Chiappini, Francesca and Michael Haugh (eds) *Face, Communication and Social Interaction* (London: Equinox) 33–54.

Arundale, Robert. (2010) 'Constituting face in conversation: Face, facework, and interactional achievement', *Journal of Pragmatics*, 42.8: 2078–2105.

Austin, John L. (1962) *How to Do Things with Words* (Oxford: Clarendon).

Bargiela-Chiappini, Francesca. (2003) 'Face and politeness: New (insights) for (old) concepts', *Journal of Pragmatics*, 35.10–11: 1453–1469.

Barish, Jonas A. (1994) 'Is there "Authenticity" in theatrical performance?' *The Modern Language Review*, 89.4: 817–831.

Barthes, R. (1977) *Image-Music-Text* (London: Fontana).

Barthes, R. (1981) 'Theory of the text', in Young, R. (ed.) *Untying the Text: A Poststructural Reader* (Boston and London: Routledge and Kegan Paul).

Bauman, Richard. (1975) 'Verbal art as performance', *American Anthropologist*, 77.2: 290–311.

Beckerman, Bernard. (1971) 'Dramatic analysis and literary interpretation: The cherry orchard as exemplum', *New Literary History*, 2.3: 391–406.

Benwell, Bethan. (2009) '"A pathetic and racist and awful character": Ethnomethodological approaches to the reception of diasporic fiction', *Language and Literature*, 18.3: 300–315.

Billington, Michael. (2003) 'Review of after Miss Julie.' *The Guardian*, 26 November 2003, accessed 28 June 2011. http://www.theguardian.com/stage/2003/nov/26/theatre.

Black, Elizabeth. (2006) *Pragmatic Stylistics* (Edinburgh: Edinburgh University Press).

Blake, Norman. (2002) *A Grammar of Shakespeare's Language* (Basingstoke: Palgrave Macmillan).

Blakemore, Diane. (1993) 'The relevance of reformulations', *Language and Literature*, 2.2: 101–120.

Blakemore, Diane. (2008) 'Apposition and affective communication', *Language and Literature*, 17.1: 37–57.

Blakemore, Diane. (2009) 'Parentheticals and point of view in free indirect style', *Language and Literature*, 18.2: 129–153.

Blakemore, Diane. (2010) 'Communication and the representation of thought: The use of audience-directed expressions in free indirect thought representations', *Journal of Linguistics*, 46.3: 575–599.

Blakemore, Diane and Robyn Carston. (2005) 'The pragmatics of sentential coordination with and', *Lingua*, 115.4: 569–589.

Blass, Regina. (2006) 'Manipulation in the speeches and writings of Hitler and the NSDAP from a relevance theoretic point of view', in de Saussure, L. and P. Schulz (eds) *Manipulation and Ideologies in the Twentieth Century: Discourse, Language, Mind* (Amsterdam: John Benjamins) 169–190.

Bogan, Louise. (1959) *Collected Poems* (New York, NY: Noonday Press).

Bohl, Inka. (1991) 'Observiere – piep – piep – Schattigen Sitzgarten – ende', *Der Literat*, 33:7, 5–7.

Booth, Wayne C. (1983) *The Rhetoric of Fiction* (Chicago: Chicago University Press).

Bourdieu, Pierre. (1993) *The Field of Cultural Production* (New York, NY: Columbia University Press).

Bousfield, Derek. (2007) ' "Never a truer word said in jest": A pragmastylistic analysis of impoliteness as banter in Henry IV, Part I', in Lambrou, M. and P. Stockwell (eds) *Contemporary Stylistics* (London: Continuum) 209–220.

Bousfield, Derek. (2008) *Impoliteness in Interaction* (Amsterdam: John Benjamins).

Bousfield, Derek and Dan McIntyre. (2011) 'Emotion and empathy in Martin Scorsese's *Goodfellas*: A case study of the "funny guy" scene', in Piazza, R., Rossi, F. and M. Bednarek (eds) *Telecinematic Discourse* (Amsterdam: John Benjamins) 105–124.

Bousfield, Derek and Miriam A. Locher. (eds) (2008) *Impoliteness in Language* (Berlin: Mouton de Gruyter).

Bowen, Elizabeth. (1929) *The Last September* (London: Constable & Co. Ltd. [Vintage, 1998]).

Bowen, Elizabeth. (1942) *Bowen's Court* (London: Longmans, Green and Co. [Vintage, 1999]).

Bowen, Elizabeth. (1952) 'Preface to the second U.S. edition of The Last September', in Lee, Hermione (ed.) (1986) *The Mulberry Tree* (London: Virago) 122–126.

Bowen, Elizabeth. (1986) 'The most unforgettable character I've met', in Lee, Hermione (ed.) *The Mulberry Tree* (London: Virago) 254–265.

Braddon, Mary Elizabeth. (1998 [1861]) *Lady Audley's Secret* (London: Penguin).

Branscombe, Nyla R., Ellemers, Naomi, Spears, Russell and Bertjan Doosjie. (1999) 'The context and content of social identity threat', in Ellemers, N., Spears, R., and B. Doosjie (eds) *Social Identity: Context, Commitment, Content* (Oxford: Wiley-Blackwell) 35–58.

Brantlinger, Patrick. (1982) 'What is "sensational" about the "sensation novel"?', *Nineteenth-Century Fiction*, 37.1: 1–28.

Bridgeman, Teresa. (2005) 'Thinking ahead: A cognitive approach to prolepsis', *Narrative*, 13.2: 125–159.

Brook, Peter. (1990) *The Empty Space* (Harmondsworth: Penguin).

Brown, Matthew. (2012) 'Strange associations: Elizabeth Bowen and the language of exclusion', *Irish Studies Review*, 20.1: 3–24.

Brown, Penelope and Stephen C. Levinson. (1978) 'Universals in language usage: Politeness phenomena', in Goody, E. (ed.) *Questions and Politeness* (Cambridge: Cambridge University Press), 56–311.

Brown, Penelope and Stephen C. Levinson. (1987) *Politeness: Some Universals in Language Usage* (Cambridge: Cambridge University Press).

Brustein, Robert. (1962) 'Male and female in August Strindberg', *The Tulane Drama Review*, 7.2: 130–174.

Bursey, Jeff and Anne Furlong. (2006) 'Cognitive gothic: Relevance theory, iteration and style', in Tabbi, J. and R. Shavers (eds) *Paper Empire: William Gaddis and the World System* (Tuscaloosa, AL: University of Alabama Press).

Byckling, Liisa. (2006) 'A Finnish Nora in St Petersburg: Ida Aalberg in Ibsen's *A Doll's House* (1882–1902)', *Toronto Slavic Quarterly*, 16: 1–20.

Caink, Andrew. (2012) 'Experiencing meanings in Spark's *The Prime of Miss Jean Brodie*', *Journal of Literary Semantics*, 41.2: 121–138.

Caink, Andrew and Billy Clark. (eds) (2012) 'Special issue on inference and implicature in literary interpretation', *Journal of Literary Semantics*, 41.2.

Carnell, Jennifer. (2000) *The Literary Lives of Mary Elizabeth Braddon: A Study of Her Life and Work* (Hastings: The Sensation Press).

Carston, Robyn. (2002) *Thoughts and Utterances: The Pragmatics of Explicit Communication* (Oxford: Wiley-Blackwell).

Carston, Robyn. (2010) 'Metaphor: ad hoc concepts, literal meaning and mental images', *Proceedings of the Aristotelian Society*, 110.3: 295–321.

Chapman, Siobhan. (2012) 'Towards a neo-Gricean stylistics: Implicature in Dorothy L. Sayers's *Gaudy Night*', *Journal of Literary Semantics*, 41: 139–153.

Chapple, Eliot D. and Martha Davis. (1988) 'Expressive movement and performance: Toward a unifying theory', *The Drama Review*, 32.4: 53–79.

Chatman, Seymour. (1980) *Story and Discourse: Narrative Structure in Fiction and Film* (Ithaca and London: Cornell University Press).

Chaudhuri, Una. (1993) 'Private parts: Sex, class, and stage space in *Miss Julie*', *Theatre Journal*, 45.3: 317–332.

Cheesman, Tom. (2006) 'Juggling burdens of representation: Black, red, gold and turquoise', *German Life and Letters*, 59.4: 471–487.

Chekhov, Anton. (2002) (first Russian version published in 1899, revised version in 1903). *The Lady with the Little Dog*, in *The Lady with the Little Dog and Other Stories, 1896–1904*, translated by Ronald Wilks, introduction by Paul Debreczeny (London: Penguin) 223–240.

Christie, Chris. (2007) 'Relevance theory and politeness', *Journal of Politeness Research*, 3: 269–294.

Clark, Billy. (1996) 'Stylistic analysis and relevance theory', *Language and Literature*, 5.3: 163–178.

Clark, Billy. (2009) 'Salient inferences: Pragmatics and the inheritors', *Language and Literature*, 18: 173–212.

Clark, Billy. (2014) 'Pragmatics and inference', in Stockwell, P. and S. Whiteley (eds) *Cambridge Handbook of Stylistics* (Cambridge: Cambridge University Press) 300–314.

Clark, Billy. (2013) *Relevance Theory* (Cambridge: Cambridge University Press.)

Cleese, John and Connie Booth. (2001) *The Complete Fawlty Towers* (Cambridge: Da Capo).

Coates, Jennifer. (1996) *Women Talk: Conversation between Women Friends* (Oxford: Wiley-Blackwell).

Cohn, Dorrit. (1999) *The Distinction of Fiction* (London: John Hopkins University Press).

Collins, Wilkie. (2011, originally published 1868) *The Moonstone* (Harmondsworth: Penguin).

Connor, Catherine. (1999) 'The preceptistas and beyond: Spectators making 'meanings' in the Corral de Comedias', *Hispania* 82.3: 417–428.

Cooper, Marilyn. (1998) 'Implicature, convention and *The Taming of the Shrew*', in Culpeper, J., Short, M. and P. Verdonk (eds) (1998) *Exploring the Language of Drama* (London: Routledge) 54–66.

Corcoran, Neil. (2004) *Elizabeth Bowen: The Enforced Return* (Oxford: Oxford University Press).

Cosmides, Leda and John Tooby. (2000) 'Consider the source: The evolution of adaptations for decoupling and metarepresentations' in Sperber (ed.) 2000: 53–115.

Croft, William and D. Alan Cruse. (2004) *Cognitive Linguistics* (Cambridge: Cambridge University Press).

Cruse, D. Alan. (1986) *Lexical Semantics* (Cambridge: Cambridge University Press).

Cruse, Alan. (2011) *Meaning in Language: An Introduction to Semantics and Pragmatics* (Oxford: Oxford University Press).

Culpeper, Jonathan. (1996) 'Towards an anatomy of impoliteness', *Journal of Pragmatics*, 25.3: 349–367.

Culpeper, Jonathan. (1998) '(Im)politeness in dramatic dialogue' in Culpeper, J., Short, M. and P. Verdonk (eds) (1998) *Exploring the Language of Drama* (London: Routledge) 83–95.

Culpeper, Jonathan. (2001) *Language and Characterisation: People in Plays and other Texts* (London: Longman).

Culpeper, Jonathan. (2011) *Impoliteness: Using Language to Cause Offence* (Cambridge: Cambridge University Press).

Culpeper, Jonathan and Dan McIntyre. (2010) 'Activity types and characterisation', in Eder, J., Fotis, J. and R. Schneider (eds) *Characters in Fictional Worlds: Understanding Imaginary Beings in Literature, Film and Other Media* (Berlin: De Gruyter) 176–207.

Dancygier, Barbara and Eve Sweetser. (2005) *Mental Spaces in Grammar: Conditional Constructions* (Cambridge: Cambridge University Press).

Davies, David. (2009) 'Rehearsal and Hamilton's "Ingredients Model" of theatrical performance', *The Journal of Aesthetic Education*, 43.3: 23–36.

Dawkins, Richard. (1976) *The Selfish Gene* (Oxford: Oxford University Press).
de Beaugrande, Robert and Wolfgang Dressler. (1981) *Introduction to Text Linguistics* (London: Longman).
Dennett, Daniel. (1969) *Content and Consciousness* (London: Routledge).
Devlin-Glass, Frances. (2001) 'More than a reader and less than a critic: Literary authority and women's book-discussion groups', *Women's Studies International Forum*, 24.5: 571–585.
Dickens, Charles. (2003 [1853]) *Bleak House* (London: Penguin).
Dickinson, Emily. (1998) *The Poems of Emily Dickinson* (Cambridge, MA: Harvard University Press).
Ducrot, Oswald. (1984) *Le dire et le dit (Propositions)* (Paris: Minuit). Durant, Alan. (2010) *Meaning in the Media* (Cambridge: Cambridge University Press).
Dylan, Bob. (1992) *Good as I Been to You* (Columbia Records).
Ebel, Martin. (1991) 'Wie skandalös darf Literatur sein, wie belanglos? Eine schwache Jury, viele schwache Texte: Zum 15. Mal bewarben sich in Klagenfurt Autoren um den Ingeborg-Bachmann-Preis', *Badische Zeitung*, 16.
Eckert, Penelope. (2000) *Linguistic Variation as Social Practice* (Oxford: Wiley-Blackwell).
Eckert, Penelope and Sally McConnell-Ginet. (1992) 'Communities of practice: Where language, gender, and power all live', in Hall, K., Bucholtz, M. and B. Moonwomon (eds) *Locating Power: Proceedings of the Second Berkeley Women and Language Conference* (Berkeley, CA: Berkeley Women and Language Group) 89–99.
Edelsky, Carole. (1981) 'Who's got the floor?', *Language in Society*, 10: 383–421.
Eder, Jens, Jannidis, Fotis and Ralf Schneider. (2010) 'Characters in fictional worlds: An introduction' in Eder, J., Jannidis, F. and R. Schneider (eds) *Characters in Fictional Worlds: Understanding Imaginary Beings in Literature, Film and Other Media* (Berlin/New York: De Gruyter) 3–66.
Edwards, Derek. (2007) 'Managing subjectivity in talk', in Hepburn, A. and S. Wiggins (eds) *Discursive Research in Practice: New Approaches to Psychology and Interaction* (Cambridge: Cambridge University Press) 31–49.
Eliot, Thomas Stearns. (1924) 'Four Elizabethan dramatists.' *Selected Essays* (New York: Harcourt, Brace and Company) 91–99.
Elton, Ben. (1989) *Stark* (London: Black Swan).
Emmott, Catherine. (1997) *Narrative Comprehension: A Discourse Perspective* (Oxford: Oxford University Press).
Ergin, Meliz. (2013) 'Emine Sevgi Özdamar's translingual poetics in Mutterzunge', *Seminar*, 49.1: 20–37.
Escandell-Vidal, Victoria. (1996) 'Towards a cognitive approach to politeness', *Language Sciences*, 18: 629–650.
Escandell-Vidal, Victoria. (1998) 'Politeness: A relevant issue for relevance theory', *Revista Alicantina de Estudios Ingleses*, 11: 45–57.
Essif, Les. (1998) 'Teaching literary-dramatic texts as culture-in-progress in the foreign language theatre practicum: The strategy of combining texts', *ADFL (Association of Departments of Foreign Languages) Bulletin*, 29.3: 24–33.
Esty, Jed. (2007) 'Virgins of empire: *The Last September* and the antidevelopmental plot', *Modern Fiction Studies*, 53: 257–275.
Evans, Vyv. (2006) 'Lexical concepts, cognitive models and meaning-construction', *Cognitive Linguistics*, 17.4: 491–534.

Evans, Vyv. (2007) 'Towards a cognitive compositional semantics: An overview of LCCM theory', in Magnusson, U., Kardela, H. and A. Glaz (eds) *Further Insights into Semantics and Lexicography* (Lublin: Wydawnictwo UMCS).

Evans, Vyv. (2009) *How Words Mean: Lexical Concepts, Cognitive Models, and Meaning Construction* (Oxford: Oxford University Press).

Evans, Vyv. (2010) 'Figurative language understanding in LCCM theory', *Cognitive Linguistics*, 21.4: 601–662.

Fabb, Nigel. (1995) 'The density of response: A problem for literary criticism and cognitive science', in Payne, J. (ed.) *Linguistic Approaches to Literature: Papers in Literary Stylistics* (Birmingham: English Language Research, University of Birmingham) 143–157.

Fabb, Nigel. (2002) *Language and Literary Structure* (Cambridge: Cambridge University Press).

Fairclough, Norman. (1992a) 'Discourse and text: Linguistic and intertextual analysis within discourse analysis', *Discourse and Society*, 3.2: 193–217.

Fairclough, Norman. (1992b) *Discourse and Social Change* (Cambridge: Polity).

Fairclough, Norman. (2003) *Analysing Discourse* (London: Routledge).

Fauconnier, Gilles. (1985) *Mental Spaces: Aspects of Meaning Construction in Natural Language* (Cambridge, MA: MIT Press).

Fillmore, Charles J. (1982) 'Frame semantics', in Linguistic Society of Korea (eds), *Linguistics in the Morning* (Seoul: Hanshin Publishing Co).

Fillmore, Charles J. (1985) 'Frames and the semantics of understanding', *Quaderni di Semantica*, 6.2: 222–254.

Fish, Stanley. (1981) 'What is stylistics and why are they saying such terrible things about it?' in Freeman, D. (ed.) *Essays in Modern Stylistics* (London: Methuen).

Fludernik, Monika. (2009) *An Introduction to Narratology* (London: Routledge).

Ford, Richard. (1998) 'Why we like Chekhov', in Ford, R. (ed.) *The Essential Tales of Chekhov*, translated by Constance Garnett (London: Granta Books) vii–xx.

Ford, Richard. (2007) 'Introduction to' in Ford, R. (ed.) *The New Granta Book of the American Short Story* (London: Granta Books) vii–xxvi.

Foucault, Michel. (1981 [1970]) 'The order of discourse', in Young, Robert (ed.) *Unifying the Text: A Post-structuralist Reader* (London: Routledge), 51–78.

Fowler, Roger. (1977) *Linguistics and the Novel* (London: Methuen).

Freadman, Anne. (2002) 'Uptake', in Coe, Richard, Lingard, Lorelei and Tatiana Teslenko (eds) *The Rhetoric and Ideology of Genre* (Cresskill, NJ: Hampton Press) 39–53.

Frye, Rinda. (1997) 'Review of *Miss Julie* at the Actors Theatre of Louisville, 26 January 1997', *Theatre Journal*, 49.4: 532–534.

Fuller, Danielle and DeNel Rehberg Sedo. (2006) 'A reading spectacle for the nation: The CBC and "Canada Reads" ', *Journal of Canadian Studies*, 40.1: 5–36.

Furlong, Anne. (1996) 'Relevance theory and literary interpretation', PhD dissertation (London: University College London).

Furlong, Anne. (2008) 'You can't put your foot in the same river once: Relevance stylistics and rereading', *Proceedings of the stare of Stylistics 26th Annual Meeting of the Poetics and Linguistics Association* (Amsterdam: Rodopi) 283–302.

Gabbay, Dov M. and Heinrich Wansing. (eds) (1999) *What is Negation?* (Dordrecht: Kluwer Academic Publishers).

Gallagher, Catherine and Greenblatt, Stephen. (2000) *Practicing New Historicism* (Chicago, IL: University of Chicago Press).
Gardiner, Michael and Willy Maley. (eds) (2010) *The Edinburgh Companion to Muriel Spark* (Edinburgh: Edinburgh University Press).
Gautam, Kripa and Manjula Sharma. (1986) 'Dialogue in *Waiting for Godot* and Grice's conception of implicature', *Modern Drama*, 29: 580–586.
Gee, James Paul. (1990) *Social Linguistics and Literacies: Ideology in Discourses. Critical Perspectives on Literacy and Education* (London: The Falmer Press).
Genette, Gérard (1972 [1980]) *Narrative Discourse* (Ithaca, NY: Cornell University Press).
Genette, Gérard. (1980) *Narrative Discourse: An Essay in Method* (Ithaca and London: Cornell University Press).
Genette, Gérard. (1992) *The Architext: An Introduction* (Berkeley, CA: University of California Press).
Genette, Gérard. (1997) *Palimpsests: Literature in Second Degree* (Lincoln, NE: University of Nebraska).
Geurts, Bart. (1998) 'The mechanisms of denial', *Language*, 74.2: 274–307.
Geurts, Bart. (2010) *Quantity Implicatures* (Cambridge: Cambridge University Press).
Giora, Rachel. (2006) 'Anything negatives can do affirmatives can do just as well, except for some metaphors', *Journal of Pragmatics*, 38: 981–1014.
Giora, Rachel, Balaban, Noga and Inbar Alkabets. (2004) 'Negation as positivity in disguise', in Colston, H. L. (ed.) *Figurative Language Comprehension: Social and Cultural Influences* (Mahwah: Lawrence Erlbaum Associates) 233–257.
Giora, Rachel, Fein, Ofer, Aschkencizi, Keren and Inbar Alkabets. (2007) 'Negation in context: A functional approach to supression', *Discourse Processes*, 43.2: 153–172.
Giora, Rachel, Fein, Ofer, Ganzi, Jonathan, Levi, Natalie Alkeslassy and Hadas Sabah. (2005) 'On negation as mitigation: The case of negative irony', *Discourse Processes*, 39.1: 81–100.
Givón, Talmy. (2001) *Syntax: An Introduction* (Amsterdam: John Benjamins).
Glendinning, Victoria. (1988) 'Introduction' in Bowen, Elizabeth (ed.) *The Last September* (London: Vintage, 1998) 1–6.
Goffman, Erving. (1955) 'On face-work: An analysis of ritual elements of social interaction', *Psychiatry: Journal for the Study of Interpersonal Processes*, 18: 213–233.
Goffman, Erving. (1967) *Interaction Ritual Essays on Face to Face Behavior* (New York: Pantheon).
Goffman, Erving. (1981) 'Footing', *In Forms of Talk* (Philadelphia, PA: University of Pennsylvania Press) 124–159.
Gramling, David. (2010) 'The Caravanserai turns twenty; or, new German literature – turns Turkish?', *AlmanDili ve Edebiyati Dergisi/Studien zur Deutschen Sprache und Literatur*, 24: 55–83.
Grice, H. Paul. (1975) 'Logic and conversation', in Cole, P. and J. Morgan (eds) *Syntax and Semantics*, Volume 3 (New York: Academic Press) 41–58. Reprinted in Grice (1989): 86–116.
Grice, H. Paul. (1989) *Studies in the Way of Words* (Cambridge, MA: Harvard University Press) 22–40.
Grotowski, Jerzy. (2002) *Towards a Poor Theatre* (New York, NY: Routledge).

H.D. (1984) *Collected Poems* 1912–1944 (Manchester: Carcanet).

Halliday, Michael A. K. (1971) 'Linguistic function and literary style: An inquiry into the language of William Golding's *The Inheritors*', in Chatman, S. (ed.) *Literary Style: A Symposium* (New York: Oxford University Press).

Hamilton, James R. (2001) 'Theatrical performance and interpretation', *The Journal of Aesthetics and Art Criticism*, 59.3: 307–312.

Hamilton, Craig and Peter Crisp. (2013) 'L'allégorie implicite dans Les Mouches de Sartre', in Schnyder, P. and F. Toudoire-Surlapierre (eds) *Ne Pas Dire: Pure Une Étude du Non-Dit dans la Littérature et la Culture Européenes* (Paris: Classiques-Garnier) 353–367.

Hartley, Jenny. (2001) *Reading Groups* (Oxford: Oxford University Press).

Henderson, Diana. (2009) 'Re-contextualising literary education: A multi-variable experiment in learning and performance', *English Language Notes*, 47.1: 105–114.

Herman, David. (ed.) (2010) *Muriel Spark: 21st Century Perspectives* (Baltimore: John Hopkins University Press).

Hidalgo-Downing, Laura. (2000) *Negation, Text Worlds, and Discourse* (Stamford CT: Ablex).

Hoey, Michael. (2005) *Lexical Priming: A New Theory of Words and Language* (London: Routledge).

Hogan, Patrick Colm. (2003) *Cognitive Science, Literature and The Art: A Guide for Humanists* (London: Routledge).

Hollander, Anne. (1971)'The clothed image: Picture and performance', *New Literary History*, 2.3: 477–493.

Holt, Elizabeth. (1996) 'Reporting on talk: The use of direct reported speech on conversation', *Research in Language and Social Interaction*, 29.3: 219–245.

Horn, Laurence R. (1972) On the Semantic Properties of Logical Operators in English (PhD thesis, University of California, Los Angeles).

Horn, Laurence R. (1984) 'Towards a new taxonomy for pragmatic inference: Q- and R-based implicature', in Schiffrin, D. (ed.) *Meaning, Form, and Use in Context: Georgetown University Round Table on Languages and Linguistics* (Washington, DC: Georgetown University Press) 11–42.

Horn, Laurence R. (1985) 'Metalinguistic negation and pragmatic ambiguity.' *Language*, 61.1: 121–174.

Horn, Laurence R. (1988) 'Pragmatic theory', in Newmeyer, F. (ed.) *Linguistics: The Cambridge Survey. Volume 1: Linguistic Theory: Foundations* (Cambridge: Cambridge University Press) 113–145.

Horn, Laurence R. (1989) *A Natural History of Negation* (Chicago, IL: University of Chicago Press).

Horn, Laurence R. (1997) 'Presupposition and implicature', in Lappin, S. (ed.) *The Handbook of Contemporary Semantic Theory* (Oxford: Wiley-Blackwell) 299–320.

Horn, Laurence R. (2004) 'Implicature', in Horn, L. R. and G. Ward (eds) *The Handbook of Pragmatics* (Oxford: Wiley-Blackwell) 3–28.

Horn, Laurence R. (2006) 'The border wars: A neo-Gricean perspective', in von Heusinger, Klaus and Ken Turner (eds) *Where Semantics Meets Pragmatics* (Amsterdam: Elsevier) 21–48.

Horn, Laurence R. (2007) 'Neo-Gricean pragmatics: A Manichaean manifesto', in Burton-Roberts, Noel. (ed.) *Pragmatics* (Basingstoke: Palgrave Macmillan) 158–183.

Horrocks, David and Eva Kolinsky. (1996) '"Blackeye and his donkey". A multicultural experience', with introduction and commentary by David Horrocks and Frank Krause, in *Turkish Culture in German Society Today* (Oxford: Berghan) 55–70.

Huddleston, Rodney and Geoffrey K. Pullum. (2002) 'Negation', in Huddleston, R. and G. Pullum (eds) *The Cambridge Grammar of the English Language* (Cambridge: Cambridge University Press) 785–850.

Hughes, Ted. (1998) *Birthday Letters* (London: Faber and Faber).

Irvin, Sherri. (2009) 'Theatrical performance and the works performed', *The Journal of Aesthetic Education* 43.3: 37–50.

Irwin, William. (2004) 'Against intertextuality', *Philosophy and Literature*, 28.2: 227–242.

Israel, Michael. (2011) *The Grammar of Polarity* (Cambridge: Cambridge University Press).

Jakobson, Roman. (1960) 'Closing statement', in Sebeok, T. (ed.) *Style in Linguistics* (Cambridge, MA: MIT Press.) 350–377.

Jankowsky, Karen. (1997) '"German" literature contested: The 1991 Ingeborg-Bachmann-Prize debate, "Cultural Diversity" and Emine Sevgi Özdamar', *The German Quarterly*, 70:3: 261–276.

Jary, Mark. (1998) 'Relevance theory and the communication of politeness', *Journal of Pragmatics*, 30: 1–19.

Jeffries, Lesley. (2000) 'Don't throw out the baby with the bathwater: In defence of theoretical eclecticism in stylistics', PALA Occasional Papers, available at: http://www.pala.ac.uk/resources/op/index.html.

Jeffries, Lesley. (2010) *Critical Stylistics* (Basingstoke: Palgrave Macmillan).

Johnson, Sheila. (2001) 'Transnational Aesthetik des türkischen Alltags: Emine Sevgi Özdamar's "Das Leben ist eine Karawanserei"', *The German Quarterly*, 74.1: 37–57.

Keeble, David. (2005) 'Interpretive representation: A relevance-theoretic analysis of the opening paragraph of Carlyle's Chartism', *Journal of Literary Semantics*, 34.1: 41–59.

Kermode, Frank. (2000) *Shakespeare's Language* (New York, NY: Farrar, Straus, and Giroux).

Kitzinger, Celia. (2008) 'Conversation analysis: Technical matters for gender research', in Harrington, K., Litosseliti, L., Sauntson, H. and J. Sunderland (eds) *Gender and Language Research Methodologies* (Basingstoke: Palgrave Macmillan) 119–139.

Klein, Julie Thompson. (2005) *Humanities, Culture, and Interdisciplinarity: The Changing American Academy* (New York, NY: State University of New York Press).

Knight, Stephen. (2010) *Crime Fiction Since 1800: Detection, Death, Diversity* (2nd edn) (Basingstoke: Palgrave Macmillan).

Knulst, Wim and Andries van den Broek, A. (2003) 'The readership of books in times of de-reading', *Poetics*, 31.3–4: 213–233.

'Lady Audley's Secret' *The Morning Post*, 17 October 1862: 6 (19th Century British Library Newspapers).

Lakoff, George. (1987) *Women, Fire and Dangerous Things: What Categories Reveal About The Mind* (Chicago, IL: Chicago University Press).

Lambrou, Marina and Peter Stockwell. (eds) (2007) *Contemporary Stylistics* (London: Continuum).

Lamm, Martin. (1924, 1971) '*Miss Julie*', in Reinert, O. (ed.) *Strindberg: A Collection of Critical Essays* (Englewood Cliffs, NJ: Prentice-Hall, Inc.) 105–116.

Lane, Harry. (1982) 'Review of *Miss Julie* at the Royal Dramatic Theatre, Stockholm, 15 May 1981', *Theatre Journal*, 34.3: 406–440.

Langacker, Ronald W. (1987) *Foundations of Cognitive Grammar*, Volume 1 (Stanford, CA: Stanford University Press).

Larkin, Philip. (2012) *The Complete Poems* (London: Faber and Faber).

Lassner, Phyllis and Paula Derdiger. (2009) 'Domestic gothic, the gothic primitive, and gender relations in Elizabeth Bowen's *The Last September* and *The House in Paris*', in McGarrity, Maria, and Claire Culleton (eds) *Irish Modernism and The Global Primitive* (New York, NY: Palgrave Macmillan) 195–214.

Lave, Jean and Etienne Wenger. (1991) *Situated Learning: Legitimate Peripheral Participation* (Cambridge: Cambridge University Press).

Law, Graham. (2006) 'The professional writer and the literary marketplace', in Bourne Taylor, J. (ed.) *The Cambridge Companion to Wilkie Collins* (Cambridge: Cambridge University Press) 97–111.

Lee, Harper. (2001/1960) *To Kill a Mockingbird* (London: Arrow Books).

Leech, Geoffrey. (1969) *A Linguistic Guide to English Poetry* (London: Longman.)

Leech, Geoffrey. (1983) *The Principles of Pragmatics* (London: Longman).

Leech, Geoffrey and Mick Short. (1981) *Style in Fiction* (2nd edn 2007) (London: Longman).

Lerner, Gene H. (2002) 'Turn-sharing: The choral co-production of talk-in-interaction', in Ford, C. A., Fox, B. A. and S. A. Thompson (eds) *The Language of Turn and Sequence* (Oxford: Oxford University Press) 225–256.

Levine, George L. (2008a) *How to Read the Victorian Novel* (Oxford: Wiley-Blackwell).

Levine, George L. (2008b) *Realism, Ethics and Secularism: Essays on Victorian Literature and Science* (Cambridge: Cambridge University Press).

Levine, William H. and Joel A. Hagaman. (2008) 'Negated concepts interfere with anaphor resolution', *Intercultural Pragmatics*, 5.4: 471–500.

Levinson, Stephen C. (1987) 'Minimization and conversational inference', in Verschueren, J. and M. Bertuccelli-Papi (eds) *The Pragmatic Perspective* (Amsterdam: John Benjamins) 61–129.

Levinson, Stephen C. (2000) *Presumptive Meanings* (Cambridge: Cambridge University Press).

Lim, Tae-Seop. (1994) 'The structure of face and the determinants of face needs in Korea', *Korean Journal of Journalism and Communication Studies*, 32: 207–247.

Lim, Tae-Seop and John W. Bowers. (1991) 'Facework solidarity, approbation, and tact', *Human Communication Research*, 17: 415–450.

Locher, Miriam and Sage L. Graham (eds). (2010) *Intercultural Pragmatics* (Berlin and New York: de Gruyter Mouton).

Loney, Glenn. (1971) 'Review of *A Doll's House*, Playhouse Theater, New York' *Educational Theatre Journal*, 23.2: 205–206.

Long, Beverly W. (1977) 'Evaluating performed literature', in Doyle, E. (ed.) *Studies in Interpretation*, Volume 2 (Amsterdam: Rodopi) 267–283.

Long, Elizabeth. (2003) *Book Clubs* (Chicago, IL: University of Chicago Press).

Lyons, John. (1977) *Semantics* (Cambridge: Cambridge University Press).

McAuley, Gay. (1988) 'Performance analysis: Theory and practice', *About Performance: Performance Analysis*, 4: 1–12.
MacMahon, Barbara. (1996), 'Indirectness, rhetoric and interpretive use: Communicative strategies in Browning's *My Last Duchess*', *Language and Literature*, 5: 209–223.
MacMahon, Barbara. (2001) 'Relevance theory and the use of voice in poetry', *Belgian Journal of Linguistics*, 15: 11–34.
MacMahon, Barbara. (2007) 'The effects of sound patterning in poetry: A cognitive pragmatic approach', *Journal of Literary Semantics*, 36.2: 103–120.
MacMahon, Barbara. (2009a) 'Metarepresentation and decoupling in *Northanger Abbey*: Part I', *English Studies*, 90.5: 518–544.
MacMahon, Barbara. (2009b) 'Metarepresentation and decoupling in *Northanger Abbey*: Part II', *English Studies*, 90.6: 673–694.
MacMahon, Barbara. (2012) 'How literature means: A cognitive pragmatic perspective', in Daiber, J., Konrad, E. M., Petraschka, T. and H. Rott (eds) *Understanding Fiction* (Paderborn: Mentis).
Mahaffey, Vicki. (2010) 'Portal to forgiveness: A tribute to Ibsen's Nora', *South Central Review*, 27.2: 54–73.
Malarcher, Jay. (1994) 'How is it played? The actor as literary critic', Didaskalia: *The Journal of Ancient Drama*. Supplement: Proceedings of the Conference at Texas A&M 1.6, accessed 27 June 2011. http://www.didaskalia.net/issues/supplement1/malarcher.html.
Malcolm, Janet. (2001) *Reading Chekhov* (New York, NY: Random House).
Marcus, Gary. (2008) *Kluge: The Haphazard Construction of the Human Mind* (London: Faber & Faber).
Martin, Mathew R. (2008) 'Maltese psycho: Tragedy and psychopathology in *The Jew of Malta*', *Literature Interpretation Theory*, 19: 367–387.
Matthews, Brander. (1908) 'The legitimacy of the closet-drama', *The North American Review*, 187.627: 213–223.
McCarthy, Cormac. (2006) *The Sunset Limited: A Novel in Dramatic Form* (New York, NY: Knopf Doubleday Publishing Group).
McConachie, Bruce A. (2007) 'Falsifiable theories for theatre and performance studies', *Theatre Journal*, 59.4: 553–577.
McConnell-Ginet, Sally. (2003) ' "What's in a name?" Social labeling and gender practices', in Holmes, J. and M. Meyerhoff (eds) *The Handbook of Language and Gender* (Oxford: Wiley-Blackwell) 69–97.
McElhattan Williams, Julia. (1995) ' "Fiction with the texture of history": Elizabeth Bowen's *The Last September*', *Modern Fiction Studies*, 41, 219–242.
Mey, Jacob. (1999) *When Voices Clash: A Study in Literary Pragmatics* (Berlin: Mouton de Gruyter).
Mey, J. L. (2001) 'Literary pragmatics', in Schiffrin, D., Tannen D. and H. E. Hamilton (eds) *The Handbook of Discourse Analysis* (Malden: Blackwell Publishing).
Mey, Jacob L. (2001) 'Literary pragmatics', in Schiffrin, D., Tannen, D. and H. E. Hamilton (eds) *The Handbook of Discourse Analysis* (Oxford: Wiley-Blackwell).
Meyer, Leonard B. (1971) 'Critical analysis and performance: The theme of Mozart's A Major Piano Sonata', *New Literary History*, 2.3: 461–476.

Miestamo, Matti. (2005) *Standard Negation: The Negation of Declarative Verbal Main Clauses in a Typological Perspective* (The Hague: Mouton de Gruyter).

Moeschler, Jacques. (1992) 'The pragmatic aspects of linguistic negation: Speech act, argumentation and pragmatic inference', *Argumentation,* 6: 51–76.

Morini, Massimiliano. (2009) *Jane Austen's Narrative Techniques* (Farnham: Ashgate).

Müller, Wolfgang G. (1991) 'Interfigurality: A study on the interdependence of literary figures' in Plett, H.F. (ed.), *Intertextualities* (Berlin: de Gruyter) 101–121.

Myers, Greg. (1999) 'Unspoken speech: Hypothetical reported discourse and the rhetoric of everyday talk', *Text,* 19.4: 571–590.

Nardin, James. (1965) 'Modern criticism and the closet drama approach,' *College English,* 26.8: 591–597.

Neely, James H. (1977) 'Semantic priming and retrieval from lexical memory: Roles of inhibitionless spreading activation and limited-capacity attention', *Journal of Experimental Psychology: General,* 106.3: 226–254.

Nemiro, Jill. (1997) 'Interpretive artists: A qualitative exploration of the creative process of actors', *Creativity Research Journal,* 10.2–3: 229–239.

Nestruck, J. Kelly. (2011) 'No small feat: Getting *Miss Julie* almost right', *The Globe and Mail* 28 January 2011, accessed 2 February 2011. http://www.theglobeandmail.com/arts/theatre-and-performance/no-small-feat-getting-miss-julie-almost-right/article627794/.

Nicolle, Steve and Billy Clark. (1998) 'Phatic interpretations: Standardisation and conventionalisation', *Revista Alicantina de Estudios Ingleses,* 11, 183–191.

Nolke, Henning. (2006) 'The semantics of polyphony (and the pragmatics of realisation)', *Acta Linguistica Hafniensia,* 38: 137–160.

Nørgaard, Nina. (2007) 'Disordered collarettes and uncovered tables: Negative polarity as a stylistic device in Joyce's "Two Gallants"', *Journal of Literary Semantics,* 36.1: 35–52.

Nowik, Ewa K. (2005) 'Politeness of the impolite: Relevance theory, politeness and banter', in Korzeniowska, A. and M. Grzegorzewska (eds) *Relevance Studies in Poland,* Volume 2 (Warszawa: The Institute of English Studies, University of Warsaw) 157–166.

Nowik, Ewa K. (2008) 'Banter – an attempt at a relevance-theoretic account', in Walaszewska, E., Kisielewska-Krysiuk, M., Korzeniowska, A. and M. Grzegorzewska (eds) *Relevant Worlds: Current Perspectives on Language, Translation and Relevance Theory* (Newcastle: Cambridge Scholars Publishing) 105–118.

Ohmann, Richard. (1971) 'Speech, action and style', in Chatman, S. (ed.) *Literary Style* (Oxford: Oxford University Press).

O'Keefe, Anne. (2002) 'Exploring indices of national identity in a corpus of radio phone-in data from Irish radio', in Sánchez Macarro, A. (ed.) *Windows on the World: Media Discourse in English* (València: Universtat de València) 91–113.

Owen, Wilfred. (1965) *The Collected Poems of Wilfred Owen* (New York, NY: New Directions Books).

Özdamar, Emine Sevgi. (1992) *Das Leben ist eine Karawanserei, hat zwei Türen, aus einer kam ich rein, aus der anderen ging ich raus* (Cologne: Kiepenheuer and Witsch).

Özdamar, Emine Sevgi. (1993) 'Schwarzauge und sein Esel', *Die Zeit*, 26 February 1993, accessed 15 December 2013. http://www.zeit.de/1993/09/schwarzauge-und-sein-esel.

Özdamar, Emine Sevgi. (1994 [1990]) *Mother Tongue*, translated by Craig Thomas (Toronto: Coach House Press).

Padilla Cruz, Manuel. (2007) 'Metarepresentations and phatic utterances: A pragmatic proposal about the generation of solidarity between interlocutors', in Cap, P. and J. Nikakowska (eds) *Current Trends in Pragmatics* (Newcastle: Cambridge Scholars Publishing) 110–128.

Pagano, Adriana. (1994) 'Negatives in written texts' in Coulthard, M. (ed.) *Advances in Written Text Analysis* (London: Routledge) 250–265.

Palmer, Alan. (2004) *Fictional Minds* (Lincoln, NE: University of Nebraska Press).

Palmer, Alan. (2010) *Social Minds in the Novel* (Columbus, OH: Ohio State University Press).

Panagiotidou, Maria-Eirini. (2010) *Mapping Intertextuality: Towards a Cognitive Model*. Online proceedings of the annual conference of the Poetics and Linguistics Association (PALA), accessed 18 March 2012. http://www.pala.ac.uk/resources/proceedings/2010/panagiotiodou2010.pdf.

Panagiotidou, Maria-Eirint. (2012) 'An introduction to the semantics of intertextuality', *Journal of Literary Semantics*, 41.1: 47–65.

Pennycook, Alastair. (1994) 'The politics of pronouns', *ELT Journal*, 48.2: 172–178.

Peplow, David. (2011) ' "Oh, I've known a lot of Irish people": Reading groups and the negotiation of literary interpretation', *Language and Literature*, 20.4: 295–315.

Peplow, David. (2012) Negotiating Literary Interpretation in the Reading Group. PhD thesis, University of Nottingham.

Peplow, David. (forthcoming) *Talk About Books: A Study of Reading Groups* (London: Bloomsbury).

Petrey, Sandy. (1990) *Speech Acts and Literary Theory* (London: Routledge).

Pilkington, Adrian. (1991) 'Poetic effects', in Sell, Roger (ed.) *Literary Pragmatics* (London: Routledge) 44–61.

Pilkington, Adrian. (1992) 'Poetic effects', *Lingua*, 87: 29–51.

Pilkington, Adrian. (2000) *Poetic Effects: A Relevance Theory Perspective* (Amsterdam: John Benjamins).

Poe, Edgar Allen. (2000) *Complete Poems* (Urbana, IL: University of Illinois Press).

Pomerantz, Anita. (1984) 'Agreeing and disagreeing with assessments: Some features of preferred/dispreferred turn shapes', in Atkinson, J. M. and J. Heritage (eds) *Structures of Social Action: Studies in Conversation Analysis* (Cambridge: Cambridge University Press), 57–101.

Potter, Jonathan. (1996) *Representing Reality: Discourse, Rhetoric and Social Construction* (London: SAGE).

Pratt, Mary Louise. (1977) *Toward a Speech Act Theory of Literary Discourse* (Bloomington, IN: Indiana University Press).

Propbay.com. 'Ridley Scott's personal shooting script for *Alien*', accessed 15 December 2013. http://www.propbay.com/original/alien-color-coded-schooting-script-alien-1979-film-production-2001.html.

Pustejovsky, James. (1995) *The Generative Lexicon* (Cambridge, MA: MIT Press).

Pykett, Lyn. (2006) 'Collins and the sensation novel', in Bourne Taylor, J. (ed.) *The Cambridge Companion to Wilkie Collins* (Cambridge: Cambridge University Press), 50–64.

Rabkin, Gerald. (2002) 'Is there a text on this stage? Theatre, authorship, interpretation', in Schneider, R. and G. Cody (eds) *Direction: A Theoretical and Practical Guide* (London: Routledge) 142–159.

Radford, Andrew. (2009) *Victorian Sensation Fiction* (Basingstoke: Palgrave Macmillan).

Raymond, G., and Heritage, J. (2006) 'The epistemics of social relationship: Owing grandchildren', *Language in Society*, 35.5: 677–705.

Rehberg Sedo, DeNel. (2003) 'Readers in reading groups: An online survey of face-to-face and virtual book clubs', *Convergence*, 9.1: 66–90.

Reynolds, Lorna. (1992) '*The Last September* – Elizabeth Bowen's *Paradise Lost*', in Rauchbauer, Otto. (ed.) *Ancestral Voices: The Big House in Anglo-Irish Literature* (Hildesheim: Georg Olms Verlag) 149–156.

Riffaterre, Michael. (1978) *The Semiotics of Poetry* (Bloomington, IN: Indiana University Press).

Riffaterre, Michael. (1980) 'Interpretation and undecidability', *New Literary History*, 12.2: 227–242.

Sauer, David Kennedy. (1995) ' "Speak the speech, I pray you," or suiting the method to the moment: A theory of classroom performance of Shakespeare' *Shakespeare Quarterly*, 46.2: 173–182.

Sauerland, Uli. (2004) 'Scalar implicatures in complex sentences', *Linguistics and Philosophy*, 27, 367–391.

Saury, Jean-Michel G. (2008) 'The Phenomenology of negation and its expression in natural language', in *Phenomenology and the Cognitive Sciences*, 8: 245–260.

Sell, Roger. (1985) 'Tellability and politeness in "The Miller's Tale": First steps in Literary Pragmatics', *English Studies*, 66: 496–512.

Sell, Roger. (ed.) (1991) *Literary Pragmatics* (London: Routledge).

Semino, Elena. (2007) 'Mind style 25 years on', *Style* 41.2: 153–203.

Şenocak, Zafer. (2006) 'Authentische Türkinnen', *tageszeitung*, 10 June 2006, accessed 17 December 2009. http://www.taz.de/1/archiv/archiv/?dig=2006/06/10/a0321.

Seyhan, Azade. (2000) *Writing Outside the Nation* (Princeton and Oxford: Princeton University Press).

Shafi, Monika. (2003) 'Joint ventures: Identity politics and travel in novels by Emine Sevgi Özdamar and Zafer Senocak', *Comparative Literature Studies*, 40:2: 193–214.

Shelley, Percy Bysse. (1991) *Posthumous Poems, 1824* (Oxford: Woodstock).

Sidiropoulou, Avra. (2011) *Authoring Performance: The Director in the Contemporary Theatre* (New York, NY: Palgrave Macmillan).

Simpson, Paul. (1989) 'Politeness phenomena in Ionesco's *The Lesson*', in Carter, Ronald and Paul Simpson (eds) *Language, Discourse and Literature* (London: Unwin Hyman) 171–193.

Simpson, Paul. (1993) *Language, Ideology and Point of View* (London: Routledge).

Simpson, Paul. (2010) 'Point of view', in McIntyre, D. and B. Busse (eds) *Language and Style* (Basingstoke: Palgrave Macmillan) 293–310.

Simpson, Paul and Geoff Hall. (2002) 'Discourse analysis and stylistics', *Annual Review of Applied Linguistics*, 22: 136–149.

Smiley, Jane. (2006) *Thirteen Ways of Looking at a Novel* (London: Faber & Faber).
Snuggs, Henry L. (1947) 'The comic humours: A new interpretation', *PMLA* 42.1: 114–122.
Spark, Muriel. (1957) *The Comforters* (London: Macmillan).
Spark, Muriel. (1960) *The Ballad of Peckham Rye* (London: Macmillan).
Spark, Muriel. (1961) *The Prime of Miss Jean Brodie* (London: Macmillan).
Spark, Muriel. (1981) *Loitering with Intent* (London: Bodley Head).
Spencer, Charles. (2009) 'Review of *A Doll's House*' *The Daily Telegraph* 20 May 2009, accessed 7 April 2011. http://www.telegraph.co.uk/journalists/charles-spencer/5354252/A-Dolls-House-at-the-Donmar-Warehouse-review.html.
Spencer-Oatey, Helen. (2000) *Culturally Speaking: Culture, Communication and Politeness Theory* (London: Continuum).
Spencer-Oatey, Helen. (2005) 'Rapport management theory and culture', *Intercultural Pragmatics*, 2.3: 335–346.
Spencer-Oatey, Helen. (2007) Theories of identity and the analysis of face', *Journal of Pragmatics*, 39: 639–656.
Spencer-Oatey, Helen. (2009) 'Face, identity and interactional goals', in Bargiela-Chiappini, Francesca and Michael Haugh (eds), *Face, Communication and Social Interaction* (London: Equinox), 137–154.
Sperber, Dan. (1996) *Explaining Culture: A Naturalistic Approach* (Oxford: Wiley-Blackwell).
Sperber, Dan. (2000) 'Metarepresentations in an evolutionary perspective' in *Sperber* 2000: 117–137.
Sperber, Dan. (ed.) (2000) *Metarepresentations: A Multidisciplinary Perspective* (Oxford: Oxford University Press).
Sperber, Dan and Deirdre Wilson. (1986/1995) *Relevance: Communication and Cognition* (2nd edn 1995) (Oxford: Wiley-Blackwell).
Stockwell, Peter. (2009) *Texture: A Cognitive Aesthetics of Reading* (Edinburgh: Edinburgh University Press).
Stoppard, Tom. (1968) *Rosencrantz and Guildenstern Are Dead* (London: Faber and Faber).
Storjohann, Petra. (2009) 'Plesionymy: A case of synonymy or contrast?' *Journal of Pragmatics,* 41.11: 2140–2158.
Swann, Joan and Daniel Allington. (2009) Reading groups and the language of literary texts: A case study in social reading, *Language and Literature*, 18.3: 247–264.
Swann, Joan, Peplow, David, Trimarco, Paola and Sara Whiteley. (in press) *The Discourse of Reading Groups* (London: Routledge).
Sweetser, Eve. (2006) 'Negative spaces: Levels of negation and kinds of spaces', in Bonnefille, Stéphanie and Sébastien Salbayre (eds), *Proceedings of the Conference 'Negation: Form, Figure of Speech, Conceptualization'. Publication du groupe de recherches anglo-américaines de l'Université de Tours* (Tours: Publications Universitaires François Rabelais).
Swinney, David. (1979) 'Lexical access during sentence comprehension: (Re) Consideration of context effects', *Journal of Verbal Learning and Verbal Behavior*, 18.6: 645–659.
Talmy, Leonard. (2000) *Toward a Cognitive Semantics*, Volume 1 (Cambridge MA: MIT Press).
Templeton, Alice. (1990) '*Miss Julie* as "A naturalistic tragedy" ', *Theatre Journal*, 42.4: 468–480.

Thom, Paul. (2009) 'Works, pieces, and objects performed', *The Journal of Aesthetic Education*, 43.3: 67–79.

Thornborrow, Joanna and Shân Wareing. (1998) *Patterns in Language* (London: Routledge).

Toolan, Michael. (2001) *Narrative: A Critical Linguistic Introduction* (2nd edn) (London: Routledge).

Toolan, Michael. (2009) *Narrative Progression in the Short Story: A Corpus Stylistic Approach* (Amsterdam: John Benjamins).

Tottie, Gunnel. (1991) *Negation in English Speech and Writing: A Study in Variation* (San Diego, CA: Academic Press).

Traugott, Elizabeth Closs and Mary Louise Pratt. (1980) *Linguistics for Students of Literature* (San Diego, CA: Harcourt Brace Jovanovich Inc.).

Turner, Brian. (2005) *Here, Bullet* (Farmington: Alice James Books).

Turner, Mark. (1998) *The Literary Mind: The Origins of Thought and Language* (Oxford: Oxford University Press).

Turner, Mark. (ed.) (2006) *The Artful Mind: Cognitive Science and the Riddle of Human Creativity* (Oxford: Oxford University Press).

Ungerer, Friedrich and Hans-Jörg Schmid. (1996) *An Introduction to Cognitive Linguistics* (London: Longman).

van Dijk, Teun. (1976) 'Pragmatics and poetics', in van Dijk,Teun (ed.) *Pragmatics of Language and Literature* (Amsterdam: North-Holland Publishing) 23–57.

van Dijk, Teun. (2011) 'Introduction: The study of discourse', in van Dijk, Teun (ed.) *Discourse Studies: A Multidisicplinary Approach* (London: Sage) 1–7.

van Knippenberg, Daan and Naomi Ellemers. (2003) 'Social identity and group performance: Identification as the key to collective effort', in Haslam, S. A., van Knippenberg, D. and N. Ellemers (eds) *Social Identity at Work: Developing Theory for Organizational Practice* (Philadelphia, PA: Psychology Press) 29–42.

van Peer, Willie. (ed.) (2008) *The Quality of Literature: Linguistic Studies in Literary Evaluation* (Amsterdam: John Benjamins).

Verhagen, Arie. (2005) *Constructions of Intersubjectivity: Discourse, Syntax and Cognition* (Oxford: Oxford University Press).

Wagner, Helmut R. (1983) *Phenomenology of Consciousness and Sociology of the Life-Word: An Introductory Study* (Edmonton: The University of Alberta Press).

Walker, Julia A. (2003) 'Why performance? Why now? Textuality and the rearticulation of human presence', *The Yale Journal of Criticism*, 16.1: 149–175.

Warner, Chantelle. (2011) 'A Turkish tale: Genre, subjectivity, and the controversy around Feridun Zaimoğlu's Leyla', *Gegenwartsliteratur*, 10: 181–206.

Warner, Chantelle. (2012) *The Pragmatics of Literary Testimony: Authenticity Effects in German Social Autobiographies* (London: Routledge).

Weber, Jean Jacques. (1996) 'Towards contextualised stylistics: An overview', in Weber, Jean Jacques (ed.) *The Stylistics Reader* (London: Arnold).

Weckwerth, W. (2004) 'Playing with dolls and houses.' *Theatre*, 34.3: 134–142.

Weimann, R. (1992) '(Post)Modernity and representation: Issues of authority, power, performativity', *New Literary History*, 23.4: 955–981.

Weimann, R. (1994) 'Textual authority and performative agency: The uses of disguise in Shakespeare's theatre', *New Literary History*, 25.4: 798–808.

Wells-Lassagne, Shannon. (2007) ' "He believed in empire": Colonial concerns in Elizabeth Bowen's *The Last September*', *Irish Studies Review*, 15: 451–463.

Wenger, E. (1998) *Communities of Practice: Learning, Meaning, and Identity* (Cambridge: Cambridge University Press).

Werkhofer, Konrad T. (1992) 'Traditional and modern views: The social constitution and the power of politeness', in Watts, R. J., Ide, S. and K. Ehlich (eds) *Politeness in Language: Studies in its History, Theory and Practice* (Berlin: Mouton de Gruyter) 155–199.
Werth, Paul. (1999) *Text Worlds* (London: Longman).
Wessels, Andries. (1995) 'Elizabeth Bowen's *A World of Love*: A "cultural analysis" of the Anglo-Irish ascendancy in the twentieth century', *Canadian Journal of Irish Studies*, 21: 88–95.
Westbury, Chris. (2003) 'Negation', Semiotics Encyclopaedia Online, accessed 15 December 2013. http://projects.chass.utoronto.ca/semiotics/dse/N/negation.html.
Whiteley, Sara. (2011) 'Text world theory, real readers and emotional responses to *The Remains of the Day*', *Language and Literature*, 20.1: 23–42.
Williams, William Carlos. (1994) *Asphodel, That Greeny Flower and Other Love Poems* (New York, NY: New Directions Publishing).
Wood, Mrs. Henry. (2008, originally published 1861) *East Lynne* (Oxford: Oxford University Press).
Wooffitt, Robin. (2001) 'A socially organized basis for displays of cognition: Procedural orientation to evidential turns in psychic-sitter interaction', *British Journal of Social Psychology*, 40: 545–563.
Wooffitt, Robin. (2007) 'The dead in the service of the living', in Clift, R. and E. Holt (eds) *Reported Talk: Reported Speech in Interaction* (Cambridge: Cambridge University Press) 244–269.
Wright, Laura and Jonathan Hope. (1996) *Stylistics: A Practical Coursebook* (London: Routledge).
Yamanashi, Masa-aki. (2000) 'Negative inference, space construal and grammaticalization', in Horn, L. and Y. Kato (eds) *Negation and Polarity: Syntactic and Semantic Perspectives* (Oxford: Oxford University Press).
Yeats, William Butler. (2000) *The Collected Poems of W. B. Yeats* (Ware: Wordsworth Editions).
Young, William C. (1974) 'Review of *The Misanthrope*, and *A Doll's House*', *Educational Theatre Journal*, 26.3: 409–410.
Young, William P. (2007) *The Shack* (New York, NY: Windblown Media).
Zangwill, Nick (1999) 'Art and audience', *The Journal of Aesthetics and Art Education*, 57.3: 315–332.
Zegarac Vlad. (1998) 'What is 'phatic communication'?', in Rouchota, V. and A. Jucker (eds) *Current Issues in Relevance Theory* (Amsterdam: John Benjamins) 327–362.
Zegarac, Vlad and Billy Clark. (1999) 'Phatic interpretations and phatic communication.' *Journal of Linguistics*, 35.2: 321–346.
Zunshine, Lisa. (2006) *Why We Read Fiction: Theory of Mind and the Novel* (Columbus, OH: Ohio State University Press).
Zunshine Lisa. (2012) *Getting Inside Your Head: What Cognitive Science Can Tell Us about Popular Culture* (Baltimore, MD: Johns Hopkins University Press).

Index

Printed and bound by CPI Group (UK) Ltd, Croydon, CR0 4YY